CATALOG OF HUMAN SOULS
Book 2

HACK ANYONE'S SOUL
100 Demos Of Human Programs From The Catalog Of Human Population

Olga Skorbatyuk and Kate Bazilevsky

HPA Press

ISBN-10: 0996731210
ISBN-13: 978-0-9967312-1-8

Olga Skorbatyuk and Kate Bazilevsky

Hack Anyone's Soul: 100 Demos Of Human Programs From The Catalog Of Human Population.

Part 2 translated by Kate Bazilevsky.
All images are in the public domain unless otherwise noted.

*Dedicated to the 40th anniversary of the discovery of the
Catalog of Human Population by researcher Andrey Davydov.*

Table of Contents

PREFACE

Sketch © 2000 Andrey Davydov

We—authors of the Catalog of Human Souls book series—would like to briefly describe what these books are about right from the beginning because the topic of the Catalog of Human Population is very new for many people.

These books are dedicated to the 40th anniversary from the beginning of research that led to discovery of the Catalog of Human Population. A technology of uncovering of the individual structure of human psyche (or simply put—the soul) was created on the basis of this scientific discovery. The author of scientific discovery of the Catalog of Human Population and this technology is a researcher of ancient books, an expert in Chinese culture Andrey Davydov.

The source of knowledge about the structure of human psyche and the basis for creation of this technology is one of the most ancient and mysterious texts preserved in this civilization—the ancient Chinese monument Shan Hai Jing (translated as the Catalog of Mountains and Seas), which Andrey Davydov managed to decrypt.

After Andrey Davydov created the technology of decryption of Shan Hai Jing (Catalog of Mountains and Seas), it was found that this ancient Chinese monument contains very detailed descriptions of 293 models of human psyche and a lot of other kind of information about the structure of *Homo sapiens*. On this basis, Shan Hai Jing was qualified as the Catalog of Human Population.

In Shan Hai Jing (Catalog Mountains and Seas), the biological type "human" is described as a type divided into 293 subtype structures according to the phenological principle. It turned out that each person, belonging to one of these 293 subtypes from birth, has stable characteristics of this subtype; regardless of race, nationality and particularities of parental psychophysiological structures, which are only minor correctors.

Information about the subtype structure is implanted in the form of a program in the unconscious of a person from birth, and this program determines all of his life: his/her personal qualities and character properties, algorithms of life and functioning, hidden motivational spring, abilities, talents, preferences, inclinations, etc. Natural subtype program is that what is called "psyche", "soul."

Natural program is that individuality, which makes a person different from other people as representatives of other subtype structures of biological type *Homo sapiens*. Each individual "speaks his own language," specified by his subtype program, as the language of values, views, convictions, preferences, which are standard and unchanging for all representatives of a subtype.

In the language of science, a natural subtype program of *Homo sapiens* is called Individual Archetypal Pattern; in simple language—an Individual (Subtype) Program, an Individual Program or a Program.

A human program is recorded in the language of natural images. Images or, using the language of science, archetypes of the unconscious sphere of a person is the language of human "software." The concept of "an archetype" was introduced to psychology by Carl Gustav Jung, but as it turned out, archetypes can be not only of the collective unconscious, but also individual. Therefore, to avoid confusion, in popular texts we prefer to call the language of "software" of *Homo sapiens* by the word "image" instead of "archetype."

Programs of each of 293 human subtypes are recorded by different natural images and a different number of images, meaning that they are endemic, are not similar to one another. *Homo sapiens* is a living system, which, as it turned out, exists and functions strictly on the basis of a natural program implanted from birth, and from this it was concluded that a human is a bio-robot at the genetic level.

The conclusion that "*Homo sapiens* is a bio-robot" is confirmed by that learning someone's natural individual (subtype) program from the Catalog of Mountains and Seas as the Catalog of Human Population, it is possible to find out absolutely everything about this person in great detail; about any aspect of his life and activities, including that what he or she carefully conceals.

In addition, *Homo sapiens*, as a biosystem programmed by nature, has modes of self-regulation and regulation (control from the outside). Modes of regulation are a natural inborn mechanism, just like an individual human program. Their discoverer Andrey Davydov named these modes Individual Manipulation Modes (Manipulation Modes for short). This management tool, which can be applied to any person, also was found in the text of the ancient Chinese monument Shan Hai Jing.

It was found that for every person, as a biosystem, there are three manipulation modes: suppressing, balancing and stimulating. Manipulation modes together with an individual (subtype) program are individual structure of psyche of *Homo sapiens*. Programs and manipulation modes of each subtype differ, from one another. For this reason, people differ from each other by internal characteristics, and individual manipulation scenarios are necessary for each person.

Structure Of Psyche Of *Homo Sapiens*

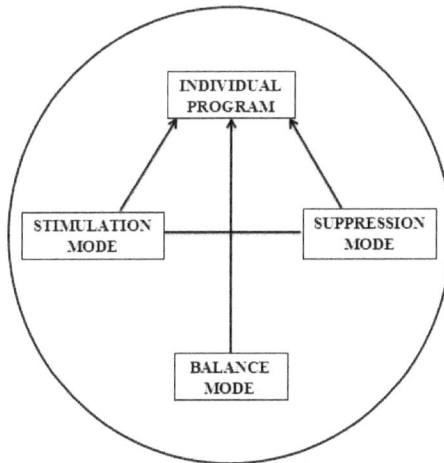

© 2015 Olga Skorbatyuk, Kate Bazilevsky

Individual program, with which a person was born, is the main segment of structure of human psyche (soul). Knowing the natural individual program allows you to find out who he/she (or you personally) is real, without masks, what motives drive this person (or you), and so on.

Suppression mode is a self-control mode, which turns on automatically as a mode of relaxation, pleasure, dream, happy oblivion (a "turn off" button). It is the individual program of people, who belong to a particular subtype.

When a manipulator acts out a personality from the suppression mode, it makes an individual experience pleasure, unconsciously get attached to the manipulator (fall in love, etc.), and on this basis obey him/her and fulfill all of his/her requests/demands.

Balance mode is a self-control mode, which turns on automatically when a person needs to become balanced, get in a harmonious, comfortable state without loss of activeness. It is the individual program of people, who belong to a particular subtype. When a manipulator acts out a personality from the balance mode, it makes an individual experience comfort in communication with him/her, trust him/her at the unconscious level and consider him/her the best friend.

Stimulation mode is a self-control mode, which turns on automatically when a person needs to stimulate himself/herself to some actions, become active. It is the individual program of people, who belong to a particular subtype. When a manipulator transmits properties of the stimulation mode in a certain way, it makes an individual experience strong irritation, up to wild rage, and on this basis he/she does that what a manipulator asks for/demands.

Natural manipulation modes described in Shan Hai Jing (Catalog of Mountains and Seas) as the Catalog of Human Population provide a key to managing any person. With the help of knowledge of human manipulation modes, it is possible to factually change a person's physical and psychological state, behavior, reactions in the desired direction.

No one is able to resist application of his personal manipulation modes because it is a natural mechanism, which is built into human psyche from birth. Therefore, information about manipulation modes of a subtype provides unlimited possibilities for influencing any individual as a representative of this subtype and allows self-control and control of any human as a biosystem.

Non-traditional psychoanalysis, a new direction in scientific psychology, allows identifying an individual's subtype structure (psyche) and manipulation modes on the basis of the Catalog of Human Population. It is called non-traditional because it does not use any of the traditional principles, approaches to the study of human psyche, as well as methods (observation, experiment, testing, biographical method, questioning, conversation) since these methods are not needed in order to obtain any kind of information about a person as a stable and identifiable biosystem.

A non-traditional psychoanalyst knows what a person is like, what problems might concern him or her and why, and how these problems can be effectively solved without any kind of contact with this person. All that a non-traditional psychoanalyst needs to know about the subject being studied is the day, the month, the year of his or her birth and the gender.

Neither race nor nationality or place of residence of the person being studied matter because the Catalog of Human Population contains descriptions of unchanging characteristics of subtypes of *Homo sapiens* of the entire human population.

For colleagues from the scientific environment we are offering our definition of what human psyche and the Catalog of Human Population are: *"The Catalog of Human Population is a description of a human as a type by subtype structures. Subtype structure ("psyche", "soul") is a combination of individual archetypes, recorded at the genetic level (principle). Expressions and interaction of subtype structures in manipulation modes and phenological algorithms are described with adjustments for gender, age and cultural differences. Information is recorded on six factors."* This definition was developed by Andrey Davydov—the author of discovery and decryption of the Catalog of Human Population.

It is also necessary to tell a bit about the main source of knowledge (knowledge of that *Homo sapiens* are bio-robots, that human psyche (soul) is "software," that "software" of any person can be easily uncovered, and so on), which was obtained in the course of our scientific research. To date, no one knows for sure who gave and preserved this knowledge, but after it was written down it got the title 山海經 Shan Hai Jing (translated from Chinese as Canon/Catalog of Mountains and Seas).

According to Artem I. Kobzev (a Russian historian of Chinese philosophy, Doctor of Philosophical Sciences, professor, author of over eight hundred scientific papers on the history of Chinese philosophy, science and culture), Shan Hai Jing is an anonymous monument, which presumably dates back to the late III century BC-early II century BC. It consists of eighteen juan (scrolls), combined into two sections: Canon/Book of the Mountains (Shan Jing) or Canon of Five Innermost Mountains (Wu Zang Jing) in five juan and Canon of the Seas (Hai Jing) in thirteen juan.

Legend claims that Shan Hai Jing was engraved on sacred vessels by Bo Yi—an assistant to the wise semi-mythical ruler of the ancient times Yu the Great, who lived in the XXIII century BC. Yu the Great entered the throne in 2205 BC. Authors of the Han epoch attribute authorship of the literary monument Shan Hai Jing to Yu the Great and his companion Bo Yi.

According to legend, Yu the Great dealt with a great flood, which fell upon earth and arranged it. The deedful ruler allegedly came to know its mountains, rivers, their spirits, as well as animals and plants. He ordered his assistant to describe everything that was seen. As a result, these recordings together with images of spirits, fantastic animals, birds and plants were engraved on nine ritual vessels-tripods. Later on, these sacred vessels were lost. However, according to historical annals, prior to their strange disappearance, the text of the Catalog of Mountains and Seas, along with amazing images of representatives of flora and fauna, spirits and deities were copied.

This answers the question why some date Shan Hai Jing back to III-II centuries BC, while others back to XXIII century BC—the Catalog of Mountains and Seas as the source of information appeared during the time of Yu the Great and it got the form of a text much later. We tend to agree with those researchers, who date Shan Hai Jing back to XXIII BC since according to Dan Zhu the Catalog of Mountains and Sea was recorded only after its long-term oral existence (this point of view is expressed in his commentaries to the famous monument Spring and Autumn - Chunqiu). Reports that Yu the Great and his assistant Bo Yi created the Catalog of Mountains and Seas exist in, for example, Wang Chong's (27-97 AD) treatise titled Critical Essays: "When Yu and Bo Yi were taming the waters of the flood—Yu was engaged in calming the water, while Bo Yi in recording information about various "things." And, they created the Catalog of Mountains and Seas."

We will add that apparently in mythologies of almost all cultures of the world (those, which to continue to exist, as well as those, which already sank into oblivion) exist facts, which show that the Catalog of Human Population was present in these cultures. This is not difficult to trace by carefully studying the ancient, archaic cultural layers. However, the source itself was preserved only in one culture—the culture of China. This is not surprising since Chinese culture is not only ancient, but also, in spite of everything, the Chinese manage to preserve it and their traditions from the ancient times to the present day (unlike representatives of other cultures).

This was a brief description of the main points, about which you will be able to learn in detail from the Catalog of Human Souls book series.

*****

In essence, the Catalog of Human Souls book series is one book divided into five parts. All these parts are devoted to a single topic—scientific discovery made by researcher Andrey Davydov, the Catalog of Human Population. Division into five parts was done because materials for this book are quite non-uniform in content and style.

The book Catalog of Human Souls is divided into five parts since fundamental research being carried out by Andrey Davydov and our colleagues is interdisciplinary, and the field of research is wide and multifaceted (psychology, gender relations, sociology, political science, linguistics, sinology and so on), and also because we present results of this research not only in the language of science, but also in the language of popular science.

In addition, we (authors of Catalog of Human Souls books), who are presenting research and discoveries of our laboratory's research supervisor Andrey Davydov, found it necessary to include some information about him as well. It seemed to us that the story of discovery of the Catalog of Human Population might be of interest not only to those, who are already familiar with it, but also to those, who are just learning about the Catalog.

Also, in order not to sound groundless, we decided to offer readers to get acquainted with some of materials from the Catalog of Human Population. These materials are provided in the form of brief demonstration versions from descriptions of natural programs of people. We are of the opinion that presentation of any, even the most captivating scientific theory is, as the saying goes, not worth even a straw, if this theory cannot be tested and used on practice.

Demos that we presented certainly are very short and they are by no means complete descriptions of individuals. However, perhaps they will be quite enough for independent testing, which even a non-professional in the field of psychology will be able to do and get a confirmation that the Catalog of Human Souls (a nonscientific title of the Catalog of Human Population) really exists. And, this means that now he or she can use this Catalog in daily life.

We—authors of the Catalog of Human Souls book series—have the honor to not only tell about some of the research done by our laboratory's research supervisor Andrey Davydov and our colleagues, but also to participate in the development of the Catalog of Human Population. However, it must be stated right away that in all sections where we tell about the technology, methodology of non-traditional psychoanalysis—we are only narrators. Technology of decryption of the ancient Chinese monument Shan Hai Jing was created over 20 years ago and its authorship belongs to Andrey Davydov.

*****

The Catalog of Human Souls book series contains the following five books:

Book 1. *Homo Sapiens* Are Bio-Robots. Human "Software" (by Olga Skorbatyuk and Kate Bazilevsky). This book tells about the new method of obtaining information from the unconscious sphere of a human and about the Catalog of Human Population in the form of answers to the most frequently asked questions. In this book, we also presented three hundred selected research topics, which were developed in our laboratory between 1974 and 2014.

Book 2. Hack Anyone's Soul. 100 Demos Of Human Programs From The Catalog Of Human Population (by Olga Skorbatyuk and Kate Bazilevsky). In this book, we are offering one hundred brief demonstration versions taken from descriptions of human programs in the Catalog of Human Population. Of course, these descriptions are only a tiny fraction of information that the Catalog contains about each person. However, we think that this is enough for independent testing and to obtain confirmation of existence of the Catalog of Human Population.

Book 3. Human Manipulation Modes. Either You Are Manipulating Or You Are Being Manipulated (by Olga Skorbatyuk and Kate Bazilevsky). This book is entirely devoted to manipulation modes—the natural toolkit for controlling a system called "a human," which was discovered in the ancient Chinese monument Shan Hai Jing (which turned out to be the Catalog of Human Population). In this book, we explain what individual manipulation modes are and how to use them to manipulate people. After all, with the discovery of the Catalog of Human Population, only two positions in society are left—either you are manipulating or you are being manipulated. And, as proof of that this is really so, in this book we provided the scenario of suppression mode for manipulation of people, who were born on October 12th of leap years or October 13th of common years. Despite that this is only one of four modes of manipulation of those people, who were born on the dates indicated—it will be sufficient for testing.

Book 4. Non-Traditional Psychoanalysis. Selected Scientific Articles And Presentations at Conferences (by Andrey Davydov and Olga Skorbatyuk). This book presents some of the scientific articles and presentations at scientific conferences done by Andrey Davydov, the author of scientific discovery of the Catalog of Human Population. It also includes several scientific articles (which are also chapters of the textbook titled Archetypal Pattern. Fundamentals of Non-Traditional Psychoanalysis.), authors of which are founders of non-traditional psychoanalysis: Andrey Davydov and his colleague—psychologist Olga Skorbatyuk.

Book 5. Shan Hai Jing—A Book Covered With Blood. The Story Of Developers of the Catalog of Human Population (by Kate Bazilevsky). This book uncovers the story of developers of the Catalog of Human Population—Andrey Davydov and Olga Skorbatyuk— that is related to obtaining of political asylum in the United States of America due to many years of persecution by the Federal Security Service of Russian Federation (FSB, former KGB) and attempts to kill them in order to take possession of their research product—the Catalog of Human Population.

*****

From the beginning, as authors of the book series Catalog of Human Souls, we would like to apologize for the lack of a single language style and popular language. Our colleagues from the scientific environment, professional psychologists or those, who are interested in scientific psychology, can satisfy their curiosity about the theory that lies at the basis of technology that we use to identify the individual structure of psyche in Book 4 of this series (Non-Traditional Psychoanalysis. Selected Scientific Articles And Presentations At Conferences.).

The other four books in this series are intended for the widest audience. From our point of view, any person, regardless of education level, must have an opportunity to get acquainted with results of our research. After all, Shan Hai Jing, as the Catalog of Human Population, was left to all humanity. Therefore, in many of our books (despite that they are all devoted exclusively to scientific topics) we try to use the literary language, avoiding frequent use of specific terminology. However, we were unable not to use jargon at all, and for this we beg your pardon. We are not writers, our main work is scientific research, and in books we are sharing with the audience some of the results of this activity, according to the common practice in the scientific community.

Speaking of language that we use to describe the topic of our research... It was noticed that some people are perplexed by that we use the word "soul," as it is not customary to use this word in the scientific community. However, as it was found, human soul, which is the same as psyche and subtype structure—exists. And, it exists regardless of someone's opinions about it.

Soul (psyche), as "software" of *Homo sapiens* is not a psychological, religious or metaphysical value—as it turned out, it is purely a natural value. Therefore, like any natural phenomenon (rain, wind, electricity, gravity), the soul functions regardless of whether people know about it or not, and regardless of what they think about this. People can argue as much as they want whether soul exists or not, and fantasize as much as they want about what it is, but the natural mechanism called "soul" will continue to work. In every person, while he is alive.

Therefore, every person has the right to continue debating whether or not the soul exists and fantasize about what it is, but we prefer to study the human soul as an existing phenomenon (which, by the way, is possible to see, hear, smell and touch, if you have information about individual structures of psyche) and use results of this research on practice.

We consider the question of what words to use to call the natural phenomenon "soul" unimportant when it is possible to study it as a phenomenon instead of talking about it. We use the word "soul" because in any language it accurately reflects the essence of the phenomenon—that foundation, on the basis of which any human being lives, and because of which he is alive; that what is called "closer than the body." And, unlike our colleagues-psychologists, we are not forgetting that "psychology" translated from the ancient Greek means "science about the soul" (from the ancient Greek ψυχή - "soul," λόγος - "teaching").

*****

Now, let's get back to the Catalog of Human Souls books series. Those people, who are already familiar with our research and our other books, usually have questions, to some of which we would like to provide answers in the Catalog of Human Souls book series. For example, people are interested to know who exactly is working on compiling of the Catalog of Human Population, and why it is not possible to find information anywhere, including on the Internet, about all members of our laboratory's staff. Also, people want to know how they can get information from the Catalog of Human Population about themselves or other people.

With regard to the question about developers of the Catalog of Human Population and other staff members of our laboratory, it really is difficult to find reliable information about them and here is why. This happens for two reasons: the first reason is explained using an example with the Internet in the Introduction to Book 1 of this series titled Homo sapiens Are Bio-Robots, and the second reason is confidentiality of all of this kind of information and is related to security. The number people in our laboratory, who work on compiling of the Catalog of Human Population, is not three people, as it might seem. However, unfortunately, we cannot provide any information about who these people are. Reasons for this are detailed in Book 5 of this series (Shan Hai Jing—A Book Covered With Blood. The Story Of Developers Of The Catalog Of Human Population).

Due to persecution because of the main subject of our scientific research—the Catalog of Human Population—by a group of employees of Federal Security Service of Russian Federation (FSB, former KGB), headed by colonel of Foreign Intelligence Service (data for the period 2000-2004) Andrey Dmitrievich Polonchuk, we do not have the right to provide any kind of information about our laboratory's staff. You can get acquainted with the evidence of these prosecutions in Book 5 mentioned above. Originals of documents presented there are stored in the United States Department of Homeland Security, Federal Bureau of Investigation (FBI), etc.

Therefore, if anywhere in public sources, for example on the Internet, you come across a statement that someone is an employee of the Special Scientific Info-Analytical Laboratory—Catalog Of Human Souls or the Human Population Academy, and is engaged in developments related to decryption of Shan Hai Jing and compilation of the Catalog of Human Population—it can be either disinformation or fraud, or both. However, we do have partners and affiliates. Therefore, it is always best to check with us.

Beware that some research works of Andrey Davydov (the author of discovery of the Catalog of Human Population) and the Special Scientific Info-Analytical Laboratory—Catalog Of Human Souls led by him were stolen by a group of employees of the Federal Security Service of Russia (formerly KGB) headed by Andrey Dmitrievich Polonchuk—colonel of SVR FSB of Russian Federation (information about his rank refers to 2000-2004). Therefore, it is possible to find offers on the Internet (in different languages) to purchase information from the Catalog of Human Population, even though this information is in no way related to the Catalog or to natural human "software."

Such offers can be found at the following websites: in Russian – Mountains and Seas of Self-Knowledge http://mountaseas.com, Catalog of Human Population (Catalog of Mountains and Seas) http://vk.com/chp_lab, Find The Answer Within Yourself http://www.facebook.com/groups/mountaseas.2905/, Catalog of Human Population http://vk.com/googlite; in English – Shan Hai Jing Lab/Shan Hai Jing Laboratory http://www.facebook.com/SHJLab/info, http://twitter.com/SHJLab and http://shjlab.wordpress.com; etc.

It is extremely dangerous to buy products offered by fraudsters. Since some time back Andrey Davydov suspected that sooner or later, in one form or another piracy will occur and made some inaccuracies in materials related to Shan Hai Jing; without taking them into account it is impossible to correctly put together the base material.

Perhaps, after realizing this A. D. Polonchuk's group decided to get at least some, at least material benefits from stolen works and this is how a strange, ugly product was born, which has nothing to do with information from the Catalog of Human Population as the decrypted ancient Chinese monument Shan Hai Jing.

The consequence of this is that those, who get information from fraudsters cause irreparable damage to their health; both physical and psychical. Unfortunately, our laboratory already has a significant amount of information about cases when people, who requested information from the Catalog of Human Population from those, who officially have nothing to do with this research, experienced serious damage in various matters and of varying degree of severity. The reason for this is the fact that human psychophysiology functions on the basis of images. Therefore, if a person receives images and decryptions (which essentially are images as well), which are in no way related to his/her personal psychophysiology and begins to use this information on practice, then consequences might be as follows:

- psychical disorders of any kind, which cannot be cured
- somatic disorders of any kind, which cannot be cured

- death, as a result of psychical and physiological disorders

Therefore, please be careful. You have every right to turn to anyone for information from the Catalog, but we issued this warning and we will not be held responsible in any way for possible consequences of your decisions.

You can get information from the Catalog of Human Population about yourself or any other person directly from our laboratory right now. For convenience of our clients, the system of issuance of any kind of information directly from developers of the Catalog of Human Population is made in such a way that they do not need to contact us. Anyone can view prices and pay for an order here - https://www.humanpopulationacademy.org/pricing/.

And, for those people, who would like to not just get materials from the Catalog of Human Population sold on our website, but also contact us (for example, with a business proposal, to order of some specific services, to get consultations, to become a student, etc.)—please refer to Human Population Academy's Contacts page at https://www.humanpopulationacademy.org/breakthrough-discovery/contacts/.

Purchasing information from the Catalog through our website or by contacting us are the only ways to get information from the Catalog of Human Population directly from its developer without the risk of coming across fraudsters.

It should be noted that no one ever persecuted our clients; they never were and are not in any danger because those who persecuted and continue to persecute us were never interested in our clients as they do not have information about the technology of decryption of Shan Hai Jing. In addition, we always respect confidentiality of any person, who turns to us for information from the Catalog and we never share information about our clients with anyone.

*****

In conclusion, we would like to state the principled position that we adhere to as authors of books (and, currently there are over three hundred of them)—we do not in any way claim to be gurus; we are more comfortable with the position of students. However, due to the fact that we engaged and continue to engage in research work, we are able to obtain information that can be interesting and useful not only to us. And, we are just legalizing this information for those, who prefer not to believe, but to know. To know how the world works and what is his or her own, personal structure.

Another principal point is that in our books, we do not share our personal opinions, hypotheses. Everything that we state is information from the ancient sources that we are studying and facts obtained during the course of our research activities, which have been tested, as it is customary in scientific practice. We prefer to keep to ourselves our opinions and fantasies, as insignificant in comparison with that what is stated in our books.

Also, on behalf of our colleagues from the laboratory and ourselves, in celebration of the 40th anniversary since the beginning of research of the ancient Chinese monument Shan Hai Jing as the Catalog of Human Population, we would like to express deep gratitude to all of our relatives, friends, acquaintances and colleagues from the scientific environment, as well as to all others, whom we happened to come across in life, for that they failed to prevent us from carrying out this research.

Olga Skorbatyuk and Kate Bazilevsky
Los Angeles, California
June 2015

INTRODUCTION

WHY IT IS NOT WORTH IT TO CONFUSE THE CATALOG OF HUMAN POPULATION WITH A HOROSCOPE

Sketch © 2000 Andrey Davydov

"Seppuku is a private matter of each samurai."
Humorous Russian saying

Before proceeding with presentation of this uneasy topic (due to that for the vast majority of readers it is absolutely new), we consider it necessary to make a brief introduction. We think that this introduction should help readers understand what the Catalog of Human Population is before they begin their acquaintance with descriptions of human programs from this Catalog.

Since, as mentioned above, we are celebrating the 40th anniversary from the beginning of research that led to scientific discovery of the Catalog of Human Population, during this period we accumulated a huge baggage of a variety of reactions to this discovery. However, with all the variety of these reactions, there is one "like a blueprint," which we came across in those, who are not engaged in scientific research work.

For this reason, by publishing one hundred short demo versions of individual programs of *Homo sapiens* from the Catalog of Human Population in this book, we can predict with high probability the initial reaction of some readers to this information. Of course, it is very likely that this reaction will be reexamined after acquaintance with demo versions of descriptions, which will show matches with character qualities of real people whom a person has met. However, jumping to a conclusion from this category can prevent some readers from getting closely acquainted with demo versions and from testing them on practice.

We have long noticed that no matter how much an average person is told about the science called "phenology," about that in nature each type of living organism is born in a strictly specific time period, and that the Catalog of Human Population has nothing to do with neither numerology nor astrology—for some reason, his first reaction is: "It resembles a horoscope." Perhaps in their overwhelming majority, ordinary people are so far from analysis of incoming information that the simple thought that something that resembles some other thing, might not be that thing usually does not occur to them.

It is characteristic of a human to draw conclusions according to the principle of an analogy, when the conclusion about an object gets built on the basis of its similarity to another object. In itself, this method of learning about the world is not bad, but in some situations, such as this one, it does not work. The reason is that in this civilization there is nothing equivalent, of equal value or similar to the ancient source of knowledge, which turned out to be the Catalog of Human Population. Due to this, probably, it is pointless to try to compare the Catalog to something familiar.

Another question is that fans of horoscopes could draw a different parallel and, for example, compare the Catalog of Human Population to encyclopedias about animals or plants, the periodic table, which describes the chemical elements, or an anatomical atlas. However, as our practice has shown, such comparisons usually do not come to minds of average people, as they are not familiar with the periodic table and anatomical atlases, do not study encyclopedias of plants and animals, and are familiar only with horoscopes, numerological descriptions of individuals, and psychological descriptions from popular glossy magazines.

This is the difference between average people and those, who are involved in scientific research. Scientific research work requires a higher level of education and general knowledge about the world, on open mind, and completely other interests. People involved in scientific research usually do not study horoscopes.

However, we think that all this is not our problem.

We adhere to the position that any person has the right to try to fence himself off from the fact that the Catalog of Human Population exists and tell himself that descriptions from this Catalog are similar to another horoscope. Any person has the right to try to fence himself off from the fact that he is a bio-robot and tell himself that Shan Hai Jing is a fantasy of the ancients. Any person has the right to consider us, developers of the Catalog of Human Population, the next oddballs, who are telling about that what they thought-up due to their desire to appear original. We do not object to this. However, there is one "but." These people are the ones, who will suffer from such actions. And, we will explain below why this is so in great detail and with examples.

Descriptions from the Catalog of Human Population are different from any horoscope not only in that they were put together without taking into account any influence of stars, planets, etc. on a human. Since they have no relation to astrology or astronomy, and the orientation on the date of birth is due to natural phenological cycles. These descriptions are different from numerology not only in that they were not made based on influence of numbers on a human (which so far has not been proven by anyone) and take into account leap/common year of birth of a person being studied. These descriptions are different from all other kinds of personality descriptions, including psychological that are made on the basis of results of traditional methods of psychological studies. And, they are different not only in that they are systematized by six factors (intellectual, physical, nutritional, emotional, sexual and environmental), but also in that they are based on an objective source of this information, meaning that they are not fruits of opinions and conclusions made by researchers. And so on. However, this is not what is important. The important thing is that underneath each characteristic of a person in these descriptions are images of his/her individual program or manipulation mode from Shan Hai Jing. And, these images are nothing other than the language of "software" of *Homo sapiens*.

Developers of the Catalog of Human Population get images from a source called the Catalog of Mountains and Seas, decrypt them using a technology specially created for this and, as a result, obtain descriptions of a particular individual, as a representative of a subtype of *Homo sapiens*.

By the way, no one has ever heard that astrologists, numerologists or traditional psychologists describe an individual on the basis of his (or a group's) belongingness to a particular subtype of *Homo sapiens*. Neither we nor anyone else came across astrologists, numerologists and traditional psychologists, who ever mentioned the existence of subtypes within the biological type "human." While the date of birth of an individual from a description, which is made on the basis of decryption of Shan Hai Jing, refers not to the date of birth of a separate individual, but to the date of birth of the entire *Homo sapiens* subtype (there are about three hundred subtypes); therefore, with human population being over seven billion people—there are about twenty million representatives of one subtype.

However, let's get back to images, as the language of human "software."

For those, who are not yet familiar with the Catalog of Human Population on practice, brief information about what Shan Hai Jing, individual programs and manipulation modes of *Homo sapiens* are is provided in the Preface. And, one can learn more about them from the first book in this series titled *Homo Sapiens* Are Bio-Robots. Human "Software" (by Olga Skorbatyuk and Kate Bazilevsky). As for images (individual archetypes), as the language of human unconscious—in order to sufficiently cover this topic, it is required to devote at least a whole book to it, not simply a chapter. However, we will, of course, explain in a nutshell what an image is and its impact on human psychophysiology. And, we will clarify this right here in the Introduction.

Those people, who are already familiar with the Catalog of Human Population and already use it in their daily lives, can see images from Shan Hai Jing (which are behind the individual characteristics of a described person) in descriptions. And, these people are well aware of that knowing information about images of the natural program of some person, as the language spoken by his unconscious and his entire psychophysiology, it is possible to influence him and there will be very serious consequences for his psyche and body.

In essence, this is exactly in what descriptions, which are made on the basis of decryption of images from Shan Hai Jing, differ from any other descriptions; and, not only astrological, but also psychological, which are made on the basis of results of traditional psychological tests and other traditional methods. Since behind descriptions done by traditional psychologists is anything, including their subjective opinions and conclusions, but not an objective source of knowledge about a human and about the structure of his psyche (such is Shan Hai Jing), and not images of human "software."

*****

In itself the ancient Chinese monument Shan Hai Jing (Catalog of Mountains and Seas), decryption of which showed that it is a description of the archaic layers of human psyche, is the richest collection of images. And, any person can easily confirm this by opening the book titled Catalog of Mountains and Seas. However, these images are not some mythological, fairy-tale characters, as researchers before us believed, but the language of... human "software."

Meaning that it is the language of human psyche, the language of unconscious of *Homo sapiens*—language as the key, as the pass into these most archaic layers of psyche of a subject of interest. And, this key, as the saying goes, "opens the doors of the soul" of a person, who someone decided to seriously influence; these doors open wide—as the saying goes, "come in and take whatever you want."

Anyone, who found out from Shan Hai Jing images of the program of a person he is interested in, can easily enter his "holy of holies"—his psyche, his soul. And, through this penetration he can do whatever he wants with this person; without warning and without asking anyone's permission. After all, knowing a particular language, there is always a possibility to speak it, right?

As stated above, behind each of descriptions from the Catalog of Human Population are images of, if we use the computer language, "software of soul" of a human. That is, images of his individual program and manipulation modes. Knowing images that are behind descriptions of an individual, it is possible to do anything you want with this person—good and evil. As mentioned above, this makes descriptions from the Catalog of Human Population cardinally different from descriptions of an individual from the category of astrological and numerological descriptions, which are made on the basis of traditional psychological tests (in our view, these are essentially the same, and we already explained why above).

And, what is most notable is that having such a degree of influence on another person is now possible even for a non-professional in the field of psychology. After all, as it turned out, all information about any person is recorded in his unconscious by natural images, including by images of those natural objects and phenomena, which we can observe around us: mountains, rivers, lakes, rocks, minerals, metals, fauna and flora, winds, rains, tornadoes, floods, drought, and so on.

Therefore, after finding out by images of which natural objects the program of a person of interest is recorded—any person, who knows how to read, can open up encyclopedias of plants, animals, metals, stones, minerals, etc., and find out what specific factors influence images that are in the personal program of this particular person.

Moreover, this influence occurs at the level of life support. And, there is nothing surprising here since images of the unconscious work specifically at this level. A person can imagine himself as anyone in his fantasies—Batman, Superman or even God. However, natural mechanisms that are "mounted" into his psyche exist from birth. These mechanisms work at the level of inborn reflexes and instincts, and not a single "superman" can influence or control their work. Not even a little bit.

To some extent, regulation of work of these natural mechanisms can be done by a person, who knows images of his own natural program and manipulation modes from the Catalog of Human Population and works with this information in a certain way. However, even then there are certain limits. What is left to others, who are not familiar with information from the Catalog about their natural structure, is to twitch on strings of their reflexes and instincts like marionettes; including when someone is skillfully pulling those strings.

Now there is no need to have psychological knowledge, skills, and access to super-secret psychotechnologies in order to "pull the strings" of another person competently. All that "a manipulator of another's soul" has to do is to find out by which images the natural program of a person whom he wants to seriously affect is recorded and read about them in an ordinary encyclopedia. Moreover, in our time, it is easy to do without going to a scientific library; for example, one can visit Internet websites devoted to biology, botany, mineralogy, etc.

After this, it is not a problem to affect the entire system of life support of a person, whom you want to influence in one direction or another. And, this influence will have consequences, which, as it seems to us, are simple to guess when taking about the life-support system. With this kind of influence, it is possible to reanimate, bring a person back to life, as well as to destroy him; moreover, to destroy him physically. Since images, by which natural programs and manipulation modes are recorded in human psyche are the key to his entire psychophysiology—soul and body. Any influence through these images, as the most powerful effect through psyche, certainly will reflect on physiology of a person, on whom this kind of influence is being made.

An image, as it turned out, is the basis for management of a system called "human." However, that is another story and more details about this are included in the third book of this series titled Human Manipulation Modes. Either You Are Manipulating Or You Are Being Manipulated (by Olga Skorbatyuk and Kate Bazilevsky). Here, it is more important to state that individual programs of different people are recorded by different natural images.

Moreover, each subtype program of Homo sapiens contains not one or two images, but approximately thirty to one hundred (and sometimes more). After all, humans did not evolve from apes, have nothing in common with primates, and by their psychophysiological structure are not as primitive, as it is customary to think (even in the scientific community). Natural bio-programs of Homo sapiens might have several different animals, as well as birds, fish, reptiles, plants and many other natural objects, which were mentioned above. This gives a person a greater survival rate compared to other natural objects on this planet.

Not having knowledge of images of the natural program of a person, using an old-fashioned method of "hit or miss" and trying to guess how to influence someone with serious consequences is absolutely useless. The trouble is that even the most wonderful horoscope, "psychic" or "clairvoyant" will not provide this information. Using traditional psychological methods it is impossible to find out by which images individual natural program of a subject of interest is recorded. It is also impossible to guess this (meaning, figure out intuitively).

On the outside, all representatives of biological type *Homo sapiens* look principally the same: two hands, two legs, no tail, hooves, horns, scales, wings, etc. Differences such as eyes, hair or skin and the overall exterior will not answer the question—what are the psychological characteristics, inner qualities of this person, and how he differs from others, who look similar.

Differences between one individual and another are invisible, hidden from the eyes because they are in the psyche; or, to be more specific, in images, by which a particular human program is recorded. As it was discovered, "secret buttons" of control of a person are in the same place. However, as many thousands of years of history of this civilization have shown, it is impossible to figure this out without turning to Shan Hai Jing as the Catalog of Human Population. No one yet has been able to obtain information of this kind because it is a priori impossible. And, this means that it would be impossible to influence someone with a guaranteed result, let alone to influence at the level of life support.

However, in life of absolutely any person situations occur when it is vital to get a working tool to manage another person; but, except for those, who use the Catalog of Human Population, no one knows how to do it quickly, effectively, and, most importantly, with a one hundred percent guarantee. This is not surprising because information about images, as the language of natural "software" of *Homo sapiens*, together with the tool that makes any person one hundred percent manageable, cannot be obtained anywhere except from Shan Hai Jing.

And, in general, this is easily observable simply by looking around. For example, without knowledge of images of a person's natural program from the Catalog of Human Population, it is possible to get rid of an unwanted subject exclusively with the help of criminal actions from the category of "an ax over the head," or actions related to the medical-pharmacological legalized murder. There is no other way.

Even a child is capable of "driving someone up the wall", "provoking to a white rage," frightening, upsetting, making "run on the ceiling" or hysterical. This type of manipulation is primitive and does not require any special knowledge, skills or specific information about a person. However, by nature any human being has a huge reserve of endurance and a great survival rate.

And, what is also important, the influence described above is mainly on the emotional factor, while human psyche, as it turned out, also includes intellectual, physical, nutritional, sexual and environmental factors. The result is that a manipulator, who uses such primitive methods will achieve very little besides a defensive reaction and often aggression towards him from the subject of manipulation.

A different matter is when a person knows images of another person's "software" from the Catalog of Human Population. In this case, it really is possible to do anything with psyche and body of any person; and to do it absolutely unnoticeably, and therefore safely for the manipulator. After all, the subject of attack will not be able to put up any resistance. And, the manipulator will not be punished because actions that need to be made in order to physically destroy a person using knowledge about images of his program are not criminal, are not subject to criminal penalties in any criminal code of any country in the world.

If we continue with examples of actions aimed at physical destruction of an unwanted subject, then if someone has information about images of "software" of this subject—actions will often be very simple to execute, will not require major financial means, and will appear absolutely innocent. Any super-investigator or coroner will not be able to connect a person's death with consequences of such actions.

For example, what is the crime in that one person left another person without access to water for a relatively short period of time? Absolutely nothing, but with a small caveat—if images of natural individual program of this other person do not have, for example, the image "fish." By the way, if necessary, it is very easy to make such person a chronic alcoholic, who, supposedly, "became a drunk on his own and died because of that." Beforehand it is possible to find out from images of manipulation modes of this person (to be more specific, from images of his suppression mode) what alcoholic beverages to offer him, so that he would not be able to say "no" to them. Since a huge number of subtype structures have the image "fish" and all have different preferences in this regard.

Or, for example, what is so criminal in that someone felt that the room was stuffy at night, opened a window in this room where someone else slept as well, it became a little colder than usual, and that someone became a bit cold in his sleep? Also nothing, you will answer, and you will be right. However, the trouble is that there are plants and animals, which die even when there are small changes in temperature. And, what if this is done regularly, and someone opens a window when a person, who is a carrier of such images, is already fast asleep, and then closes the window right before that person wakes up?

Yes, *Homo sapiens* is not a fish and not a flower. By nature he has a much greater margin of strength in comparison with any of animals or plants on this planet. However, if unsuitable life conditions from the standpoint of images of the natural program of a person are constantly created, then psychophysiology of absolutely any *Homo sapiens* will begin to slowly, but surely "fall apart"—one physiological system will fall apart after another until the natural program of utilization turns on.

Here is another example. There are, for example, reptiles that do not eat anything except animal feed such as meat, fish and eggs. We think that you can guess that we are talking about snakes. What can be easier than making a person, who is a carrier of the image "snake," and who does not know his natural program, follow a strict vegetarian diet? No matter under what sauce—religious, health improvement, or to lose weight, for example. Then, all that will be necessary is to wait a little until the entire psychophysiology of this person becomes completely broken due to that his organism is not getting the necessary nutrients from food. Meanwhile, another person does not have similar types of images-carnivores in his program, but has, for example, such images as "a horse", "a deer", "a cow," etc., and therefore, he can be a one hundred percent vegetarian and this will only strengthen his health.

As for a person, who has "a stone" as one of images of his program—it is not very difficult to destroy his entire psychophysiology. All that is necessary in order to do this is only to make him regularly experience strong emotions without the possibility of sharing them with someone. Or to regularly create sudden and abrupt temperature changes, for example, having convinced him that alternations of a hot sauna and cold water are good for him. In these cases all that will be left is to wait until his health begins to "burst at the seams" and finally breaks down. By the way, this image is found in human programs quite often.

In conclusion, we will provide a more in-depth example. A woman decides to take revenge on her man for being unfaithful, and she knows images of his natural program. She knows that, one of these images, among many others, is a natural object reindeer. Therefore, all that she needs to do to understand how to take revenge on this man with the maximum harm to his health is to open an encyclopedia and read about reindeer.

Having learned from an encyclopedia that a reindeer falls into madness simply from being excessively terrorized by mosquitoes, it is not difficult for this woman to guess that all that is needed to carry out an action that is most simple to execute, but which will have terrible consequences in terms of making great damage to psyche and physiology of this men—is a piece of glass wool, gloves and access to the offender's pants. It does not get any simpler.

The financial side of this does not deserve any attention, as costs are minimal. As for the tactical side—it is not a problem for any woman to get access to pants of any man because very few people will say "no" to sex, especially when acting wisely. While the subject of revenge is, for example, in the shower, his pants get turned inside out and the inner side gets coated with a thin layer of glass wool. This layer will not be noticeable while a man puts them on, but once the pants are on—thousands of finest glass fibers will get under the skin of the subject of revenge.

Now imagine a real reindeer, the skin of which got attacked by millions of mosquitoes... Interim results in the form of inflammation of the skin, pain, screams, squeals, tears, rushing to the doctors—do not count because it will be traumatic for any person if the inside of his pants got covered with glass wool. In this example, no one is talking about the result of these actions at the level of physical health of an individual. In this case, the main result will be constantly growing derangement of the psychical sphere of this man.

This, unlike effects from traditional women's manipulation toolkit, like groundless accusations, claims, snotty hysterics and other cheap tricks, is guaranteed to lead to gradual breakdown of a man's physiology.

This example considers an opportunity to make serious damage to physiology of an unwanted subject through derangement of his psyche, which occurred not as a consequence of damage to his skin, by as a consequence of effecting the program image of this man—"reindeer." A man, who does not have this specific image in his natural individual program, would simply have to be treated for purely somatic disorders in such a situation, but these actions would not cause such a serious psychical trauma. Moreover, a trauma, which with time will have a negative impact on his physiology.

Of course, these examples are very primitive and are not methods of quick liquidation of an unwanted subject. Without doubts, there are scenarios that have a quick effect in damaging human physiology by impacting his physiology through psyche (and, psychologists can continue arguing about what is primary—psyche or physiology, but we have found out a long time ago that psyche is primary). However, we do not consider it ethical to share such recipes with the audience.

We are categorically against any violence. We just wanted to warn that it is not a good idea to consider the Catalog of Human Population a horoscope or something similar to that.

After all, none of you are safe from that one day not too wonderful for you— you can become the subject of an attack from this category. And, you will not even notice this because you have no chance to notice this, as you do not know your natural program and images, by which this program is recorded in your unconscious. And, this means that if someone really needs to, by using knowledge about images of your natural program and manipulation modes from the Catalog of Human Population that someone will take away from you not only money, health, loved ones, or something else that you value, but your life.

Sadly, regardless of what anyone declares, people of this civilization love one another obviously unchristianly, otherwise during its history humanity would not have come up with such a huge number of most varied, most devious methods of destruction of "thy neighbour:" from magic spells to the atomic bomb. Therefore, it is very naïve to hope that with discovery of the Catalog of Human Population (from which it is possible to get any kind of information about any person) this information will not be used, including in order to get rid of an unwanted subject from one's path. And, you have no guarantee that this unwanted subject will not be you personally.

Since now in order to physically destroy someone it is no longer necessary to have "ground-to-ground" missiles, to invent most complicated poisons or hellish killing machines. It is enough to simply have information about images of the individual program of a person, who is, as the saying goes "stepping on the tail" and interfering with one's life. Any impact made on psyche of an individual through these images will automatically lead to changes in his physiology (any, including fatal).

Therefore, we repeat that we are in no way opposed to someone considering the Catalog of Human Population a horoscope. Every person has the right to be mistaken. However, as decent people, we are obligated to warn about the possible consequences of such kinds of mistakes. After all, regardless of what opinion we, developers of this research product, have about such cruel, inhuman actions—we are not able to control or affect the process of use of the Catalog of Human Population by separate individuals.

In such situation, we think that every person should worry about his safety himself. All that we can help with is to warn and say that in this situation it would be most wise to find out images of your own individual natural program and manipulation modes from the Catalog of Human Population, so that no one would be able to do with your psychophysiology that what will inflict irreparable damage. As the saying goes, "forewarned is forearmed." And, whether or not you value your own life and lives of your loved ones—is not for us do decide. As the saying goes, "Seppuku is a private matter of each samurai."

After all, regardless of what anyone thinks, no one is safe from a situation where he drives someone so high up the wall that this someone will hate him to death. The reason is simple: natural manipulation modes. After all, natural arranged it so that the individual program of any person is the stimulating mode for someone. And, the stimulating mode is the strongest irritant for any person. Therefore, any person can become the subject of hatred at any point in time. And, in order to avoid this, it is not enough to be "an angel in the flesh:" meek and friendly, affectionate and caring, try to please and appease other people, treat them with kindness, respect. This will not help you.

Another question is that maybe you will be lucky and no one will want to destroy you physically. However, you are not safe if someone will want to turn you into his personal resource. A resource for anything: for getting money or other material assets, free services, help, sex, childbirth, and so on. Whether you like the idea of being used by someone or not—we do not know. However, if you do not understand what the Catalog of Human Population is and why this Catalog was left to humanity, if you do not know your natural program and your natural images, then you now have only two prospects: to become utilized or to become a resource. And, we honestly told you about these prospects.

*****

Now it is time to move on to the main topic of this book—descriptions of individual programs of *Homo sapiens* from the Catalog of Human Population. However, we want to warn you that in these descriptions you will not find information about images, by which programs of these people are recorded—this information can be obtained only by contacting us. We have already stated how to do this in the Preface.

However, first, it probably makes sense to say a few words about what this information is, where it was obtained, why it is needed, and how to use it on practice. This will be discussed in Part 1 of this book.

PART 1

ANYONE CAN NOW
GET INTO YOUR SOUL
WITHOUT YOUR PERMISSION

Sketch © 2000 Andrey Davydov

CHAPTER 1

YOUR LIFE IS NOT PRIVATE ANYMORE

Over many millennia in this civilization, a human got used to considering himself unique and unknowable. This is not surprising "thanks" to efforts of psychologists, who still cannot provide an unambiguous and detailed answer to the question: what is the soul? Although who if not they should know this since "psychology," translated from the ancient Greek, means "science about the soul," and psyche and soul are synonymous.

However, the situation has changed. The Catalog of Human Population was discovered along with the answer to the question "What is psyche and what is its structure?" Thanks to this discovery, which was made in the 80s of the XX century by a Russian researcher and an expert in Chinese culture—Andrey Davydov, it became known that the soul exists.

And, the soul is not some metaphysical, religious or philosophical magnitude, but a natural magnitude—the soul is a biological program. And, human soul is identifiable. In connection with this, all those, who continue to consider themselves unique and unknowable should know that it will be possible to try to defend their uniqueness to some extent, but their unknowability will have to be forgotten. Forever.

You will have to accept that the so-called personal, private life no longer exists and will not exist for any one of you. Before now "privacy" could be bought, ensured by a status in society. Or the opposite could be done: a person could become worthless and poor, so that it would not even occur to anyone to show interest in him or her. Now, the former or the latter will not help people to continue to lovingly preserve their "skeletons in a closet."

All "closets" are open. Human psyche was opened like a tin can. Now anyone can, as the saying goes, "get into the soul" of a subject of interest and see what he or she hides there: what he/she thinks, wants, intends to do, seeks and so on in reality.

According to dictionaries, "to get into one's soul" means to find out secret thoughts and feelings of another person, to ferret out something about someone's personal life, to gain someone's sympathy by any means, to gain trust, to try to evoke a strong feeling of attachment, respect, love in another person towards yourself. All this specifically became possible with discovery of the Catalog of Human Population: now you can find out who the person you are interested in really is (behind self-presentation masks and shows, which are aimed at concealing true motives) and make it so that he/she treats you in the way that you need and does that what you need.

And, with discovery of the Catalog of Human Population, now this can be done to anyone, regardless of race, nationality, social status and other factors, which are minor compared with natural structure of psyche. Humanity has gotten that what it has been waiting for—the "era of global equality" has finally come. Now, a monarch and a janitor are absolutely equal in that any person can get instructions to them like to a coffee maker, and then study and use these instructions according to his or her goals and objectives.

Besides, in order to do this it no longer necessary to meet with a person or to spy on him or her. It is enough to simply read about him or her in a certain encyclopedia in the same way that you read encyclopedias about animals or plants. The name of this encyclopedia is the Catalog of Human Population. This encyclopedia is about people, about *Homo sapiens*; including, about you personally.

It is easy and simple to find out from the Catalog of Human Population who people really are without their masks and self-presentations. Moreover, the Catalog contains details and particulars. What is so surprising in this? This is what the Catalog of Human Population allows. After all, if you open, for example, a professional reference book about dogs—you will find out everything about a dog regardless of its breed, including how to influence its behavior and how to train it. Things are analogues when it comes to *Homo sapiens*.

From the Catalog of Human Population it is possible not only to find out that what you want to know about someone, but you can also use information about this person on practice; for example, in manipulation. Manipulating someone now also became quite simple. All you need to know is exactly what needs to be done in order for another person to begin to obey you and act in a way that you need. In essence, all that you need to do is to act out a certain role. And, in this civilization everybody knows how to act, even non-professional actors.

However, there is a secret. By nature human—bio-robot, as a biological system, is arranged in such a way that he can become one hundred percent manageable, but as it turned out, for every person his own manipulation scenario is necessary, and this scenario is different from scenarios of influence on other people. Numerous seekers of management methods of a system called "a human" have failed because they did not know this secret.

Yes, we know that we live the society of manipulators and that the topic of management of another person is always of a great interest to any person, who learns about the discovery of the Catalog of Human Population because from this Catalog it is possible to easily get the tool for managing absolutely any person. However, here we will not tell about manipulation in detail because this book is dedicated to natural individual human programs, and not to manipulation modes. You can find out about individual manipulation modes and how to use them from the third book of this series: Human Manipulation Modes: Either You Are Manipulating Or You Are Being Manipulated.

CHAPTER 2

WHO IS BEHINDS MASKS?

At all times people try to hide some particularities of their nature from others. As psychological and universal practices clearly show—any person is not in a hurry to reveal to others his or her true thoughts, feelings, intentions, goals, and desires. True motives of a person often remain hidden behind his numerous masks; even from people closest to him.

And, those people, who managed to convince themselves that their souls are "open like a book," that they have nothing to hide, that they are absolutely honest, sincere and open should know that now such fairy-tales are suitable only for children, very naïve adults and traditionally-oriented psychologists. Since psychologists, who do not know about the Catalog of Human Population and human "software," have nothing to orient themselves on except words, self-presentations and other external manifestations of people.

Throughout their waking hours, men and even more so women are busy trying to ensure that others never guess true motives of their behavior. Hence, a well-known fact: on the inside, people are very different from how they want to be perceived. Their true desires, intentions, thoughts, feelings are always hidden deeply within themselves behind countless masks and self-presentations. And, no one wants to voluntarily disclose them.

Very likely this is connected with that at the current level of development of humanity, true motives of *Homo sapiens* are so not far from motives of animals that a person is simply ashamed "to show his true face." So, people are forced to regularly fool everyone around them. And, first of all, they fool themselves since a person can act out a conceived "character" most truthfully only after fooling himself about his own motives. This is how masks, as the saying goes, "adhere to a face."

There is only one main problem encountered not only by psychologists and managers, but also in domestic, personal relationships: how to find out true qualities, motives, intentions of others? How to find out his true moods, attitudes toward other people and events? How to find out what he really intends to do and why? In short, how to ferret out from a person that what, as he thinks, should not become known to anyone else under any circumstances?

With such all-common orientation towards deceit and secrets, getting needed information out of a subject of interest is practically an impossible task even for professional "soul-experts." Since psychologists are usually "feed" with responses to questions and results of tests, which have nothing to do with real motivations of an individual. And, psychologists have nothing left to do except to "eat" this: listen to tales told by their clients, and watch their "shows" with masks and self-presentations.

What to say about the regular people. The only thing that remains to them is to live in fantasies about each other. However, psychologists at least get money for self-deception and "attending shows," which their clients put on, but simple people regularly have to pay for their fantasies themselves. And, the price is often very high. Since the price for incorrect understanding of true motivations of other people, as it is known, can be various troubles, problems and any kind of damage to the one, who was unable to "guess" correctly.

And, guessing this is impossible in principle because a human is a system with a very complex psychical structure. Even today in the XXI century, psychologists, ideologists, advertisers, etc. are trying to solve the riddle of this structure practically without any success. Yes, they learned how to train *Homo sapiens* like a dog since nature did not deprive a human of instincts and reflexes. However, they could not and still cannot "get into the soul" of a human.

Things are not at all easier for regular people from that even professionals are baffled by the riddle of human psyche. Knowledge about the true motives of another person is necessary in daily life of any human. And, sometimes it is vital to have a possibility to influence other people. What to do?

In the Middle Ages there were attempts to resolve this problem with the help of brutal tortures. Not without reason information that people try to hide from others very hard is called by the word "podnogotnaja" (lowdown, background, ins and outs, secret, the whole truth, carefully guarded secrets, etc.) in the Russian language. In essence, this word means secrets, hidden details about something. It originated from the ancient torture of sticking needles or nails under a person's fingernails in order to ferret out that what he keeps deep inside.

"To know the complete lowdown of a person" in Russian language means to know all of his or her secret wishes and desires, passions and predilections, secrets and mysteries, true thoughts, plans, and intentions. In other words, to know those motives, which drive this person. After all, it only seems that people act arbitrarily, "just because." In reality, any actions of any person are always driven by invisible springs, or, using the modern computer language, by programs; invisible programs.

Unfortunately, even today some public structures are not averse to the use of medieval "ways of gaining knowledge" about true motives of people. However, from our point of view, this is typical neanderthalism. Neanderthalism as primitivism, as a consequence of being poorly informed, lack of elementary culture, and lack of knowledge about the structure of human psyche and what psyche is in general.

When one has all this information, any Neanderthal actions simply become unnecessary. Since today any information about any person (including that what he or she carefully hides) can be found out from the Catalog of Human Population—open it and read. It is only necessary to open this Catalog and read the description of any person you are interested in, a person of any gender, any race, any nationality, place of residence, social status, level of education, religious views, and so on. As already mentioned, this is as simple as reading an encyclopedia, for example, about any animal or plant.

The Catalog of Human Population contains any information about any person: what his personal qualities are, how, based on what, and what for he lives, what his natural functions and abilities, goals and objectives, passions and predilections are. In other words, any motives that drive human behavior can be found out from the Catalog of Human Population; about any person. After reading the description of a particular person in this Catalog of Human Souls (not a scientific title, but a popular title of the Catalog of Human Population) and without use of any kind of torture, one knows the entire "lowdown", "lining," in other words—the true essence of the person of interest, everything that he or she hides.

With the Catalog of Human Population, any person becomes like an open book—open the book, read and use received information on practice. If you wish, you can simply prognosticate another's behavior and on this basis build a relationship with this person or, if you want, you can manipulate him, influence, change and model his behavior depending on your personal needs, goals and objectives.

You will ask: is this possible? We are offering you not only to learn about the existence of the Catalog of Human Souls, but also to test whether it exists in reality or not. Right now. However, before you begin to study one hundred demos that we provided for this testing in Part 2 of this book, we think that it makes sense to tell a little bit more about the Catalog of Human Population.

CHAPTER 3

BRIEFLY ABOUT THE CATALOG
OF HUMAN POPULATION

As stated above, the Catalog of Human Population was discovered by Russian researcher, specialist in Chinese culture Andrey Davydov back in the 80s of the XX century. In one the most ancient texts preserved in this civilization, which is titled the Catalog of Mountains and Seas (Shan Hai Jing), Andrey Davydov found about three hundred very detailed descriptions of human characters, algorithms of life activities and functioning, as well as the toolkit for managing the system called "a human."

Conclusions were drawn from this that humanity is a biological type, divided into subtypes, representatives of which cardinally differ from each other by structure of psyche, and that Shan Hai Jing is nothing other than the Catalog of Human Population.

After selecting keys to decrypt the Catalog of Mountains and Seas, Andrey Davydov got an opportunity to get acquainted with contents of this ancient text, which has been written entirely in the language of the ancient mythological images; images, which previous researchers could not understand without decipherment. The result of years of research that he carried out was that by decrypting this ancient Chinese monument he began to obtain descriptions of different people from it. And, he began to find out in detail what these people are really like, what motives they are driven by, and much more. This confirmed the initial hypothesis of the researcher that Shan Hai Jing describes the structure of human psyche.

Also, thanks to the decryption technology of Shan Hai Jing, which was specially developed by Andrey Davydov, it was found that some of the other ancient texts, for example, Tao Te Ching and I Ching, are commentaries to the Catalog of Mountains and Seas as the Catalog of Human Population. A lot of other interesting information was found as well.

After systematizing information about *Homo sapiens* that was being obtained from Shan Hai Jing according to the unique author's system, which he created for this specially and which allows to describe human psyche on six factors (intellectual, physical, nutritional, emotional, sexual and environmental), Andrey Davydov began to create the Catalog of Human Population as the catalog of biological type *Homo sapiens*.

This refers to the Catalog of Human Population in that form, in which any person can get acquainted with it—decrypted, understandable and practically usable. All work on compilation of the Catalog, which as a source existed for millennia before it was discovered by Andrey Davydov, consists only of one thing: translation the language of the ancient images from the Catalog of Mountains and Seas into the language of modern psychological descriptions of individuals.

According to Andrey Davydov's calculations, the decrypted Catalog of Human Population should contain quite detailed descriptions of 293 subtypes of biological type *Homo sapiens*. At minimum. This is not counting descriptions of the next levels of development of representatives of this biological type, which are after the level of primary programs. The next stages of development, as it turned out, are also programmed from the beginning, from birth, and are described in detail in Shan Hai Jing.

By the way, with the discovery of descriptions of levels of development of *Homo sapiens* in Shan Hai Jing, it was found out that if a person follows the path of development, and not the path of degradation, then the program, with which an individual was born, gets replaced by another program. And, this must happen a few times. There are seven stages described in the Catalog of Mountains and Seas, and they are different for each human subtype. All these stages are directed at qualitative transformation of a bio-robot, as a segmental being, into a Human.

One can call these levels (stages) of development by different words "self-perfecting", "spiritual growth"—whatever one prefers, as it does not change the essence. Therefore, for those, who do not want to live their entire lives as a primitive animal, there is no sense in losing any more time in search for themselves and methods of self-perfecting, as all these methods were left to us in the text, which is the Catalog of Human Population.

In view of the above, being born in human form one should not rush to consider himself/herself a human. According to information from the ancient sources, this would be an extremely hasty conclusion. These sources state there that in order to open up one's own human potential, meaning—to become a human, one must study and learn. And, first of all, learn to be himself and not another clone "molded" by the environment, meaning—by parents, mentors and society. However, it is impossible to do this without having knowledge of your own natural individual (subtype) program from the Catalog of Human Population.

As history of development of this civilization has shown, without this knowledge and study directed at opening up a person's own natural qualities and functions—he lives his entire life like an animal. That is, he lives on primitive instincts and reflexes: food, easing of nature, search for food (in the case of a human—work, professional activity), social interactions (communication, entertainment, games, self-presentation, competition), sex, caring for offspring, etc. And, that what should be done, as it turns out, in order to become a human people in this civilization do not do. However, that is a different story.

*****

To conclude this chapter, it should be noted that for many readers the expression "human subtype" might seem unusual. However, on the other hand, what is so surprising in this formulation? There are subtypes within many of the biological types, and this is well known from biology classes taught in schools. Biological type *Homo sapiens*, as it turned out, is not an exception to this rule.

As you know from biology, a biological type (Lat. *species*) is the basic unit of classification of living organisms (animals, plants, microorganisms). It is a group with common morpho-physiological, biochemical and behavioral properties, capable of interbreeding, which produces fertile offspring. And, a subtype means totality of separate populations of a biological type, in which all or most representatives differ by one or several (morphological) attributes that distinguish them from representatives of other subtypes of that same type. In nature, representatives of different subtypes of the same type can interbreed and produce fertile offspring.

Note that the same is observed within the "human" biological type: a representative of one subtype is externally similar to a representative of another subtype, while they have different qualities of personality, behavior, abilities, and life algorithms. At the same time, problems with interbreeding within the single human biological type are also not observed.

However, unlike it is, for example, in the animal world, human children are not antenna-like continuations of their parents. Meaning that, in essence, in most cases people reproduce and raise not their "own blood", "their continuation," as they think, but representatives of other subtypes. In most cases, children are not copies of their parents, as they have a completely different natural program (except for when a child is a representative of the same subtype as one of his parents—a mother or a father), and this causes parents' frustration.

Another "stumbling block" is that children do not need their parents' experience because it is not the experience of their subtype; therefore, this experience gets rejected and this irritates parents. These are far from all problems that exist in parent-child relations in civilization, which existed without the Catalog of Human Population for so many thousands of years (more on the topic of parents-children can be found in the third part of the first book in this series (*Homo Sapiens* Are Bio-Robots. Human "Software.") titled Ahnenerbe: Your Killer Is Under Your Skin). However, this does not at all influence the continuation of human race.

There is really only one problem with human subtypes: subtype characteristics of representatives of the biological type *Homo sapiens* (meaning that what makes one person different from another person, even though they have the same external attributes) are hidden inside, in the psyche. It is not possible to see them, unlike it is in the animal world. For this reason, even for very insightful people with a huge bundle of knowledge, good analytical apparatus and extensive life experience, it is not possible to learn about a particular person anywhere except from the Catalog of Human Population, where all these hidden springs of human behavior are described in great detail.

This is how it is arranged by nature. And, why engage in guessing, if you can know instead, and for this our ancestors left us Shan Hai Jing, the Catalog of Human Population?

As clearly shown by experiments (which were conducted in Russian scientific institutions in order to verify how the technology of obtaining information from the unconscious sphere of a human using Shan Hai Jing works), the percentage of learning of true qualities and motives of a person without the use of the Catalog of Human Population is not large; even when cases are taken on by professional psychologists. The only things left are needles under fingernails and other not very humane methods of obtaining knowledge or self-deception.

However, we think that instead of this it is wiser to look in the Catalog of Human Population and find out who has what, using the computer language, "software" "installed" by nature inside. We think that this is both simpler and more humane.

CHAPTER 4

SIMPLICITY IS WORSE THAN ROBBERY

Catalog of Human Population—sounds very interesting, but too complicated, you say? Well, such reaction is not original. And, apparently, we should give some attention to this fact in this book.

It is known that the level of education and the level of difficulty of tasks solved professionally significantly help a person understand any new, complex information. And, help him determine how obtained information can be used by a person in daily life.

Intellect of a human is as trainable as his muscular system, and if training does not occur, then normal work of the intellectual factor will not occur. It is long noticed that those people, who are far from scientific research activities, or from professional activities such as, for example, security services, but mainly those, who are far from having a sufficient educational level—are sometimes unable to immediately distinguish the Catalog of Human Population from a horoscope, numerology, etc. And, this is not surprising.

Professional activities, which require one to solve global tasks such as foreign policy, force him not only to think globally, but also worry about consequences of his decisions and actions. Such a person understands very well that any mistake could cost him not only his position and status in society, but often his life as well. Probably due to this reason, for example, major politicians and businessmen, officials, not to mention employees of security services, usually do not take long to understand what the Catalog of Human Population is, what they need it for, and how it can be used on practice. These people highly value any opportunity to get reliable, precise information about people, who interest them. And, they know exactly what they need it for, and they also know what will happen if they will not have this information. Therefore, they usually do not take long to ponder the question: do they need to have the instrument to influence other people or not.

However, from our point of view, the Catalog of Human Population (also known as the Catalog of Human Souls) is that kind of heritage of ancestors, which belongs to each one of over seven billion people living on planet Earth. However, at the same time, for example, a housewife, a cashier or a plumber by definition do not have the same level of education as an analyst at an intelligence agency, a major politician or a university professor. And, for many people things really are quite difficult to understand.

The absence of a sufficient level of education and people not engaging in self-enlightenment (sometimes they do not even read books), led to that quite a high percentage of the human population, regardless of nationality, not only have difficulty with, so to speak, "adding two plus two," but even, as it turned out, have difficulties with reading texts and comprehending what they read.

In addition, so-called "ordinary, simple citizens" tend to think that they do not really need knowledge about other people and the ability to manage their behavior. Although in reality this is not true at all. Consider, for example, a housewife who, is at home all day long, "surrounded by four walls," usually has a husband, children, relatives, with whom she communicates every day and with whom she constantly has problems. And, these problems exist simply because she has nowhere to get information on how to correctly interact with them and she does not know for sure what they need and what they do not need, what they want and what they do not want. She is unable to correctly identify reasons behind their actions, their true motives, let alone qualitatively affect them (even her children). (This is how it is in reality, even though in one hundred percent out of one hundred cases, women prefer not to admit their complete helplessness in this matter, even to their own selves.)

However, even if big-scaled plans, high aspirations and ambitions are not inherent in a person (since this is not implanted in some of the subtype programs) each person still has something to lose. And, who knows for whom consequences will be more severe—for example, for a woman with children, whose husband left due to her illiterate treatment of him or for an official, who got fired from his job due to his illiterate behavior in contact with someone superior. The latter usually at least has something to live on (his "savings"), while a recently single mother might not, and in this case she and all her "brood" fall into the public "millstones," where they are, figuratively speaking, made into ground-meat. Or consider, for example, a simple clerk, who has a wife and multiple children, getting fired from his job only because he was unable to correctly communicate with colleagues and bosses, even though he executed his duties properly. And so on and so forth.

Of course, one can simply not trouble himself with finding out true qualities and motivations of other people. For example, a person can trust everyone, basing on principles of the so-called "universal love," which does not exist in nature and has never existed, or, on the contrary, fear everyone. However, this never saved anyone either. After all, no matter how long you persuade a shark that it is a goldfish, it might try to eat you anyway. Probably it is best to know in advance that before you is a shark because at some point it might already be too late to learn about "your neighbor."

As it turned out, the only thing that can serve as reliable help and protection in interaction with another person is knowledge of exactly what specific qualities of personality and natural functions he has; and, use of this knowledge to operate in all relationships, which must be built with every person individually, taking into account specific natural characteristics of the opponent. As experience shows, such knowledge can be obtained only from an objective source, which is Shan Hai Jing, the Catalog of Human Population.

In fact, for the sake of keeping or gaining his own well-being, a major politician or a businessman need to do exactly the same thing as a housewife: know people, with whom he/she communicates, know how to communicate with them correctly instead of random guessing, and be able to manipulate people. Nothing more. The principle and the process are the same everywhere. In this sense, all people are the same: from a president of a country to a representative of the lowest social strata.

It should also be noted that the so-called "highest strata" of human society began to use the Catalog of Human Population a long time ago. What about you? If not, we suggest that you try it out.

CHAPTER 5

DO NOT TRUST, BUT TEST INSTEAD

In the next part of this book you will find demo versions of human programs. These demos are very short excerpts from descriptions of natural programs of different subtypes of *Homo sapiens*, which were found in the text of the ancient Chinese monument Shan Hai Jing and decrypted by its researcher Andrey Davydov.

We presented these demos because, as researchers of the Catalog of Human Population, we do not call to believe in that this Catalog exists and in that we really are capable of decrypting the ancient Chinese monument, which is the Catalog. We are not apologists for another religion where faith is required. We are engaged in science, and science always required, requires and will require proof. And, proof can be obtained only as a result of testing of provided information, and this is what we are offering to anyone, who wishes to do so by using presented demos of human programs from the Catalog of Human Population.

Of course, descriptions are very brief, but these are demos, meaning examples, and are not detailed descriptions. From them you will find out what described people are really like, without masks; although it will certainly be quite difficult to see this completely because you are getting only a tiny piece of information about described people. After all, in all descriptions from the Catalog of Human Population the most interesting and shocking details come after the general description of an individual (which is also much longer than two pages).

However, this is not a problem because by contacting us any interested person can get complete descriptions of a person he or she is interested in. We explained how to do this in the Preface. Moreover, in this book we are providing only one hundred descriptions, while their number is much greater since there are three hundred and sixty five days in a year, and, taking leap years into account, this number is multiplied by two. Developers of the Catalog of Human Population have information about any person, even if you did not find it among demos.

Now that you have these one hundred demos from the Catalog of Human Population, we think that it will not be difficult for you to compare these descriptions to real people, their qualities, life algorithms, actions, and behavior. You can compare them to those people, who live close to you, your family members and relatives, neighbors, friends, colleagues, acquaintances, those you communicate with via the Internet, and so on. Try it and you might learn something new that you did not know before about people, who you think you know. However, most importantly, you will partially or fully recognize these people in provided descriptions and with that you will get a confirmation that the Catalog of Human Souls, meaning the Catalog of Human Population, exists.

However, first we would like to warn you about something. That what is presented in these demos are only very, very small fragments taken from full texts of decryptions of human programs. Therefore, it would be wrong to think that qualities and characteristics of personality presented in any particular demo version are the only ones inherent in described people.

Each person is a huge kaleidoscope of qualities. And, demos present only one or two, so to speak, "pebbles" of this big "kaleidoscope."

One should not expect to find out absolutely everything about a person, whose description you received in a demo. It is very naïve to think that since this is not a horoscope. Figuratively speaking, you will see only a part of an ear, an eye, a horn, a leg or a tail in the picture with an image of some animal. To be even more precise, you will be able to find out only a very small piece of information about a particular individual. And, you should know about this from the beginning.

CHAPTER 6

A HUMAN IS NOT A DOG
AND NOT AN IRON

A human always amazed researchers by the complexity of his structure, both physiological and psychological. However, what to do—a human really is not a dog and not an iron. Even if someone really wants to think that a human is more primitive than an iron. Yes, by nature *Homo sapiens* is a bio-robot, as animals are, for example. However, this does not put him on the same level as animals.

Human "software" is not only absolutely unique in the case of each human subtype, but also contains a wide range of qualities, functions. Due to that natural programs of humans have such a wide diapason of properties and functionality, by nature on the inside of every individual is a rich multicolor of characteristics, properties of character, particularities, motivations, functions, possibilities, abilities, and talents. Therefore, one should not try to consider the entire diapason of a person based on a few fragments of this diapason. That would be the wrong path.

Although this path specifically is very common in civilization, which existed without the Catalog of Human Population for many millennia. Even from psychologists it is possible to hear something like: "This person is kind and decent, and that person is a rascal and a scoundrel", "This woman is a good mother and wife, and that woman is a whore", "This man is always ready to help, and that one is selfish and a fraudster", "This woman is so sweet and caring, and that woman is a cruel, cold-blooded killer." However, in reality, natural human programs easily combine qualities mentioned above in one person.

And, one can easily see this by reading descriptions of people in the Catalog of Human Population. By nature human "software" is arranged in such a way that it can include a wide variety of qualities of personality, which not only complement each other, but sometimes it seems that they contradict each other. However, this is how it is. Therefore, considering a human, figuratively speaking, as an iron that can only iron clothes and nothing else is not only naïve, to put it mildly, but also very dangerous. Since in this case, referring to example provided above, it is possible not to notice that some sweet and caring woman at the same time is a cruel, cold-blooded killer.

"Horoscopism" as the extreme stage of primitivism, hasty conclusions with so-called "labeling" of a person, intuitionism, as attempts to guess what a person is really like, as well as subjectivism as thinking-up and attributing non-existent characteristics and qualities to a person—are all very ineffective methods to classify a human. In ninety-nine percent out of one hundred this leads to mistakes, and sometimes to very tragic ones.

By nature each person has extremely complex, using a computer term, "software." And, each time a human program is a combination of a huge number of various qualities of individuality. Similar to a food processor, any person combines within himself a huge number of most different functions and characteristics.

Specifically this natural variety within each person, which constitutes the structure of human psyche, is the fundamental difference between *Homo sapiens* and any of animals. In comparison with animals, specifically this provides a human with a higher survival rate in the environment. And, most importantly, this gives *Homo sapiens*—bio-robot that natural potential, which, if realized, is able to make him into a being with qualities and possibilities like those of deities described in the mythologies, meaning—into a Human. However, that is a different topic.

A human is not as primitive as it is common to believe even in scientific psychological circles. Even though people live, function and manifest themselves very primitively—this is not an indication of their primitive psychophysiological natural arrangement. This is only an indication of their low level of development, low level of knowledge about themselves, about their natural potential and about how to open up this potential, and nothing more.

In reality, the structure of human psyche is not at all simpler than human physiology. Moreover, as it was found, it is more complex. Therefore, a human cannot be classified and described as presented in any of currently existing so-called "systems of classification." It does not matter whether it is a system of "four temperaments" known since antiquity, psychological, esoteric or horoscopic (which, from our point of view, are all the same, as their authors do not know what really lies at the basis of specific human manifestations) descriptions of so-called "psycho-types", and so on and so forth. In addition, as it turned out in the course of our scientific research, descriptions of human psychical structure cannot be the result of someone's subjectivity. Even when based on tests or other methods of traditional psychological research.

Therefore, we would like to warn readers against attempts to consider a human in a way that they are used to—meaning, from the position of horoscopes. Demo versions that we presented are not for this. These demos are presented so that any person, even without having a degree in psychology, could read the description of an individual provided in a demo and easily compare it to real people, whom he knows or can observe. Also, demos are presented so that any person could get at least some information, about people's true, natural qualities and motivations, which can be observed. In any case, some information is better than none.

CHAPTER 7

HOW TO USE INFORMATION FROM DEMO DESCRIPTIONS OF *HOMO SAPIENS*

Information from demo versions of human programs from the Catalog of Human Population can be used to compare these descriptions to real people or simply to "look behind masks" of these people and see what they are like in reality, real. It should be noted that to "look behind masks" using demos will be much easier than to try to find out what a particular person is like by personally communicating with him or by observing him.

In both cases, the only information that you need to know about a person to whom you want to compare a description beforehand is the full date of his or her birth. Knowing the exact day, month and necessarily year of birth of a person, all that remains in order for one to do the test is to carefully observe that person—qualities presented in a demo will be clearly and distinctly visible.

Date of birth of people born with a particular program is specified in the title of each demo. Please note that it is very important to know the year of birth of a person in order to get information about him or her from the Catalog of Human Population. It is important to know the year for one reason only: to understand whether it is a leap year or a common year.

To make it easier for our readers to determine whether the year of birth of a person, whom they decided to compare to one of the provided demos, is a leap year or a common year—we are including a list of leap years of XX and XXI centuries. All years in this period that are not included in this list are common years. And, if someone is interested in people, who were born before the period specified in the list or will be born after about—can find information about leap years and common years on their own.

Complete list of leap years of XX and XXI centuries:

1904, 1908, 1912, 1916, 1920, 1924, 1928, 1932, 1936, 1940, 1944, 1948, 1952, 1956, 1960, 1964, 1968, 1972, 1976, 1980, 1984, 1988, 1992, 1996, 2000, 2004, 2008, 2012, 2016, 2020, 2024, 2028, 2032, 2036, 2040, 2044, 2048, 2052, 2056, 2060, 2064, 2068, 2072, 2076, 2080, 2084, 2088, 2092, 2096.

Prior to testing information that we provided in demo versions, please make sure that you know the exact year of birth of the person to whom you decided to compare a description. Since if you read the description of people, who were born in common years and the person, to whom you decided to compare this description, was born in one of the leap years, then this person is not suitable for your test; because in most cases this is a representative of a completely different human subtype, with completely different qualities, characteristics and functions.

Coincidences, of course, do happen because the ancient Chinese monument Shan Hai Jing is not a numerological horoscope, but the Catalog of Human Population. It contains two hundred and ninety three descriptions of human programs and, as it is known, there are three hundred and sixty five days in a year. However, it is necessary to know exactly which individual (subtype) programs of *Homo sapiens* repeat multiple times in a year, but you do not have this information.

Of course, it would also best to take gender of an individual into account. However, by and large, it is not essential because representatives of one human subtype (carriers of one subtype program) of both genders differ from each other in the same way as a male and a female of one animal, bird, fish, reptile, etc. subtype (subspecies). In other words, differences are not significant.

Differences between male and female natural programs are mainly in the sexual factor of an individual, and this factor is not present in demos available in this book. (Complete descriptions of human programs always include sexual particularities, preferences and algorithms of representatives of a particular subtype structure in the Sexual Factor section.) Therefore, feel free to compare both men and women to demos from the Catalog presented here, even when a description states that information applies only to a man or only to a woman.

At this time we are not providing information about each person, who might be of interest to our readers. However, we think that this will not prevent readers from testing out our research product. After all, if among presented descriptions you did not find someone who you either know very well or have a possibility to observe, you can always find people described in our demos, for example, via the Internet. For example, in personal profiles on social networks people often include their date of birth. However, be careful with women over forty, as they often provide false data about their year of birth and this might distort results of your test.

To avoid the only complication mentioned above related to year of birth, which might arise in the process of testing of demos, we recommend that in cases when you are not sure about the year of birth—choose another person for comparison. Fortunately, approximately twenty million out of over seven billion people, who populate the earth, have the same subtype program. Among them you will certainly find those, who will help you confirm for yourself the fact that the Catalog of Human Population really exists. And, this means that you also can use this Catalog in all spheres of your life. This makes life of any person much easier, as you will understand very quickly.

CHAPTER 8

FIND OUT ABOUT YOURSELF
BECAUSE OTHERS ALREADY
KNOW ABOUT YOU

Enthusiasm for disclosure of hidden motivations of other people is very understandable. Anticipation of how information about other people's personal characteristics can be used for personal advantage also does not surprise us. However, in this we recommend not to forget that as easy as you will now be learning all the "ins and outs" of other people from the Catalog of Human Souls, it is just as simple for someone to learn about you.

And, it is not recommended even to dream of that having received information about you from the Catalog of Human Population people will not try to use it. As our long-term practice showed, having learned about someone from the Catalog of Human Population, people immediately begin to try using this information in order to influence this person. And usually, this influence is aimed at getting personal benefits for themselves by trying to get something from a person or by using him somehow; not for his good, but for their own benefit.

In this civilization people are far from ideals of the so-called "universal love." They are capable of being kind and decent in relation to another person only in words, which are not very convincing. For this reason, it probably makes sense to learn about yourself because it is possible that others already know about you. And, among them are not only your loved ones, relatives and friends, but also enemies and competitors.

*****

Besides, from our point of view, it will not hurt anyone to know his real self. Since a person, who does not know his natural self is not an individual. And, here is why.

The natural program of a human is recorded by natural images. Or, using the language of science, by individual archetypes, but a person does not know by which ones because he did not have the Catalog of Human Population, from which it would be possible to get this information.

"Individual archetypes" are an analogue of computer software. The difficulty lies in that individual archetypes are implanted in a person from birth, but in a civilization without the Catalog of Human Population, during his life he knows nothing about them. And, this is happening not only for the last few hundred years, but for thousands of years.

We do not know who and when took away the source about software of a human, as a bio-robot at the genetic level. This happened in the ancient times. A human was faced with the fact that he had to survive somehow. And, a human, creating various societies, began to try to create theories. In his time, Thomas More noted that if everything gets taken away from a human, then, first of all, he will begin to create mythology.

From mythological times to this day a huge number of theories, philosophies and religions were created and tried out. They had a sociological basis. It provided for foundation of existence of a human in society on the basis of those images, which were present in these numerous theories. If earlier comparisons with gods were used, for example, "mighty as Heracles," then now it turned into "mighty as Schwarzenegger" and "beautiful as Aphrodite" turned into "beautiful as Marilyn Monroe (or Scarlett Johansson)."

However, that is not really the point. The point is that everyone, without exception, are "schwarzeneggers" and "monroes", "barbies" and "supermen," which means that none of them are their own selves, meaning—as they were created by mother-nature from birth.

To those, who are interested in the topic of artificial and natural "software," it is recommended to read about it in the third part of the first book in this series (*Homo Sapiens* Are Bio-Robots. Human "Software.") titled Ahnenerbe: Your Killer Is Under Your Skin. Here, we just wanted to mention that probably someone is fine with being another clone, like everyone else, and that is his right. However, those, who are not satisfied with the status and fate of zombies, finally got a chance to become their real selves. And, in order to do this it is no longer necessary to look for yourself your entire life, to ask society questions like "Who am I? What am I like? What was I was born for and what am I living for? How should I live?"—and to listen to ridiculous and sometimes openly harmful opinions in response.

This is no longer needed now that there is an opportunity to turn to the heritage of our ancestors in order to get answers to these questions.

PART 2

100 DEMOS OF INDIVIDUAL NATURAL PROGRAMS OF *HOMO SAPIENS* FROM THE CATALOG OF HUMAN POPULATION

Sketch © 2000 Andrey Davydov

DEMO 1

Description Of Women Born On January 4th Of Common Years From The Catalog Of Human Population

Presented demo is a very short description. A complete description consists of a very detailed description of functioning and qualities of personality: a general description and a description on 6 factors (intellectual, nutritional, physical, emotional, sexual, and environmental).

Considered person is an ardent apologist of everything standard and common. This uncompromising woman is a border-guard, who protects precise and strict boundaries of everything that is established, rules and norms that exist in society and keeps a watchful eye to ensure that no one oversteps the bounds. As a shepherd with his sheep, she tirelessly reminds everyone that they must act always and everywhere only in a way that is accepted, customary, as they should because she is a human-standard, a person like everyone else. Since it is a common practice in society to declare principles of peace, kindness, beauty, decency, justice, and so on, most likely this is exactly what this woman will protect and preach the necessity of this for each and every person at every corner. She will insist on, enforce all of these principles, even though such declarations do not in any way reflect on the actual behavior of people and their attitudes towards one another. This woman will tell everyone around her about ideals of Christian love and kindness, moral and ethical purity, sincere faith and will tirelessly tell everyone that they must care about purity of the soul and acquisition of heavenly grace. This person will try to tell everyone about necessity and importance of salvation of the soul and suppression of passions. And, most importantly, she is convinced that anyone who will really try to achieve harmony in their life will choose to achieve it using the common ways of social laws.

This woman has a look of a faithful adept: goodly, gloomily respectable. Her whole appearance as if claims to spread good around, tries to radiate faith and love that are thick like anointing oil and adhere to others regardless of whether they want it or not. This woman seeks to exhort, persuade, and convince everyone with her warm, hearty voice, which, by the way, she uses excellently. This woman is one of those people who are able to literally, as they say, torture others with their "kindness" and wise advices, which they magnanimously and generously spread around themselves.

This woman feels that she is a born leader. Being a person with ambition and aspiration for power, she strives to be the main, leading horse in common harness, while all other people, figuratively speaking, will be only trace horses. Having the ability to take on a burden truly beyond her strength and being an incorrigible workaholic, who gives all her strength to work or an affair, this woman is convinced that without her any work will stop, will not progress, and that nothing and no one will work without her participation, presence. Just as in a team of horses, where the leading horse is the main horse, she believes that without her everything will fall apart like a house of cards. Like any leader, this person seeks to establish and maintain her dictate: she thinks that every person is obligated to live, think, act, behave, dress and so on strictly by her order, or at least under her wise guidance. She considers herself a pillar of existing rules, "faith and love" and other people are simply obliged to correspond to her perception of life. This individual allows herself to frankly, warmly tell the "truth" directly to someone's face, straight from the shoulder and she does this with a kind expression on her face. This woman advises on what to do and how to act, and she engages in this even on weekends and holidays, and totally for free. She is a generous distributor of kind advices. However, due to the fact that this is a woman-leader, it is necessary to remember that the power of her kind advices can make anyone toe the line...

DEMO 2

Description Of Women Born On January 8th Of Common Years From The Catalog Of Human Population

Presented demo is a very short description. A complete description consists of a very detailed description of functioning and qualities of personality: a general description and a description on 6 factors (intellectual, nutritional, physical, emotional, sexual, and environmental).

The character of this person strongly resembles female character types from Soviet films made between 1930s and 1950s, who were played by Lyubov Orlova, Lyudmila Tselikovskaya, Marina Ladynina, Valentina Serova and other actresses of that period: sincere, kind, open, joyful, optimistic women, who, of course, wholeheartedly believe in a bright future! Although in our time these heroines appear somewhat naïve and their smiles more remind of joy of oligophrenic nature—their appeal and attractiveness do not suffer! How can one not have sympathy for them: they are cheerful gigglers, endearing, amusing, and naughty! This woman too is a romantic dreamer, very prominent, bright in her feminine openness. Openness, which perhaps is not so typical in modern women, who mostly show off, pose, while carefully camouflaging their true face, their true essence. However, this woman, in the spirit of almost forgotten Komsomol times, is all plainly visible: "Her soul lies wide open before us!" She likes everything around her to be light, fun, with jokes, songs and dances. Being very artistic, she loves naughty genres such as drawings with prizes, skits by students, and funny and inventive competitions between teams. However, she jokes and plays with those around her in a very friendly way—she makes fun of people and jokes with them in such a way that it is simply impossible to take offense! She even cocks her nose and insists in a perky manner. Warm (sometimes even openly hot), joyful, optimistic, radiant, and glowing, she is one of those people who others often call "Sunshine." Indeed, with her strength, positive emanations she as if seeks to give people warmth like the sun. She has a creative, active, sparkling nature. Therefore, when looking at her, one might feel like saying: "She is not a woman, but a meteor!" As befits a major "luminary," she presents herself as a bright, striking, memorable person, who attracts people like a huge radiant star that is endowed with incredible energy, stunning, attractive force. This woman not only looks like that, she lives based on the principle, which was well expressed by revolutionary poet Vladimir Mayakovsky: "Always to shine, to shine everywhere, to the very deeps of the last days, to shine—and to hell with everything else! That is my motto—and the sun's!"

In her recklessness and tendency for epatage, this person looks like one of those charming barbarians in a skirt, who win people's hearts with their primordial, primeval force, expression, and straightforwardness. However, one should not forget that while she is achieving recognition as "one of us," this woman does not want to be one of many elements of the gray mass. On the contrary, she strives to stand out, to be original and unique! And, joyful barbaric behavior actually helps her achieve this! For example, she can get totally drunk together with others; engage in debauch, sometimes even physical abuse on her part; scoff; crack indecent jokes; tell incredible stories, inventing them on the go. And, she absolutely does not care that she looks like a complete goosey! Another good tool to achieve her objectives is her ability to transform, completely change her appearance. The general direction is only one—to attract attention at any cost. However, on the one hand, this is advantageous to her as a participant of her own show, but on the other hand, this can lead her to a mental disorder. In the first case, it may be extravagance on the verge of insanity that many stars have; in the latter case it can be a complete destruction of that communal niche, to which this person belongs (family, co-workers, etc.), when everything crumbles from her actions and ends in a complete failure, collapse. In yet another case, insanity can serve as an effective method for making original, non-standard decisions in situations when this person works at an emergency management agency, or as a doctor as part of ambulance crew, or is involved in localization of various social cataclysms. In this case, the use of "insanity" can be expressed in extravagant, non-standard actions, which often help to resolve difficult situations. If one day this woman begins to consciously use her qualities and control her passions, she can become a true individual, worthy of status of a leader...

DEMO 3

Description Of Men Born On January 8th Of Common Years From The Catalog Of Human Population

Presented demo is a very short description. A complete description consists of a very detailed description of functioning and qualities of personality: a general description and a description on 6 factors (intellectual, nutritional, physical, emotional, sexual, and environmental).

This man is a strongly pronounced male because he has qualities that are usually contradistinguished from qualities of females (women). He is warm (sometimes even openly hot), joyful, optimistic, radiant, and glowing. Like the sun, he as if on purpose directs all of his vital forces to giving people warmth with his joy, strength, and positive emanations. He is creative, active, sparkling—not a human, but a meteor! He presents himself as a bright, prominent, memorable person, like a huge radiant star that has incredible energy and incredible attractive force. His cheerful, incendiary nature screams to everyone around him: "Life is good!" And, adds: "...and to live well is even better!" He even cocks his nose and insists in a perky manner. Like a cheerful toastmaster at a table, he offers people toasts-slogans, calls to live deliciously, with an appetite, on a grand scale, freely, without any constraining factors and restrictions. He thinks that it is necessary to live with full force: a party should be a real party, a feast should be a real feast, work should be real work, fun should be real fun. And, he illustrates this principle by doing all of this above measure, absolutely without restraint. He is energetic, lively, upbeat and makes an impression of an honest, sincere, straightforward person with an open soul: "one of our own", "an outgoing fellow." However, he also uses his straightforwardness and "wide open soul" as a tool to achieve his goals. He certainly is sincere, though often this is a very attractive cover, behind which stands his true self, unknown not only to others, but sometimes also to himself.

This man can be described as a charismatic individual. Some of his particularities help him in this. One of them is that he always looks for some words, expressions that will put his opponent (opponents), listeners, interlocutors in a state of shock, a strong emotional experience, an ecstatic state and force them to experience brightest memories connected with pleasures. In general, his behavior (words, actions) might be in regard to complete nonsense, but by using phrases in a certain way, he is able to intuitively select them according to a particular situation, a particular person (people) just as accurately as a professional thief selects keys in order to pick a lock. This man uses words and phrases that others use everywhere all the time, and by themselves these words are comfortable, but boring and colorless. However, in his arrangement and performance they have strength, flavor, color and, as a result, force hearts to literally tremble...!

Another interesting ability that he has can be called leg length discrepancy (LLD). However, it is not at all physical, but rather at the level of emotion and movement. The fact is that this person has a particular predilection for work of his lower limbs. This is why, besides keeping track of his movements, walking, which present him in a more favorable way, he also knows how to always use his lower limbs as if he is gesturing with his... legs! With the help of his legs, he always disappears from his interlocutor's visual field. This was defined as LLD and not something else because people with normal legs have smooth amplitude of movement when they walk, and those with LLD, having unequal length of limbs, have sharp amplitude. And, this person constantly turns and spins with the help of his feet, and after he makes his opponent accustom to stationary state of his body, he suddenly begins to make sharp movements with his legs. First, he is directly in front of his listener, then turns sideways, then changes the position of his body as if he is diving and the listener is forced to look for him with his or her eyes... And so, with the help of his leg movements, he constantly changes position of his body in space. LLD also applies to emotions that he transmits. For example, first he paints a picture of how he once got so frightened that hair on his head stood up, and he does this in an extremely contagious manner, makes his audience experience the emotion of fear that he is experiencing, but as soon as people freeze in horror, he abruptly moves on to an opposite emotion. Just as contagiously and inspiringly, he tells a story about how he once laughed so hard that his stomach almost tore; and so on, from tears to laughter, from aggression and anger to hysterics, from irrepressible joy to animalistic horror... He not only experiences vibrant feelings internally, but has a talent (knows how) to very accurately transmit them to an audience using words, facial expressions, gestures, voice, tone, and other means of communication. He can do this so masterfully that his audience will experience cold sweat from horror, then become covered with goose bumps from excitement, and then immerse into joyful euphoria. In combination, all these techniques—selection of phrases, changes of body in space, evocation of sharp changes in emotions—as if turn the audience into a piece of steel that is tempered by temperature amplitudes from 0 to 1,000 degrees Celsius. As a result, this man succeeds in leaving an unforgettable impression of himself...

DEMO 4

Description Of Women Born On January 9ᵗʰ Of Common Years From The Catalog Of Human Population

Presented demo is a very short description. A complete description consists of a very detailed description of functioning and qualities of personality: a general description and a description on 6 factors (intellectual, nutritional, physical, emotional, sexual, and environmental).

This woman perceives herself a titled person, at least a duchess or a princess, but more likely a queen or an empress. Regardless of who this person is in real life, no matter what social position she occupies—her self-sentiment is that of a ruler, a sovereign; moreover, a perfect ruler: kind, wise and, of course, outstanding, superior to all. This woman might be a cashier at a supermarket, or live in a shelter for the homeless. She might have no special knowledge or even a standard required education, no extraordinary talents or any skills at all. In any case, she behaves like a queen always, everywhere and with everyone.

This individual considers herself a blue-blooded person, one who is no match for all other people. She stubbornly believes that she has all thinkable qualities that exist in nature. Since, as it is known, the status of an empress, as an expression of the essence of monarchical layer, claims the role of no more and no less than that of an intermediary between heaven (God's will) and earth (people). That is ideally, but in real life similar mission is available to very few monarchs, at least because usually they do not have some personal qualities that cardinally differentiate them from their lieges. Ideally, an empress must be the etalon carrier; she is called upon to demonstrate to her lieges that sounding of personality, which would be consonant with "music of heaven." However, more often sovereigns of this level amount to despotic petty tyrants, capricious, with claims and try to implement self-legitimized unlimitedness based on the principle "I do as I want." Exactly the same behavior can be observed in this woman (towards others as well). She is similar to a capricious blue-blooded person, who, without being something special, only by the right of her birth claims to rule over other people. She purports to do what she pleases and does not care about wishes of "some heaven." Execution of her personal will is much more important to her.

This woman considers herself as a person, who has qualities, which are the etalon for all other people, are exemplar, and most importantly—a reason for people to obey her unquestioningly. And, it does not even occur to her that these qualities might be far from real etalons. That is what she decided and it is enough. In case someone doubts her dignities and superiority, if there is a need to prove her exclusivity to someone, then this woman will stand up for herself. She will, so to speak, dig the ground with her nose and do whatever it takes to prove that she really is above all in her dignities and qualities. Even if the proof will not seem too convincing to other people, this will not in any way affect her exorbitantly high self-rating and exorbitant ambitions. All doubts will be written off as stupidity of others, that they are simply unable to evaluate her dignities because they are nobodies and can only be nobodies.

Inside herself this woman clearly knows that she is superior to other people, better than they are, and therefore she is worthy to command, dominate, control, and rule over them. In this sense, it is a waste of time to try to change her opinion in regard to her rights and dignities, or to try to challenge her actions and decisions. This woman is tends to reason more or less like this: "I consider myself wonderful no matter what, and this gives me every right to do what I want. And, all other people have the right to do only what I want."

Having this kind of sense of self, this person behaves accordingly—as a sovereign. It does not matter if she is heading to a board of directors meeting or to a store for some milk; it does not matter how she is dressed— in a suit that is worth tens of thousands of dollars and diamonds, or sweatpants stretched out at the knees. It really does not matter whether she is sitting in the back seat of a huge luxury limousine, or is steering the wheel of some old automobile covered with corrosion. It absolutely does not matter how much money she has in her bank account, and whether she has access to gold reserves of a country or a couple of crumpled dollars and some change in her wallet.

Even if she washes cars, sells gasoline at a gas station or wipes off other people's spits and scrubs off dried up gum at a public restroom—in any case, she will always find a way to show you who she is and who you are. For example, by her posture, voice, facial expressions, tone that she will use to talk to you. She might pour a bucket of dirty water over your feet as if by accident, and when you become outraged she will find a way to show you how insignificant you are compared to her.

In any situation, this person's posture is prideful, steps are measured, manners are regal, and her behavior is haughty, stately and patronizing. Just try not to get angry and make claims because if you do, you will see what it means to debate with a person who thinks that she is a person of the highest rank!...

DEMO 5

Description Of Men Born On January 11ᵗʰ Of Common Years From The Catalog Of Human Population

Presented demo is a very short description. A complete description consists of a very detailed description of functioning and qualities of personality: a general description and a description on 6 factors (intellectual, nutritional, physical, emotional, sexual, and environmental).

Considered person perceives the entire world as a world of doors, by opening which it is possible to get into some social layer or field. His objective is to find that cherished one, entering which will provide him that environment and way of life, which he seeks. In other words, like the well-known character from the tale by A. Tolstoy called Buratino, who wanted to get to the world that was painted on a canvas, this person seeks to enter that door, behind which happiness, wealth, wellbeing, public recognition in the form of numerous prizes, awards, respect, and so on await him. He reasons that since these doors exist, all that remains is to find that "golden key," which will open the necessary door; although it is possible that during some periods of his life he is not fully aware of this. For example, in his youth, being quite primitive, roughish, careless and featherheaded, not having an understanding of the purpose of studying as such, this man might cherish an illusion that the world is one open door, behind which every person anxiously awaits him. Influenced by such fantasy, this man is capable of being deeply convinced that it is not at all necessary to be someone, to study society and look for "keys"—it is enough to simply see him, to see all his, as he thinks, numerous dignities, and then all doors will automatically swing open in front of him! During this period, he is not yet aware of the fact that high opinion of oneself must also conform to reality, and that studying is a necessary condition in order to be able to get to where he wants to be; that studying is exactly that what provides the key(s) that he is so eager to have, and which opens any doors. Although very soon life experience will, of course, clearly show him how deep were misconceptions that he had during his younger years, and possibly he will quickly be removed from the list of underachievers at a school or a college and become one of quite good students. One day, this person will understand that one must also really make efforts, that a lot of persistence, utmost effort is required in order to be able to open any doors. And then, he will draw a very important conclusion for himself and decide that, first of all, it is necessary to do something and not just sit idly, in other words—to act energetically; and from that moment on the process will move forward for him. Once he understands conditions and toolkit needed to reach his objective, this person will start to, metaphorically speaking, puff like a steam engine, as he will make efforts to execute all actions energetically: whether it is learning, development of new skills, or acquisition of experience and professionalism, which, of course, are also necessary. And, this man will consider this algorithm as a guarantee of success. However, sometimes his vigor will take a bad turn since he will not just knock on the next door, but will rather try to kick it open. Of course, this will not always be successful. However, despite the understanding in his mind that in order to enter cherished doors it is not at all necessary to break them, to act highhandedly, and despite the realization that quite different rules and conditions apply here, that keys are necessary in order to enter—still he literally becomes ferocious if he experiences difficulties with some door! And, he begins to actually break it, knock it out with his shoulder, and this is not a mistake or stupidity, but simply his particularity. In itself, the idea to break most durable doors, behind which, as it seems to him, is a coveted world of wonders, causes great enthusiasm in him. And, he is ready for anything in the process: super-efforts and most desperate actions! When observed, this man literally charms, shocks, and stuns the audience by his attempts. Even though, in principle, he is one of those realistically minded people, who tend to take circumstances into account—still he can seriously deviate from this rule in the situation described above. However, the important thing is that by nature this man has a great ability to break through, and, sooner or later, he learns to act with maximum efficiency, like a skilled burglar, against whom no "door" can withstand.

In addition to his great ability to break through, this person also has other tools for "breaking-in": he is a very deft, quick-witted, inventive and resourceful man, and he does not shun to actively use one of the most effective means of communication—flattery and toadying. If necessary, he is able to not only be very amiable, but he is also not afraid to show himself as a complete amateur in some area, or be an onhanger near a higher ranked, important person for some time. He is sociable and maintains friendly relations with all of his acquaintances (classmates, fellow students, members of his social class, his guild). However, his attitude towards a particular person with whom he communicates is firmly determined by that category, to which he assigns this person: what class, what type—above or below himself. And, he will certainly take into account whether a person can somehow help him advance in his career (recommend, promote, put in a good word) or not...

DEMO 6

Description Of Women Born On January 23rd Of Common Years From The Catalog Of Human Population

Presented demo is a very short description. A complete description consists of a very detailed description of functioning and qualities of personality: a general description and a description on 6 factors (intellectual, nutritional, physical, emotional, sexual, and environmental).

Considered person has a particularity: she makes an impression of a completely self-sufficient person. She makes such impression is due to her sense of self as a self-dependent person, wholly and entirely autonomous. It seems that this woman does not manifest herself in any way and reminds of the Sphinx, calmly looking at two-legged beings that potter about, run and fuss around by its feet. Just like the above-mentioned cultural object, she literally exudes a sense of immutability. When observing her facial expression, habits, character and trajectory of movements, it seems that in front of you is a person of a high rank, who holds an authoritative position, is capable of and possesses a lot, has unlimited rights and possibilities—a person who is carrying out a mission of universal significance!.. It seems to an observer that due to some special status this woman obtained absolute internal and external calmness, and because of this now she represents an impenetrable, unattainable monolith. A sense of inner dignity of this person combined with permanent state of nirvana present her as a female-Buddha. Of course, she is capable of rushing about, while being suppressed by some unfavorable life situation, and, usually neatly groomed, neglecting her appearance when she is alone with herself, or forgetting about her calmness and greatness and pulling her hair out in distress: "My life is a failure!" Sometimes she might get lost in doubts, go on a spree, became hysterical or excessively romantic: "Oh, I dream of vast sky!" However, it is absolutely safe to say that no one will ever be able to tell this from her appearance or her face! This woman has a truly inscrutable face, it does not reflect any of her inner feelings and it is impossible to observe neither suffering, nor hesitation on it. However, it is not possible to say that this woman's appearance is just a cover. Behind a passionless mask of the Sphinx is a woman made of iron and concrete—powerful, strong, and unbendable. Once this steel-woman sets a goal, she goes towards it without any flexibility. And, no one can turn her away from it. And, she is committed to ensuring that she will always be like that, and so she does everything in order to have the strongest position in her life.

This woman is of colonial type, she aims to capture as many territories as possible, once she makes them her own—she will enforce her own order, which will also be made of iron, just like she is herself. These orders will be enforced for herself and for others. Being a wise colonizer, she takes into account the fact that others have needs and that it is necessary to satisfy them in order to get benefits for her own self. In other words, figuratively speaking, in order to get milk from a cow, it is necessary to graze it, take it to a bull, and, of course, milk it! And so, this woman patiently cultivates, feeds, and even overfeeds social areas that, from her point of view, provide a valuable product. However, she maintains her position of using strict measures, policies of blood and iron. A social territory that provides her with an opportunity to get rich is considered holy land, and she will fight for it to the last drop of blood. In addition, this woman is different in that she always does things carefully, scrupulously, in a detailed manner, and does not leave anything to chance. Similar to work of a jeweler, all her activity is based on calculations of extremely high precision. She is not like some of other people, who act according to their "intuitive knowledge of the world!" She does not make any random actions, and does not act based on principles of faith or luck. She is one hundred percent pragmatic, always very precise and very specific in her approach to any person in any life situation. This woman-general always has a detailed plan for processes that take place under her leadership, as well as clearly developed strategy and tactics.

By nature this woman is a puppet master. In any communications and situations she feels that she is in the role of Mangiafuoco and perceives others as marionettes on the stage of her puppet theater. She pre-calculates actions and directs, controls people by pulling the strings in accordance with her manipulative objectives...

DEMO 7

Description Of Men Born On January 24th Of Common Years From The Catalog Of Human Population

Presented demo is a very short description. A complete description consists of a very detailed description of functioning and qualities of personality: a general description and a description on 6 factors (intellectual, nutritional, physical, emotional, sexual, and environmental).

A characteristic particularity of this man is that he perceives himself as quite significant, and not only capable, but in his view, also destined to change this world. In other words, this person's ambitions are very high. By nature this person is very domineering, and since he is from the category of system specialists he thinks that it is necessary to review everything based on a systematic approach, to rethink and change the existing system. This person will position his proposed innovations as extremely positive: the world, he says, should be changed for the better. In general, it is characteristic of him to demonstrate brightest, most kind, pure, and good intentions. However, he is not in a hurry to take interest in someone else's opinion about his reforms; by and large, he is not interested in anyone's opinion. He considers himself to be of bigger scale than society. Hence, his conviction that society should be concerned with matching up to him and not vice versa. In this connection, it is no wonder that opinions of some, from his point of view, "bugs" in regard to anything—his plans, perceptions, views, actions, and so on—are not taken into account. Getting someone else's opinion? That is just nonsense, he thinks. Everything that does not coincide with his views, decisions, and goals can simply be ignored. This person holds the following position: he is right, always and about everything, and even when he is wrong. However, even if it occurs to someone to bring him out into the open, to prove him wrong, to show the groundlessness of his statements or something similar to that—it would be a completely useless exercise. In such situations this man is never lost and usually says that he was simply misunderstood. He will always whitewash himself, and then explain and clarify everything. As a result, the attacker will be made a fool of. Certainly, if this man does not concern himself with education and only claims to be always right, then in the eyes of a bystander he will look like a complete idiot, who makes claims, but does not correspond. However, he does not care about this either. This individual considers himself an authority. And, if he notices that the degree of his credibility, in fact, leaves much doubt—he will not be embarrassed, but rather will inflate his authority, just like a special device for inflation of balloons inflates yet another balloon. And, here he is, as he sees it—weighty and reputable, so to speak. And, as he thinks, nobody knows that on the inside he is empty, that his authority is like gold plated jewelry—phony. As he thinks, all means are good here. He might use grand gestures, exclusive expensive gifts, demonstrate attributes of an authoritative person, and so on. For example, he might get a cane to appear more respectable and walk around swaggered. Also, he is very concerned with his reputation—he wants it to be spotless. He also tends to whitewash and make up excuses for everything and everyone (first and foremost, for himself, of course). This man will not just explain anything, but will also camouflage anything at all, will present it in the best possible light. It is said about some people: "He sees things through pink glasses," and, in the same way, this person sees things through white ones. Especially, of course, the above-mentioned quality applies to his own actions: as he says, he is always pure as a virgin, innocent no matter what he had done.

By his nature this man is very active, and it is easy to observe this quality in all areas of his life. Take, for example, his relationships with the opposite sex. He is like a pioneer—always ready! Usually, there is not one and not two, but a whole herd of women! And, of course, if this man was not and is not get sick with something that is dangerous to his potency, then you will see a real stallion. After all, specifically this comparison usually comes into play in regard to manifestations of temperament demonstrated by this man. He has enough energy to not only get himself this huge "herd," but also to make sure that no woman in his "herd" is left with nothing and takes offence in regard to sexual matters. He also has enough energy to protect all his women from being bothered by other, if it is possible to say, "males" and ensure that no one dares to even lay their eyes on them. This man is extremely jealous and will not tolerate any even slightest efforts of other men in the direction of his harem—he will fight desperately! When it comes to protection of his "herd," he becomes completely, in the language of slang, turretless, and without thinking too much gets into a fight. And, by the way, it is noteworthy that his harem always grows! He does not lack energy for this either! In principle, if one wants to, he or she can easily observe such activeness in all other areas of life of this individual. He is very communicable, fiery, perky—a kind of playboy-jollier. Sun, water, yachts, sea, cheerful company, music, dancing, ladies...

DEMO 8

Description Of Women Born On January 28th Of Common Years From The Catalog Of Human Population

Presented demo is a very short description. A complete description consists of a very detailed description of functioning and qualities of personality: a general description and a description on 6 factors (intellectual, nutritional, physical, emotional, sexual, and environmental).

This person can be called by a variety of epithets, but the most accurate definition would be—"a reformer." Of course, reforms as such can be very different, but in this case, before us is a reformer as a destroyer or transformer of culture. One of the main functions of this woman is transformation, and that, as a radical remake of something, is always connected with a greater or lesser degree of destruction since in order to build something new, first of all, it is always necessary to break free from the old. In her case, transformation is not only a transition from one quality to another (sometimes the exact opposite), which, in principle, is standard, but also this transformation is directed at an individual. In other words, this woman specializes in transformation of individuals. Transformation as a process that has its own precise algorithms, rules, goals and methods, in this case is influenced by particular characteristics of this specific person. One of them is that she reshapes or gives new qualities to this or that individual by the means of acculturation. (Or rather that what she personally sees as acculturation.) Another particularity is that she gives preference only to extraordinary people, and better yet those, who fit the category of outstanding. And, the more unusual, talented, bright, metaphorically speaking, "the log" is—the more interesting this peculiar "Mastro Geppetto" considers work on transforming him or her into a "Pinocchio" in a way that she sees fit. It should be noted that the process of choosing of a subject is quite precise, as by nature this woman has an internal, built-in device, which almost unmistakably determines sizes (scale) of two or more objects and selects the larger. (Of course, sometimes even she makes mistakes, and selects as a larger object, for example, a nobody, who is bloated from his sense of self-importance or is simply a good actor, who is playing the role of someone significant. However, this does not happen often.) And, as already mentioned, the larger the scale and talent, the more majestic and grandiose a person that she meets is—the bigger the flare of her desire to change him. If this woman comes across a truly brilliant personality, then that person will be graded down and reduced to the level of, as the saying goes, gray mediocrity by any means.

There is no doubt that if she would have caught Einstein in his time, then today no one would know his name because he simply would not have become a prominent scientist. It should also be noted that this principle works in regard to groups as well: any individual, who stands out from the general mass of a community, this woman will bring, so to speak, to a common denominator by any means, or expel, or even destroy him or her. Her efforts will be directed to ensuring that a group consists of individuals, who are of equal value, absolutely equal by their mass, properties, and scale. And, from that point, these people, of course, can no longer be attributed to the category of individuals—thanks to her transformations they can now be attributed to the category of general mass of rather primitive forms, as components of a single social organism. And, all this will be referred to by the word "life." She thinks that there should not be any Einsteins in a group. She thinks that people must be transformed into a single whole, like grass on a soccer field, and if a tree will suddenly grow on that field, then, naturally, it will have to either be grubbed out or sawed. All this strongly reminds of a situation, in which a music lover remakes a truly brilliant music piece into a schlager, arguing that it would be a really folksy, mass, popular product. For example, at some research institution, this woman would regularly organize a variety of social events, factually sabotaging the main activities, distracting from the actual research work and, consequently, cutting off the possibility of someone going beyond the gray mass based on new discoveries and achievements. The goal is: to saw, to destroy, and eventually to actually reduce an individual to the scale of yet another small screw of a large mechanism called "society"; to make the subject of transformation fall under the category of gray mass, "just like everyone else," make him or her into an easy-to-use social product. Specifically this process, which is also called by the word "socialization," is the task of this woman's life. Another property of her transformations is that she acts in the role of Procrustean bed, ruthlessly breaking limbs of those who were laid in it, those who turned out to be above standards, and forcibly pulling limbs of those, who do not live up to the etalon accepted in society. In short, all actions of this woman are directed at either, so to speak, re-dyeing a white crow into the "right" color, or destroying it. And, in this her success rate could not be better...

DEMO 9

Description Of Women Born On February 6th Of Leap Years From The Catalog Of Human Population

Presented demo is a very short description. A complete description consists of a very detailed description of functioning and qualities of personality: a general description and a description on 6 factors (intellectual, nutritional, physical, emotional, sexual, and environmental).

Considered person does not belong to the category of people referred to as "lone wolves" and those, who drift, so to speak, on the waves of life in a single copy (alone), feeling quite comfortable. A metaphorical definition of the state "alone on an ice floe" is not about her and not for her since this woman was created by nature as part of a tandem, a link in some social mechanism. She cannot go through life and act successfully without having a connection with someone or something, either a person or an affair—she absolutely requires a partner or partners in affairs and in private life. That is why, if she devotes herself, for example, to musical creativity, she will definitely seek to sing or play in a duet with someone. With the same determination, she also cannot live without some affair; in her case, it might be some joint project, in which she will be able to realize herself in a pair with someone. Naturally, this will be on equal and mutually beneficial terms; she is not only for partnership type of relationships in the best sense of the word, but she herself is a good ally as well. In collaboration with someone this woman will not only function properly, precisely and cohesively, but also will manifest herself as extremely fruitful, making one magnificent creative product after another. For example, being engaging in a literary activity together with someone, she will produce a series of wonderful works; for example, romance novels or scripts for television series. Moreover, all of her creative products will be very high quality because this person does not belong to the category of people, who prefer quantity over quality; on the contrary, she is a supporter of a job well done and certainly fully completed. The fact is that this woman has a valuable quality: when she begins her work on a certain product—she struggles to finish it, does not leave it halfway done. For example, being a musician or a composer, if she writes a song, and not one, but several, then she considers it necessary to finish all of them, unlike it often happens with creative people, who leave their works in the hopes of returning to them, so to speak, "when the inspiration returns." In her case, things are different: if she began something, then she must finish it and output a quality product. It does not matter whether it is a song, a musical composition, a literary work, or something else. Her works might have varying degrees of success, they might resemble one another or be different, but it is a fact that they are fully completed, finished products. Another characteristic particularity of this woman in regard to partnerships is that once, so to speak, she clings onto someone, she remains in contact with that person only until she learns and knows how to do everything that he or she knows. Once she gains experience and knowledge of her partner, she quickly loses interest in him and at that point works in the direction of surpassing the level, knowledge and skills that he has. And, the groundwork that she obtained in the process of communication and independent work often gets used to in turn become a teacher, a mentor for someone herself; plus, to obtain a reputation of a woman, who knows everything and teaches everyone.

By nature this woman is a careerist. Therefore, even if she chooses family as the main field of her activities, anyway she will strive to make a career out of it, which in her understanding means having a significant place among couples by becoming an exemplary, model wife, who knows it all, and on this basis gives wise advices, counsel, and recommendations left and right. However, even though family is very important in this woman's life, it is not the only field of possible applications of her strength, especially considering her desire and ability to achieve mastership in quite a wide range of fields of professional activity. Some of the tools used for success are strictness and high demands in regard to her own self, as well as others, be it partners or pupils, whom she fosters with all of her might. In this process, she is not only strict, but also fair. She is direct when expressing her demands, opinions, "pro" and "contra." Very often this woman openly scolds not only children, but also adults and her work partners. As it seems to her, she does this to stimulate them to take actions, to produce and cultivate something, whether it concerns pulling out weeds, making a creative product or doing business. And, she does not save time and energy on this since it is extremely important for her to create a microclimate for a team in which her partners do not mope around, loose spirit, and stop working. Therefore, this woman is very persistent in her actions in regard to raising, so to speak, the fighting spirit of her associates and accomplices. In the process of such stimulation she might overdo it at some points and get in trouble or conflict, but this will not stop her...

DEMO 10

Description Of Women Born On February 7ᵗʰ Of Common Years From The Catalog Of Human Population

Presented demo is a very short description. A complete description consists of a very detailed description of functioning and qualities of personality: a general description and a description on 6 factors (intellectual, nutritional, physical, emotional, sexual, and environmental).

Considered person does not belong to the category of people referred to as "lone wolves" and those, who drift, so to speak, on the waves of life in a single copy (alone), feeling quite comfortable. A metaphorical definition of the state "alone on an ice floe" is not about her and not for her since this woman was created by nature as part of a tandem, a link in some social mechanism. She cannot go through life and act successfully without having a connection with someone or something, either a person or an affair—she absolutely requires a partner or partners in affairs and in private life. That is why, if she devotes herself, for example, to musical creativity, she will definitely seek to sing or play in a duet with someone. With the same determination, she also cannot live without some affair; in her case, it might be some joint project, in which she will be able to realize herself in a pair with someone. Naturally, this will be on equal and mutually beneficial terms; she is not only for partnership type of relationships in the best sense of the word, but she herself is a good ally as well. In collaboration with someone this woman will not only function properly, precisely and cohesively, but also will manifest herself as extremely fruitful, making one magnificent creative product after another. For example, being engaging in a literary activity together with someone, she will produce a series of wonderful works; for example, romance novels or scripts for television series. Moreover, all of her creative products will be very high quality because this person does not belong to the category of people, who prefer quantity over quality; on the contrary, she is a supporter of a job well done and certainly fully completed. The fact is that this woman has a valuable quality: when she begins her work on a certain product—she struggles to finish it, does not leave it halfway done. For example, being a musician or a composer, if she writes a song, and not one, but several, then she considers it necessary to finish all of them, unlike it often happens with creative people, who leave their works in the hopes of returning to them, so to speak, "when the inspiration returns." In her case, things are different: if she began something, then she must finish it and output a quality product. It does not matter whether it is a song, a musical composition, a literary work, or something else. Her works might have varying degrees of success, they might resemble one another or be different, but it is a fact that they are fully completed, finished products. Another characteristic particularity of this woman in regard to partnerships is that once, so to speak, she clings onto someone, she remains in contact with that person only until she learns and knows how to do everything that he or she knows. Once she gains experience and knowledge of her partner, she quickly loses interest in him and at that point works in the direction of surpassing the level, knowledge and skills that he has. And, the groundwork that she obtained in the process of communication and independent work often gets used to in turn become a teacher, a mentor for someone herself; plus, to obtain a reputation of a woman, who knows everything and teaches everyone.

By nature this woman is a careerist. Therefore, even if she chooses family as the main field of her activities, anyway she will strive to make a career out of it, which in her understanding means having a significant place among couples by becoming an exemplary, model wife, who knows it all, and on this basis gives wise advices, counsel, and recommendations left and right. However, even though family is very important in this woman's life, it is not the only field of possible applications of her strength, especially considering her desire and ability to achieve mastership in quite a wide range of fields of professional activity. Some of the tools used for success are strictness and high demands in regard to her own self, as well as others, be it partners or pupils, whom she fosters with all of her might. In this process, she is not only strict, but also fair. She is direct when expressing her demands, opinions, "pro" and "contra." Very often this woman openly scolds not only children, but also adults and her work partners. As it seems to her, she does this to stimulate them to take actions, to produce and cultivate something, whether it concerns pulling out weeds, making a creative product or doing business. And, she does not save time and energy on this since it is extremely important for her to create a microclimate for a team in which her partners do not mope around, loose spirit, and stop working. Therefore, this woman is very persistent in her actions in regard to raising, so to speak, the fighting spirit of her associates and accomplices. In the process of such stimulation she might overdo it at some points and get in trouble or conflict, but this will not stop her...

DEMO 11

Description Of Women Born On February 15th Of Leap Years From The Catalog Of Human Population

Presented demo is a very short description. A complete description consists of a very detailed description of functioning and qualities of personality: a general description and a description on 6 factors (intellectual, nutritional, physical, emotional, sexual, and environmental).

This woman is a ruler, who values herself very highly and considers herself head of the family, kin. This perception of self is based on her conviction that she is special, the best in general: the healthiest, the most powerful, the most beautiful, the most intelligent, the most educated, the most experienced, the most professional, the most eminent, and so on and so forth; in other words—the best of the best. According to her reasoning, she achieved everything that one can achieve: self-dependence, good earnings, and independence from others. Moreover, as it seems to her, she is an example of moral and ethical perfection (she considers herself flawless, like Caesar's wife, who, as the story goes, was "always above suspicion"). And, she thinks that she is superior to others in all respects, and since she is such a bright individual—all other members of the family, her relatives simply must look up to her, and, of course obey her. She thinks that possession of a number of outstanding qualities is enough for a lifelong right to be the head of her family. And, if someone does not agree with this conclusion, if someone does not want to notice her value, does not want to obey her, then this woman will quickly "show them who is the chief." In such situations, she takes a fighting stance with arms akimbo, and since by nature she has a loud voice—opens her mouth. In such situations, she makes such a powerful sound that probably only the penguins at the South Pole do not hear it! As a result, usually her opponent or opponents immediately understand whose opinion in the house is fundamental. She is convinced that she deserves the highest rating, respect, reverence, and even worship. This respect must be expressed by members of the household through obedience, as well as through fulfillment of her numerous requests and commands. And, of course, she thinks that family must look up to her as the etalon of way of life. To achieve the above-described position, mother nature endowed this woman with a number of qualities that help her get what she claims. For example, one of these qualities is her ability to exert pressure. Considered person is extremely importunate and extremely demanding. In connection with this, she tries to turn others into, so to speak, a high yielding class, so that they would supply her and the whole family with benefits, achievements. For example, if she cares for someone, fosters someone, nurtures someone, then she requires: "Give a result!" Produce it at once! Although it is necessary to give her credit: first and foremost, she treats her own self in the same demanding way! That is, if she planned to achieve something, then she absolutely must achieve it and get a result or results.

This woman is absolutely sure of her purpose, her leadership, her superiority, and her exclusivity. She acts as a dictator and this clearly shows in some of her phrases, for example: "I said," "I insist," "It will be as I said!" And, it should not be doubted that this woman really will do everything, so that everything goes according to her decision. In this process, she actively uses the mechanism of repressions called "a carrot and a stick." Nature endowed this woman with high energy, observing which one can hardly assume that she will not bring herself to do something, will not be able to achieve what she fights for. Looking at her, it becomes obvious that this person will not back down from her plan! And, if she decides, so to speak, to weigh someone down, then all that is left is to sympathize with the poor fellow. Very powerful energy of this woman will kick out all the folly, all the dust, and, so to speak, "roll him or her out like a rug" quickly enough. In addition, she is a person of principle and if she decides to uses her principles, then one should hold on tight. However, she knows how to be forgiving like a queen, and if someone humbly asks forgiveness, then she will forgive. Especially since she is very much drawn to justice, seeks to ensure that everything is based on truth and that everything is fair.

As the head of a kin, her main sphere of activity is family. Family is extremely important to this woman. It is important from all sides. Firstly, she would very much like to have her dynasty, preferably rich and noble. If there is nothing at all special in her family history, then she is ready to create this dynasty. And, not one that, so to speak, consists of workers and peasants, but one that is namely rich and noble. And, she has everything to be able to succeed in this because by nature she has qualities of a founder of a dynasty, family line. Secondly, she is very interested in all questions related to her relatives. She is one of those people, who know all their relatives without exception and by names, know all their forefathers and ancestors. Thirdly, this woman absolutely must be married and have a family in the form of a spouse and children...

DEMO 12

Description Of Women Born On February 16th Of Common Years From The Catalog Of Human Population

Presented demo is a very short description. A complete description consists of a very detailed description of functioning and qualities of personality: a general description and a description on 6 factors (intellectual, nutritional, physical, emotional, sexual, and environmental).

This woman is a ruler, who values herself very highly and considers herself head of the family, kin. This perception of self is based on her conviction that she is special, the best in general: the healthiest, the most powerful, the most beautiful, the most intelligent, the most educated, the most experienced, the most professional, the most eminent, and so on and so forth; in other words—the best of the best. According to her reasoning, she achieved everything that one can achieve: self-dependence, good earnings, and independence from others. Moreover, as it seems to her, she is an example of moral and ethical perfection (she considers herself flawless, like Caesar's wife, who, as the story goes, was "always above suspicion"). And, she thinks that she is superior to others in all respects, and since she is such a bright individual—all other members of the family, her relatives simply must look up to her, and, of course obey her. She thinks that possession of a number of outstanding qualities is enough for a lifelong right to be the head of her family. And, if someone does not agree with this conclusion, if someone does not want to notice her value, does not want to obey her, then this woman will quickly "show them who is the chief." In such situations, she takes a fighting stance with arms akimbo, and since by nature she has a loud voice—opens her mouth. In such situations, she makes such a powerful sound that probably only the penguins at the South Pole do not hear it! As a result, usually her opponent or opponents immediately understand whose opinion in the house is fundamental. She is convinced that she deserves the highest rating, respect, reverence, and even worship. This respect must be expressed by members of the household through obedience, as well as through fulfillment of her numerous requests and commands. And, of course, she thinks that family must look up to her as the etalon of way of life. To achieve the above-described position, mother nature endowed this woman with a number of qualities that help her get what she claims. For example, one of these qualities is her ability to exert pressure. Considered person is extremely importunate and extremely demanding. In connection with this, she tries to turn others into, so to speak, a high yielding class, so that they would supply her and the whole family with benefits, achievements. For example, if she cares for someone, fosters someone, nurtures someone, then she requires: "Give a result!" Produce it at once! Although it is necessary to give her credit: first and foremost, she treats her own self in the same demanding way! That is, if she planned to achieve something, then she absolutely must achieve it and get a result or results.

This woman is absolutely sure of her purpose, her leadership, her superiority, and her exclusivity. She acts as a dictator and this clearly shows in some of her phrases, for example: "I said," "I insist," "It will be as I said!" And, it should not be doubted that this woman really will do everything, so that everything goes according to her decision. In this process, she actively uses the mechanism of repressions called "a carrot and a stick." Nature endowed this woman with high energy, observing which one can hardly assume that she will not bring herself to do something, will not be able to achieve what she fights for. Looking at her, it becomes obvious that this person will not back down from her plan! And, if she decides, so to speak, to weigh someone down, then all that is left is to sympathize with the poor fellow. Very powerful energy of this woman will kick out all the folly, all the dust, and, so to speak, "roll him or her out like a rug" quickly enough. In addition, she is a person of principle and if she decides to uses her principles, then one should hold on tight. However, she knows how to be forgiving like a queen, and if someone humbly asks forgiveness, then she will forgive. Especially since she is very much drawn to justice, seeks to ensure that everything is based on truth and that everything is fair.

As the head of a kin, her main sphere of activity is family. Family is extremely important to this woman. It is important from all sides. Firstly, she would very much like to have her dynasty, preferably rich and noble. If there is nothing at all special in her family history, then she is ready to create this dynasty. And, not one that, so to speak, consists of workers and peasants, but one that is namely rich and noble. And, she has everything to be able to succeed in this because by nature she has qualities of a founder of a dynasty, family line. Secondly, she is very interested in all questions related to her relatives. She is one of those people, who know all their relatives without exception and by names, know all their forefathers and ancestors. Thirdly, this woman absolutely must be married and have a family in the form of a spouse and children...

DEMO 13

Description Of Women Born On February 17th Of Leap Years From The Catalog Of Human Population

Presented demo is a very short description. A complete description consists of a very detailed description of functioning and qualities of personality: a general description and a description on 6 factors (intellectual, nutritional, physical, emotional, sexual, and environmental).

Considered individual thinks that she is the keeper of the very principles of existence and that all processes revolve around her because, as she thinks, nothing in the world can exist without her. This woman is a priestess, who, due to her involvement in something higher and esoteric, claims that she has knowledge of the secret mechanisms of influence on natural objects (natural phenomena, plants, animals), as well as on people. This woman claims that she knows the laws (from laws of the Universe to corporate rules of interactions between members of this or that organization) and that she possesses professional knowledge of rituals of any social environment.

However, the main motives of the considered individual are always aimed at only one thing: getting money. It is not enough to say that she simply loves money and strives to have it. Money is her life, her animal passion, the basis of her existence, where everything is for money and for the sake of money. Like the famous cartoon character created at Walt Disney Productions—an American duck by the name of Donald Duck, this person wants to have so much money that she could open not a wallet, a chest or a safe, but a whole storehouse, walk into an ocean money and swim in it. It might seem that she is so greedy and mercenary that even when she goes to the restroom she pays herself because she is reluctant even to ease nature for free, and instead of "Good morning" she says: "How much?" Money as such, anytime, anywhere and in any amount, raises her spirit, causes unconcealed elation, sincere enthusiasm and genuine interest.

Of course, in her youth she might dream that, like the clandestine millionaire Koreiko (a well-known character from the satirical novel by Ilf and Petrov called The Golden Calf), she will now close her eyes, turn the corner and find a thick wallet with money on a sidewalk. With age, as she becomes more realistic, she begins to realize that wallets with money do not fall from the sky. However, in order to have a lot of money it is necessary to have a strong financial base; hence the saying: "money makes money." And, where is the most money? Of course, atop the social "pyramid." So, that is where this woman sets course, and, naturally, to the West. The rich, wild West, where, according to promises, anyone can become a millionaire. Or, as she thinks, it would be even better to find herself a billionaire and make him a millionaire!

This woman is an ambitious person of wide-ranging nature, who sets global goals and objectives for herself. And, it must be noted that she has a great tool to make them a reality: she is extremely goal-oriented and centripetal, sees the target clearly and hits it like a laser beam—concentrated and precise. And, she knows how to use her elbows and, so to speak, walk on people's heads, if necessary, in order to make her way towards her goal.

This woman is ready to fight fiercely for her financial well-being, money in general, and the position of the richest. She begins to grind her teeth at the slightest hint that someone in her circle is richer than she is. She will track her possible competitors meticulously and scrupulously. This woman makes a lot of acquaintances in order to realize all of her aptitudes and make her dream—a pool of cherished "papers"—come true; however, not just any acquaintances, but only those people, who, from her point of view, have satisfactory financial resources. Therefore, all of her new acquaintances are carefully filtered according to the following main criterion: can this person help improve her financial status or not? And, those who pass the selection get meticulously and scrupulously recorded in a specially created registry (organizer): who the person is, what he or she does, where he or she is from, and how he or she can be useful to her. Of particular interest to her are the so-called "powerful people in this world": presidents, dictators, monarchs, sheiks, and everyone else who became models of ideal money "bags" by sitting on natural resources and making money from them.

She thinks that all means are good when trying to get into the needed stratums. For example, if in order to enter it is necessary to demonstrate her body in some glossy magazine like Playboy—she will do it without giving it any thought. The power with which this woman is able to take money for herself from the environment can only partly be compared with a high-tech snow removal machine, or a sewage pipe cleaning machine. And, if she decides to "harvest" this or that "tree"—she will pick to the last "apple" until all that will be left to say about the subject of her financial interest would be: "stripped like a lime-tree"...

DEMO 14
Description Of Women Born On February 18th Of Common Years From The Catalog Of Human Population

Presented demo is a very short description. A complete description consists of a very detailed description of functioning and qualities of personality: a general description and a description on 6 factors (intellectual, nutritional, physical, emotional, sexual, and environmental).

Considered individual thinks that she is the keeper of the very principles of existence and that all processes revolve around her because, as she thinks, nothing in the world can exist without her. This woman is a priestess, who, due to her involvement in something higher and esoteric, claims that she has knowledge of the secret mechanisms of influence on natural objects (natural phenomena, plants, animals), as well as on people. This woman claims that she knows the laws (from laws of the Universe to corporate rules of interactions between members of this or that organization) and that she possesses professional knowledge of rituals of any social environment.

However, the main motives of the considered individual are always aimed at only one thing: getting money. It is not enough to say that she simply loves money and strives to have it. Money is her life, her animal passion, the basis of her existence, where everything is for money and for the sake of money. Like the famous cartoon character created at Walt Disney Productions—an American duck by the name of Donald Duck, this person wants to have so much money that she could open not a wallet, a chest or a safe, but a whole storehouse, walk into an ocean money and swim in it. It might seem that she is so greedy and mercenary that even when she goes to the restroom she pays herself because she is reluctant even to ease nature for free, and instead of "Good morning" she says: "How much?" Money as such, anytime, anywhere and in any amount, raises her spirit, causes unconcealed elation, sincere enthusiasm and genuine interest.

Of course, in her youth she might dream that, like the clandestine millionaire Koreiko (a well-known character from the satirical novel by Ilf and Petrov called The Golden Calf), she will now close her eyes, turn the corner and find a thick wallet with money on a sidewalk. With age, as she becomes more realistic, she begins to realize that wallets with money do not fall from the sky. However, in order to have a lot of money it is necessary to have a strong financial base; hence the saying: "money makes money." And, where is the most money? Of course, atop the social "pyramid." So, that is where this woman sets course, and, naturally, to the West. The rich, wild West, where, according to promises, anyone can become a millionaire. Or, as she thinks, it would be even better to find herself a billionaire and make him a millionaire!

This woman is an ambitious person of wide-ranging nature, who sets global goals and objectives for herself. And, it must be noted that she has a great tool to make them a reality: she is extremely goal-oriented and centripetal, sees the target clearly and hits it like a laser beam—concentrated and precise. And, she knows how to use her elbows and, so to speak, walk on people's heads, if necessary, in order to make her way towards her goal.

This woman is ready to fight fiercely for her financial well-being, money in general, and the position of the richest. She begins to grind her teeth at the slightest hint that someone in her circle is richer than she is. She will track her possible competitors meticulously and scrupulously. This woman makes a lot of acquaintances in order to realize all of her aptitudes and make her dream—a pool of cherished "papers"—come true; however, not just any acquaintances, but only those people, who, from her point of view, have satisfactory financial resources. Therefore, all of her new acquaintances are carefully filtered according to the following main criterion: can this person help improve her financial status or not? And, those who pass the selection get meticulously and scrupulously recorded in a specially created registry (organizer): who the person is, what he or she does, where he or she is from, and how he or she can be useful to her. Of particular interest to her are the so-called "powerful people in this world": presidents, dictators, monarchs, sheiks, and everyone else who became models of ideal money "bags" by sitting on natural resources and making money from them.

She thinks that all means are good when trying to get into the needed stratums. For example, if in order to enter it is necessary to demonstrate her body in some glossy magazine like Playboy—she will do it without giving it any thought. The power with which this woman is able to take money for herself from the environment can only partly be compared with a high-tech snow removal machine, or a sewage pipe cleaning machine. And, if she decides to "harvest" this or that "tree"—she will pick to the last "apple" until all that will be left to say about the subject of her financial interest would be: "stripped like a lime-tree"...

DEMO 15

Description Of Women Born On February 24ᵗʰ Of Leap Years From The Catalog Of Human Population

Presented demo is a very short description. A complete description consists of a very detailed description of functioning and qualities of personality: a general description and a description on 6 factors (intellectual, nutritional, physical, emotional, sexual, and environmental).

Considered person reminds of yeast dough, which constantly "bursts the banks" or champagne, which foams over the edge of a glass. This individual is always absorbed by something: an idea, a thought, her work, family, children, friends or laundry. When she engages in mopping and moving of furniture, a large financial project or a political campaign—she fully devotes herself to the process. It seems that she completely fills up her life with parenting, guests, rotation of men in her bed, preparation of food, and professional activities on purpose. As a result, she is in a loop, inside events, affairs and situations without beginning or end.

Everything is always very well in her life! She has plenty of everything and everything is always of excellent quality! Even if her financial abilities allow her to live only on stale bread and water, and no one in her building says "Hello" to her except the cleaning lady, still she will brag that yesterday she again had dinner at a posh restaurant with some powerful people. Her desire to build castles in the sky and to convince everyone that she lives in them is simply unstoppable! For example, after spending a summer at a country house and coming back tanned, she will din into her friends' ears about how she went on a cruise to the Canary Islands or Haiti, even though she swam in a tiny pond all summer long. Being not too modest, to put it mildly, she talks only about herself to everyone and everywhere—what a star she is and how tirelessly and unstoppably she thrives and prospers. After finally moving her face away from a huge bowl of black caviar, with drunken hiccups, she festively and proudly exclaims: "Life is good!" That is her usual self-presentation in the environment. This behavior is a kind of a call to others to join her and to luxuriate, indulge in extremes together with her! Indeed, she wants everyone around her to live calmly, happily, peacefully, be prosperous, successful and lead a lavish, from luxurious to wasteful, lifestyle.

This person has a particularity: she wants to do everything together with someone. She might be a part of any social associations: diasporas, trade unions, communities, cooperatives, clubs, schools, parties, etc. She seeks to become friends with everyone, so that she does not live in isolation. She is particularly attracted to mutual responsibility. This woman seeks to be part of a clan, wants to always be "in her environment," her circle. This clan of like-minded people, people of the same nationality, race, type, social status, cultural and educational level, profession, interests, qualification, or level of consciousness; people who share common views, tastes, an affair, an idea, etc. They do everything corporately: vacation, spend weekends, fight or laugh, rush somewhere to take care of business, celebrate holidays, disagree and make peace, and so on—all together. And, it does not matter to her what affairs to participate in, what to do, as the main thing is to live together and die together!

She thinks that it is good to be together... but only initially. And then, everything must be done to become the head of a community, to lead it in order to exploit it! She knows how to work hard in the name of her dream of becoming outstanding, renowned, and famous. However, she still really wants others to do it for her! And, for this, by hook or by crook, with a carrot and a stick, by cunning and insidiousness, ostentatious and excessive unction, gratitude or unconcealed terrorism—forces everyone to work for her.

This woman is an overseer. She is ready to pace the parapet as an overseer of her "prisoners," and use a whip and a gun "to inspire" everyone to work, shooting periodically. Her intellect works very well in this process of control—here she is genius! For instance, she is ready to present herself as almost dying under the weight of backbreaking burden of her duties and affairs in order to put some of her work (and, better yet all of it!) on someone else's shoulders. And, she is not interested in other people's problems: "Die, but do it anyway!" And, she knows how to make practically any person work for her. When others ask her for help, she always produces the same type of reaction: "I would be happy to help you, but I cannot due to objective circumstances that are beyond my control."

This woman is not very good at hiding her strength and sense of her own superiority. She perceives her place in the environment and behaves like she does not even suppose that someone could argue or compete with her— all others are weak, simply husks!..

DEMO 16

Description Of Women Born On February 25th Of Common Years From The Catalog Of Human Population

Presented demo is a very short description. A complete description consists of a very detailed description of functioning and qualities of personality: a general description and a description on 6 factors (intellectual, nutritional, physical, emotional, sexual, and environmental).

Considered person reminds of yeast dough, which constantly "bursts the banks" or champagne, which foams over the edge of a glass. This individual is always absorbed by something: an idea, a thought, her work, family, children, friends or laundry. When she engages in mopping and moving of furniture, a large financial project or a political campaign—she fully devotes herself to the process. It seems that she completely fills up her life with parenting, guests, rotation of men in her bed, preparation of food, and professional activities on purpose. As a result, she is in a loop, inside events, affairs and situations without beginning or end.

Everything is always very well in her life! She has plenty of everything and everything is always of excellent quality! Even if her financial abilities allow her to live only on stale bread and water, and no one in her building says "Hello" to her except the cleaning lady, still she will brag that yesterday she again had dinner at a posh restaurant with some powerful people. Her desire to build castles in the sky and to convince everyone that she lives in them is simply unstoppable! For example, after spending a summer at a country house and coming back tanned, she will din into her friends' ears about how she went on a cruise to the Canary Islands or Haiti, even though she swam in a tiny pond all summer long. Being not too modest, to put it mildly, she talks only about herself to everyone and everywhere—what a star she is and how tirelessly and unstoppably she thrives and prospers. After finally moving her face away from a huge bowl of black caviar, with drunken hiccups, she festively and proudly exclaims: "Life is good!" That is her usual self-presentation in the environment. This behavior is a kind of a call to others to join her and to luxuriate, indulge in extremes together with her! Indeed, she wants everyone around her to live calmly, happily, peacefully, be prosperous, successful and lead a lavish, from luxurious to wasteful, lifestyle.

This person has a particularity: she wants to do everything together with someone. She might be a part of any social associations: diasporas, trade unions, communities, cooperatives, clubs, schools, parties, etc. She seeks to become friends with everyone, so that she does not live in isolation. She is particularly attracted to mutual responsibility. This woman seeks to be part of a clan, wants to always be "in her environment," her circle. This clan of like-minded people, people of the same nationality, race, type, social status, cultural and educational level, profession, interests, qualification, or level of consciousness; people who share common views, tastes, an affair, an idea, etc. They do everything corporately: vacation, spend weekends, fight or laugh, rush somewhere to take care of business, celebrate holidays, disagree and make peace, and so on—all together. And, it does not matter to her what affairs to participate in, what to do, as the main thing is to live together and die together!

She thinks that it is good to be together... but only initially. And then, everything must be done to become the head of a community, to lead it in order to exploit it! She knows how to work hard in the name of her dream of becoming outstanding, renowned, and famous. However, she still really wants others to do it for her! And, for this, by hook or by crook, with a carrot and a stick, by cunning and insidiousness, ostentatious and excessive unction, gratitude or unconcealed terrorism—forces everyone to work for her.

This woman is an overseer. She is ready to pace the parapet as an overseer of her "prisoners," and use a whip and a gun "to inspire" everyone to work, shooting periodically. Her intellect works very well in this process of control—here she is genius! For instance, she is ready to present herself as almost dying under the weight of backbreaking burden of her duties and affairs in order to put some of her work (and, better yet all of it!) on someone else's shoulders. And, she is not interested in other people's problems: "Die, but do it anyway!" And, she knows how to make practically any person work for her. When others ask her for help, she always produces the same type of reaction: "I would be happy to help you, but I cannot due to objective circumstances that are beyond my control."

This woman is not very good at hiding her strength and sense of her own superiority. She perceives her place in the environment and behaves like she does not even suppose that someone could argue or compete with her—all others are weak, simply husks!..

DEMO 17

Description Of Women Born On March 4ᵗʰ Of Leap Years From The Catalog Of Human Population

Presented demo is a very short description. A complete description consists of a very detailed description of functioning and qualities of personality: a general description and a description on 6 factors (intellectual, nutritional, physical, emotional, sexual, and environmental).

This woman can be characterized as a person who lives by the principle of a pendulum that swings from side to side. She can be described as a person of algorithm, contrasts because all personality characteristics of this woman, her whole life are subject to perpetual changes and fluctuations, which lead to completely opposite states. Due to pendulum algorithms, this woman has a dual personality. Fluctuations that occur within her, "torn rhythm" of her internal states define functioning of mechanisms of all her life activity— from physiology to worldview. Everywhere and in everything, in one way or another she transitions from one extreme to another: her genius neighbors with stupidity; sublime thoughts, feelings and aspirations—with rudeness, ordinariness and vulgarity; subtle abstract matters—with brute material basis; deep submergence into herself changes to absorption by external events. Presence of a double bottom of this individual is clearly seen among these contrasts and is emphasized by her stable desire to present herself in the best light. Although she has a habit of discoursing on topics of sublime matters, other worlds and spirituality aloud—in real life this woman is guided purely by material principles and very ordinary motives. She constantly transitions from one of her own hypostasis to another; first, she appears as an individual from the other world, who communicates with spirits, and then as a person with mentality of an ensign and jokes worthy of a soldiers' dining facility. Despite declarations of this woman about primacy of the spirit over the body, she cannot imagine her life without vanity of being, and, in this, she does not principally differ in anything from other people, who do not think about the spirit. The behavior of this individual is ambiguous, misleading and confusing: first, she expresses a deep philosophical thought, and then she suddenly makes a terrible mistake, forcing others to doubt that she is the person with whom they were talking a half an hour ago. Life of this woman is a continuous contrast: periods of absolutely unimaginable activeness, when she literally darts through the air, alternate with periods of inactivity. Sharp and powerful emotions are suddenly replaced by a state of complete calmness, gluttony is replaced by a complete refusal to eat, and desire to commit suicide suddenly changes to optimism. To an observer, all her life seems like an amplitude with sharp peaks of pluses and minuses.

This individual is able to appear as a hereditary witch, a sorceress, a psychic, or a great astrologer. She might present herself as a woman, who not only has a mystical perception of the world and is seriously into esoterism, but also applies her knowledge in a variety of mysterious areas in practice. Concepts like "destiny", "fate", "karma" and so on occupy a huge place in her life and worldview. It might seem that she is not only interested in, but also is seriously engaged in various occult sciences, and not only studies, but also follows various kinds of esoteric systems. She might be a part of some secret sects, attend various mystical communities like schools, ashrams, and so on, or she might not be a part of anything and might not attend any such institutions, while successfully engaging in all this in her own kitchen.

This woman has a very important psychophysiological particularity: she has enormous sexual needs. Her internal understanding of this matter, as well as self-sentiment of this woman can be described like this: in life, first of all, there is sex, and then everything else. Therefore, her "shaman," and her "general" (this woman loves to command very much), and all her other qualities get strung on her mad, passionate, constantly present sexual desire, as if on a rod. Her desire never begins because it never ends; first, it continues from dawn until dusk, and then from dusk until dawn. And, this mode does not stop throughout her life. This individual has hypertrophied sexual needs by nature. She can and wants to have sexual relations with the opposite sex always, anywhere, regardless of anything, longer, more, more often, and most importantly—without stopping. Life under such "degree" of sexual desire forms this person's philosophy: "My life credo? Always!!!" Despite the fact that sexual relations give this woman a lot of pleasure, she is haunted by the idea of a sin. Figuratively speaking, this thought jumps out of bed right after she does, and it does not cease to haunt her all the way to the next bed. She subjectively perceives such situation as a fly in the ointment, when, after spending a wild night of continuous, non-stop pleasure, she suddenly begins to think about her perversity, licentiousness, and most importantly—uncontrollability. If she adheres to religious beliefs, then this individual might try to go to a priest for a piece of advice or a confession, as well as visit several monasteries and a dozen of ashrams in search of a reliable method to pacify her sexual appetites. However, all of her attempts in this direction are doomed to failure...

DEMO 18

Description Of Women Born On March 5ᵗʰ Of Common Years From The Catalog Of Human Population

Presented demo is a very short description. A complete description consists of a very detailed description of functioning and qualities of personality: a general description and a description on 6 factors (intellectual, nutritional, physical, emotional, sexual, and environmental).

This woman can be characterized as a person who lives by the principle of a pendulum that swings from side to side. She can be described as a person of algorithm, contrasts because all personality characteristics of this woman, her whole life are subject to perpetual changes and fluctuations, which lead to completely opposite states. Due to pendulum algorithms, this woman has a dual personality. Fluctuations that occur within her, "torn rhythm" of her internal states define functioning of mechanisms of all her life activity—from physiology to worldview. Everywhere and in everything, in one way or another she transitions from one extreme to another: her genius neighbors with stupidity; sublime thoughts, feelings and aspirations—with rudeness, ordinariness and vulgarity; subtle abstract matters—with brute material basis; deep submergence into herself changes to absorption by external events. Presence of a double bottom of this individual is clearly seen among these contrasts and is emphasized by her stable desire to present herself in the best light. Although she has a habit of discoursing on topics of sublime matters, other worlds and spirituality aloud—in real life this woman is guided purely by material principles and very ordinary motives. She constantly transitions from one of her own hypostasis to another; first, she appears as an individual from the other world, who communicates with spirits, and then as a person with mentality of an ensign and jokes worthy of a soldiers' dining facility. Despite declarations of this woman about primacy of the spirit over the body, she cannot imagine her life without vanity of being, and, in this, she does not principally differ in anything from other people, who do not think about the spirit. The behavior of this individual is ambiguous, misleading and confusing: first, she expresses a deep philosophical thought, and then she suddenly makes a terrible mistake, forcing others to doubt that she is the person with whom they were talking a half an hour ago. Life of this woman is a continuous contrast: periods of absolutely unimaginable activeness, when she literally darts through the air, alternate with periods of inactivity. Sharp and powerful emotions are suddenly replaced by a state of complete calmness, gluttony is replaced by a complete refusal to eat, and desire to commit suicide suddenly changes to optimism. To an observer, all her life seems like an amplitude with sharp peaks of pluses and minuses.

This individual is able to appear as a hereditary witch, a sorceress, a psychic, or a great astrologer. She might present herself as a woman, who not only has a mystical perception of the world and is seriously into esoterism, but also applies her knowledge in a variety of mysterious areas in practice. Concepts like "destiny", "fate", "karma" and so on occupy a huge place in her life and worldview. It might seem that she is not only interested in, but also is seriously engaged in various occult sciences, and not only studies, but also follows various kinds of esoteric systems. She might be a part of some secret sects, attend various mystical communities like schools, ashrams, and so on, or she might not be a part of anything and might not attend any such institutions, while successfully engaging in all this in her own kitchen.

This woman has a very important psychophysiological particularity: she has enormous sexual needs. Her internal understanding of this matter, as well as self-sentiment of this woman can be described like this: in life, first of all, there is sex, and then everything else. Therefore, her "shaman," and her "general" (this woman loves to command very much), and all her other qualities get strung on her mad, passionate, constantly present sexual desire, as if on a rod. Her desire never begins because it never ends; first, it continues from dawn until dusk, and then from dusk until dawn. And, this mode does not stop throughout her life. This individual has hypertrophied sexual needs by nature. She can and wants to have sexual relations with the opposite sex always, anywhere, regardless of anything, longer, more, more often, and most importantly—without stopping. Life under such "degree" of sexual desire forms this person's philosophy: "My life credo? Always!!!" Despite the fact that sexual relations give this woman a lot of pleasure, she is haunted by the idea of a sin. Figuratively speaking, this thought jumps out of bed right after she does, and it does not cease to haunt her all the way to the next bed. She subjectively perceives such situation as a fly in the ointment, when, after spending a wild night of continuous, non-stop pleasure, she suddenly begins to think about her perversity, licentiousness, and most importantly—uncontrollability. If she adheres to religious beliefs, then this individual might try to go to a priest for a piece of advice or a confession, as well as visit several monasteries and a dozen of ashrams in search of a reliable method to pacify her sexual appetites. However, all of her attempts in this direction are doomed to failure...

DEMO 19

Description Of Women Born On March 9th Of Leap Years From The Catalog Of Human Population

Presented demo is a very short description. A complete description consists of a very detailed description of functioning and qualities of personality: a general description and a description on 6 factors (intellectual, nutritional, physical, emotional, sexual, and environmental).

If we try to compare this woman to a natural phenomenon—she resembles a strange black hole, which tries to take in everything that is within her reach. This black hole attracts, pulls in and eventually absorbs. The fact is that this woman also tries to maximally take in a maximum number of objects of the external world: various information, rumors, people, events, impressions, advices, admonitions, and so on. To draw an analogy with household appliances: in this respect, she can be compared to a vacuum cleaner, which sucks in whatever it comes across.

Like a vacuum cleaner, this person absorbs everything that is in the environment, and, in this sense, she can also be compared to a paper towel that absorbs liquid instantly. Once she begins to do something, this woman cannot stop. For example, if she picks up a book and starts to read it, then she will read, read and read without stopping, both day and night. If she starts to get some experiences, some information from communication with friends, then she will stay with them until late night. If she turns on a television, then she cannot tear herself away from it. Due to these personal peculiarities, this woman always strives to be in places where it is possible to get large amounts of varied information (the press, the Internet, people, books, videos, television and radio broadcasts, etc.). She pays a lot of attention to the most varied literary works, ranging from scientific to popular-science literature (of course, if her education allows).

Of course, unlike the black hole as a natural phenomenon, this person has her own capabilities to take in large amounts of information and experiences, but in comparison with many other people—she can take in huge amounts. On the one hand, in this case, everything she comes across is subject to absorption, but, on the other hand, there are priorities. One of them is all that is secret, dark, mystical, and otherworldly—in other words, all that is concealed or simply unclear. She is also interested in so-called "skeletons in closets," that is—the secret, other side of people, phenomena and events; various esoteric and mystical systems, secret teachings and similar things. In this sense, she is omnivorous. Therefore, along with really serious research on occultism and esotericism, such as studies of Manly

Hall, she will read about some green beings, karmic astrology, black magic of a village sorceress, and other frank delirium of mystically minded citizens. By the way, this woman might consider herself a witch, a sorceress by nature, who can jinx anyone. She might think that there is something infernal in her, or, to put it simply—something out of this world.

She might consider herself an individual who possesses demonic force, which can influence men; or a shaman, who has an ability to communicate with spirits from parallel worlds. The next directions of her interest are various philosophical, religious, psychological, scientific, and cultural systems, which she absorbs in incredible amounts. For example, today she extensively and seriously studies Islam, tomorrow—Nietzsche, and the day after—she is carried away by the Renaissance culture, and so on. She seriously studies everything: revelations of the holy Christian elders, stories from lives of Buddhist monks, along with the works of Hitler, Hegel or Freud, Vedanta and Encyclopedia of philosophy of England and France.

While she studies various cultural directions, for example, Renaissance paintings, then she will not only study works of painters, but also the history, the context, in which they created their art; she will not only study the techniques that great artists used, but also certainly will try to find out their philosophy. Since all of her hunting for information and its absorption in unimaginable amounts are necessary to the considered individual in order to find as many variants of various recipes of life as possible.

This woman is a peculiar collector of life positions. She actively seeks peculiar recipes of Existence based on different worldviews, various value systems, both in society and in cultural layers: literature, music, painting, science, philosophy...

DEMO 20

Description Of Women Born On March 10th Of Common Years From The Catalog Of Human Population

Presented demo is a very short description. A complete description consists of a very detailed description of functioning and qualities of personality: a general description and a description on 6 factors (intellectual, nutritional, physical, emotional, sexual, and environmental).

If we try to compare this woman to a natural phenomenon—she resembles a strange black hole, which tries to take in everything that is within her reach. This black hole attracts, pulls in and eventually absorbs. The fact is that this woman also tries to maximally take in a maximum number of objects of the external world: various information, rumors, people, events, impressions, advices, admonitions, and so on. To draw an analogy with household appliances: in this respect, she can be compared to a vacuum cleaner, which sucks in whatever it comes across.

Like a vacuum cleaner, this person absorbs everything that is in the environment, and, in this sense, she can also be compared to a paper towel that absorbs liquid instantly. Once she begins to do something, this woman cannot stop. For example, if she picks up a book and starts to read it, then she will read, read and read without stopping, both day and night. If she starts to get some experiences, some information from communication with friends, then she will stay with them until late night. If she turns on a television, then she cannot tear herself away from it. Due to these personal peculiarities, this woman always strives to be in places where it is possible to get large amounts of varied information (the press, the Internet, people, books, videos, television and radio broadcasts, etc.). She pays a lot of attention to the most varied literary works, ranging from scientific to popular-science literature (of course, if her education allows).

Of course, unlike the black hole as a natural phenomenon, this person has her own capabilities to take in large amounts of information and experiences, but in comparison with many other people—she can take in huge amounts. On the one hand, in this case, everything she comes across is subject to absorption, but, on the other hand, there are priorities. One of them is all that is secret, dark, mystical, and otherworldly—in other words, all that is concealed or simply unclear. She is also interested in so-called "skeletons in closets," that is—the secret, other side of people, phenomena and events; various esoteric and mystical systems, secret teachings and similar things. In this sense, she is omnivorous. Therefore, along with really serious research on occultism and esotericism, such as studies of Manly

Hall, she will read about some green beings, karmic astrology, black magic of a village sorceress, and other frank delirium of mystically minded citizens. By the way, this woman might consider herself a witch, a sorceress by nature, who can jinx anyone. She might think that there is something infernal in her, or, to put it simply—something out of this world.

She might consider herself an individual who possesses demonic force, which can influence men; or a shaman, who has an ability to communicate with spirits from parallel worlds. The next directions of her interest are various philosophical, religious, psychological, scientific, and cultural systems, which she absorbs in incredible amounts. For example, today she extensively and seriously studies Islam, tomorrow—Nietzsche, and the day after—she is carried away by the Renaissance culture, and so on. She seriously studies everything: revelations of the holy Christian elders, stories from lives of Buddhist monks, along with the works of Hitler, Hegel or Freud, Vedanta and Encyclopedia of philosophy of England and France.

While she studies various cultural directions, for example, Renaissance paintings, then she will not only study works of painters, but also the history, the context, in which they created their art; she will not only study the techniques that great artists used, but also certainly will try to find out their philosophy. Since all of her hunting for information and its absorption in unimaginable amounts are necessary to the considered individual in order to find as many variants of various recipes of life as possible.

This woman is a peculiar collector of life positions. She actively seeks peculiar recipes of Existence based on different worldviews, various value systems, both in society and in cultural layers: literature, music, painting, science, philosophy...

DEMO 21

Description Of Women Born On March 13ᵗʰ Of Leap Years From The Catalog Of Human Population

Presented demo is a very short description. A complete description consists of a very detailed description of functioning and qualities of personality: a general description and a description on 6 factors (intellectual, nutritional, physical, emotional, sexual, and environmental).

Considered individual can be compared to the Antarctic, the pole—in essence, the "center of the universe," from which everything begins and where everything ends. It is not surprising that this woman is clearly egocentric since, as it is known, a compass is calibrated based on the earth's poles! She feels that she is one of these poles, and since all roads lead to Rome—they must all lead to her as to a peculiar center of the universe. In fact, this woman's sense of self is that of a type of a post that represents zero miles, a mark, from which the count begins. This quality is manifested in all factors. With her family, for example, it is expressed in that she expects that all members of the household (except, perhaps, children) are obligated, first of all, to consider and take into account her needs and desires, and only then remember their own. How else? After all, as it seems to her, everything revolves around her! She is the compass for everyone! In this case, a compass is a person, who indicates the direction, the course and is a walking pointer ("You go here, and you go there!"), who determines actions, movement of other people. Maybe it is due to such sense of self that she constantly recommends something to someone, instructs, commands in various forms, manages, and directs. Such behavior is combined with another one of her peculiarities: if she, so to speak, trapped someone (something), that is—took for personal use, considered her own, then it will be impossible to get him/her (it) out of her hands by any means! This quality makes her related to an octopus, which has spread its tentacles and now firmly holds its prey.

This woman is not just the center of the universe, but also, at a minimum, is the Queen of Sheba. In fact, it is necessary for the considered person to somehow differ from the general gray mass, "the herd" around her. After all, any herd is kept in some enclosure, within limits, while by nature this person is extremely proud, audacious, unrestricted, daring, and self-willed. She has a very despotic character, along with all related peculiarities. On the one hand: "Everybody stand up, drop down and squeeze! Put the money on the table!" And, on the other hand: "Everybody dance, I will treat you!" Wastefulness, generosity, and petty tyranny are woven together. This can manifest all the way to a lack of all restraint and outright rudeness towards others. So what? Nothing is shameful for a great person, whom she considers herself. Everything is forgivable! Especially since she does not quite know what shyness is. Quite often, she allows herself to behave arrogantly due to, at times, a hypertrophied sense of self-worth. Sometimes, she behaves defiantly. Therefore, artificial limits invented by someone are absolutely of no use to her. Moreover, the considered individual perceives herself as a person, who is capable of a lot. She considers herself an outstanding person, and, in principle, it is not so important to her what to be outstanding in: beauty, talents, strength, mind, power, wealth, or something else. It does not matter whether to become a coryphaeus of literature or a war hero, an influential person or even a gangster "moll." Any means are good—the main thing is to not be a worthless, gray person, one among many. Therefore, no matter what turn her life takes, regardless of what environment she is in—she will strive to go beyond the average statistical variant. The question is: how is it possible to do this? She thinks that the most effective ways are the following. The first one is to do something heroic, some deed or a series of deeds, which will bring her the status of an unusual, unordinary woman. And, as it is known, there are no heroes in "a herd." That is why quite often, she plans something along the lines of the famous character Baron Munchausen: "Every day between noon and dinnertime I will perform a feat!" As an individual who is not bound by conventionalities, this woman is always ready for, so to speak, a mighty gust. (All that can let her down in this pursuit are set life routes, which will be discussed is other sections...)

DEMO 22

Description Of Women Born On March 14ᵗʰ Of Common Years From The Catalog Of Human Population

Presented demo is a very short description. A complete description consists of a very detailed description of functioning and qualities of personality: a general description and a description on 6 factors (intellectual, nutritional, physical, emotional, sexual, and environmental).

Considered individual can be compared to the Antarctic, the pole—in essence, the "center of the universe," from which everything begins and where everything ends. It is not surprising that this woman is clearly egocentric since, as it is known, a compass is calibrated based on the earth's poles! She feels that she is one of these poles, and since all roads lead to Rome—they must all lead to her as to a peculiar center of the universe. In fact, this woman's sense of self is that of a type of a post that represents zero miles, a mark, from which the count begins. This quality is manifested in all factors. With her family, for example, it is expressed in that she expects that all members of the household (except, perhaps, children) are obligated, first of all, to consider and take into account her needs and desires, and only then remember their own. How else? After all, as it seems to her, everything revolves around her! She is the compass for everyone! In this case, a compass is a person, who indicates the direction, the course and is a walking pointer ("You go here, and you go there!"), who determines actions, movement of other people. Maybe it is due to such sense of self that she constantly recommends something to someone, instructs, commands in various forms, manages, and directs. Such behavior is combined with another one of her peculiarities: if she, so to speak, trapped someone (something), that is—took for personal use, considered her own, then it will be impossible to get him/her (it) out of her hands by any means! This quality makes her related to an octopus, which has spread its tentacles and now firmly holds its prey.

This woman is not just the center of the universe, but also, at a minimum, is the Queen of Sheba. In fact, it is necessary for the considered person to somehow differ from the general gray mass, "the herd" around her. After all, any herd is kept in some enclosure, within limits, while by nature this person is extremely proud, audacious, unrestricted, daring, and self-willed. She has a very despotic character, along with all related peculiarities. On the one hand: "Everybody stand up, drop down and squeeze! Put the money on the table!" And, on the other hand: "Everybody dance, I will treat you!" Wastefulness, generosity, and petty tyranny are woven together. This can manifest all the way to a lack of all restraint and outright rudeness towards others. So what? Nothing is shameful for a great person, whom she considers herself. Everything is forgivable! Especially since she does not quite know what shyness is. Quite often, she allows herself to behave arrogantly due to, at times, a hypertrophied sense of self-worth. Sometimes, she behaves defiantly. Therefore, artificial limits invented by someone are absolutely of no use to her. Moreover, the considered individual perceives herself as a person, who is capable of a lot. She considers herself an outstanding person, and, in principle, it is not so important to her what to be outstanding in: beauty, talents, strength, mind, power, wealth, or something else. It does not matter whether to become a coryphaeus of literature or a war hero, an influential person or even a gangster "moll." Any means are good—the main thing is to not be a worthless, gray person, one among many. Therefore, no matter what turn her life takes, regardless of what environment she is in—she will strive to go beyond the average statistical variant. The question is: how is it possible to do this? She thinks that the most effective ways are the following. The first one is to do something heroic, some deed or a series of deeds, which will bring her the status of an unusual, unordinary woman. And, as it is known, there are no heroes in "a herd." That is why quite often, she plans something along the lines of the famous character Baron Munchausen: "Every day between noon and dinnertime I will perform a feat!" As an individual who is not bound by conventionalities, this woman is always ready for, so to speak, a mighty gust. (All that can let her down in this pursuit are set life routes, which will be discussed is other sections...)

DEMO 23

Description Of Women Born On March 18ᵗʰ Of Leap Years From The Catalog Of Human Population

Presented demo is a very short description. A complete description consists of a very detailed description of functioning and qualities of personality: a general description and a description on 6 factors (intellectual, nutritional, physical, emotional, sexual, and environmental).

Considered person has a stable desire to have her own family. Whatever it takes. She seeks family life, family coziness. However, this woman wants to make a family not as some kind of formal or semi-formal union, but to create a union based on deep mutual understanding between spouses, who would be almost inseparable from each other. She wants this marriage to last a lifetime, according to the principle: "They lived happily ever after, and died on the same day."

Although this tendency, by and large, is only a manifestation of her basic motivation: to realize the principle of pairing, as the desire to have two copies of everything, to do everything in a pair with someone. Therefore, this tendency is traceable throughout her life. For example, in the physical factor, this woman seeks to have several interchangeable and sometimes even identical clothing items in her wardrobe. As far as selection of dresses, shoes, accessories, or any other elements of her appearance—she also uses the above principle, in the sense that her spouse, boyfriend, lover, the one who makes her pair must necessarily be involved in the search and the purchasing process. And, during this process, she usually acquires not one, but two pairs of shoes; the same applies to stockings, heels, dresses, and so on. The following peculiarity of her personality is closely related to the desire of this woman to always be in a pair with someone: she constantly tries to "tie" someone to herself, whether it is one of her friends, children, or a future husband.

This aspiration manifests in actions directed at connecting with a person whom she chose by creating a dependency on her. By doing this (that is—by tying and uniting with someone), this person organizes the process of their interaction in such a way that they can do the maximum number of things in this tandem: sets a common goal, assigns responsibilities to each, synchronizes actions of partners, and so on. These might be house chores, which are divided between spouses or a parent and a child, where one does laundry, irons, vacuums, cleans and washes the floors, and the other does grocery shopping, cooks, cleans the kitchen; or something else, for example, work related processes, common business, and so on.

This woman seeks to be always young, fresh, blooming, bright, flawless, and brilliant. The environment in which she resides and everything in that environment must correspond as well. The aspiration of this woman to adhere to such concept is expressed in her appearance (she is always well groomed, styles her hair and dresses according to the latest fashion trend) and in much more. For example, in her speech. She thinks that not only the form should be beautiful and graceful, but the content of her self-expression through speech must also be of high style. This is expressed not only in the beauty of syllable and elegance of verbal cobwebs, but also in that she actively declares ideals of goodness, beauty, humanism, world peace, and so on. In the intellectual factor, as well as in her general behavior, in any situation this person seeks to adhere to the style of women's salons of the century before last, in which enlightened ladies of noble blood played musical instruments, declared poetry, prose, displayed their own artwork. In short, the style of aristocracy is very close to her, and an aristocrat, as it is known, will be an aristocrat everywhere, always and in everything. Therefore, this woman's requirements, manners, behavior are similar in all other factors. For example, the nutritional factor. It can hardly be assumed that an aristocrat, or a person who aspires to be an aristocrat, would agree to have food in some cheap cafeteria, where the air is full of disgusting miasmas: sour cabbage soup, stale food or lumpens sitting at neighboring tables; or that she would dine at a table covered with a piece of paper with thick pieces of sausage served on it instead of a clean table with nicely served food. That is very unlikely. And, this is exactly what happens with this woman: situations mentioned above might result in loss of appetite or refusal to eat in such conditions. In her case, even a common and loved by many event like barbeque out in the nature might cause her displeasure: "Smoke, dirt, peasant-like style! Yuck!" However, she has high demands not only to the outside world, but also to herself: she always strives to be the best, to know everything, to be able to do everything, to have time for everything. This woman strives for perfection. Using the language of psychology, she has a high motivation for achievement, seeks to reach the peak in everything that she engages in. In principle, she is not interested in all intermediate stages, in stages from zero to the last one. The main thing is to turn up at the top. At any cost...

DEMO 24

Description Of Women Born On March 19th Of Leap Years From The Catalog Of Human Population

Presented demo is a very short description. A complete description consists of a very detailed description of functioning and qualities of personality: a general description and a description on 6 factors (intellectual, nutritional, physical, emotional, sexual, and environmental).

Considered person has a stable desire to have her own family. Whatever it takes. She seeks family life, family coziness. However, this woman wants to make a family not as some kind of formal or semi-formal union, but to create a union based on deep mutual understanding between spouses, who would be almost inseparable from each other. She wants this marriage to last a lifetime, according to the principle: "They lived happily ever after, and died on the same day."

Although this tendency, by and large, is only a manifestation of her basic motivation: to realize the principle of pairing, as the desire to have two copies of everything, to do everything in a pair with someone. Therefore, this tendency is traceable throughout her life. For example, in the physical factor, this woman seeks to have several interchangeable and sometimes even identical clothing items in her wardrobe. As far as selection of dresses, shoes, accessories, or any other elements of her appearance—she also uses the above principle, in the sense that her spouse, boyfriend, lover, the one who makes her pair must necessarily be involved in the search and the purchasing process. And, during this process, she usually acquires not one, but two pairs of shoes; the same applies to stockings, heels, dresses, and so on. The following peculiarity of her personality is closely related to the desire of this woman to always be in a pair with someone: she constantly tries to "tie" someone to herself, whether it is one of her friends, children, or a future husband.

This aspiration manifests in actions directed at connecting with a person whom she chose by creating a dependency on her. By doing this (that is—by tying and uniting with someone), this person organizes the process of their interaction in such a way that they can do the maximum number of things in this tandem: sets a common goal, assigns responsibilities to each, synchronizes actions of partners, and so on. These might be house chores, which are divided between spouses or a parent and a child, where one does laundry, irons, vacuums, cleans and washes the floors, and the other does grocery shopping, cooks, cleans the kitchen; or something else, for example, work related processes, common business, and so on.

This woman seeks to be always young, fresh, blooming, bright, flawless, and brilliant. The environment in which she resides and everything in that environment must correspond as well. The aspiration of this woman to adhere to such concept is expressed in her appearance (she is always well groomed, styles her hair and dresses according to the latest fashion trend) and in much more. For example, in her speech. She thinks that not only the form should be beautiful and graceful, but the content of her self-expression through speech must also be of high style. This is expressed not only in the beauty of syllable and elegance of verbal cobwebs, but also in that she actively declares ideals of goodness, beauty, humanism, world peace, and so on. In the intellectual factor, as well as in her general behavior, in any situation this person seeks to adhere to the style of women's salons of the century before last, in which enlightened ladies of noble blood played musical instruments, declared poetry, prose, displayed their own artwork. In short, the style of aristocracy is very close to her, and an aristocrat, as it is known, will be an aristocrat everywhere, always and in everything. Therefore, this woman's requirements, manners, behavior are similar in all other factors. For example, the nutritional factor. It can hardly be assumed that an aristocrat, or a person who aspires to be an aristocrat, would agree to have food in some cheap cafeteria, where the air is full of disgusting miasmas: sour cabbage soup, stale food or lumpens sitting at neighboring tables; or that she would dine at a table covered with a piece of paper with thick pieces of sausage served on it instead of a clean table with nicely served food. That is very unlikely. And, this is exactly what happens with this woman: situations mentioned above might result in loss of appetite or refusal to eat in such conditions. In her case, even a common and loved by many event like barbeque out in the nature might cause her displeasure: "Smoke, dirt, peasant-like style! Yuck!" However, she has high demands not only to the outside world, but also to herself: she always strives to be the best, to know everything, to be able to do everything, to have time for everything. This woman strives for perfection. Using the language of psychology, she has a high motivation for achievement, seeks to reach the peak in everything that she engages in. In principle, she is not interested in all intermediate stages, in stages from zero to the last one. The main thing is to turn up at the top. At any cost...

DEMO 25

Description Of Women Born On March 19ᵗʰ Of Common Years From The Catalog Of Human Population

Presented demo is a very short description. A complete description consists of a very detailed description of functioning and qualities of personality: a general description and a description on 6 factors (intellectual, nutritional, physical, emotional, sexual, and environmental).

Considered person has a stable desire to have her own family. Whatever it takes. She seeks family life, family coziness. However, this woman wants to make a family not as some kind of formal or semi-formal union, but to create a union based on deep mutual understanding between spouses, who would be almost inseparable from each other. She wants this marriage to last a lifetime, according to the principle: "They lived happily ever after, and died on the same day."

Although this tendency, by and large, is only a manifestation of her basic motivation: to realize the principle of pairing, as the desire to have two copies of everything, to do everything in a pair with someone. Therefore, this tendency is traceable throughout her life. For example, in the physical factor, this woman seeks to have several interchangeable and sometimes even identical clothing items in her wardrobe. As far as selection of dresses, shoes, accessories, or any other elements of her appearance—she also uses the above principle, in the sense that her spouse, boyfriend, lover, the one who makes her pair must necessarily be involved in the search and the purchasing process. And, during this process, she usually acquires not one, but two pairs of shoes; the same applies to stockings, heels, dresses, and so on. The following peculiarity of her personality is closely related to the desire of this woman to always be in a pair with someone: she constantly tries to "tie" someone to herself, whether it is one of her friends, children, or a future husband.

This aspiration manifests in actions directed at connecting with a person whom she chose by creating a dependency on her. By doing this (that is—by tying and uniting with someone), this person organizes the process of their interaction in such a way that they can do the maximum number of things in this tandem: sets a common goal, assigns responsibilities to each, synchronizes actions of partners, and so on. These might be house chores, which are divided between spouses or a parent and a child, where one does laundry, irons, vacuums, cleans and washes the floors, and the other does grocery shopping, cooks, cleans the kitchen; or something else, for example, work related processes, common business, and so on.

This woman seeks to be always young, fresh, blooming, bright, flawless, and brilliant. The environment in which she resides and everything in that environment must correspond as well. The aspiration of this woman to adhere to such concept is expressed in her appearance (she is always well groomed, styles her hair and dresses according to the latest fashion trend) and in much more. For example, in her speech. She thinks that not only the form should be beautiful and graceful, but the content of her self-expression through speech must also be of high style. This is expressed not only in the beauty of syllable and elegance of verbal cobwebs, but also in that she actively declares ideals of goodness, beauty, humanism, world peace, and so on. In the intellectual factor, as well as in her general behavior, in any situation this person seeks to adhere to the style of women's salons of the century before last, in which enlightened ladies of noble blood played musical instruments, declared poetry, prose, displayed their own artwork. In short, the style of aristocracy is very close to her, and an aristocrat, as it is known, will be an aristocrat everywhere, always and in everything. Therefore, this woman's requirements, manners, behavior are similar in all other factors. For example, the nutritional factor. It can hardly be assumed that an aristocrat, or a person who aspires to be an aristocrat, would agree to have food in some cheap cafeteria, where the air is full of disgusting miasmas: sour cabbage soup, stale food or lumpens sitting at neighboring tables; or that she would dine at a table covered with a piece of paper with thick pieces of sausage served on it instead of a clean table with nicely served food. That is very unlikely. And, this is exactly what happens with this woman: situations mentioned above might result in loss of appetite or refusal to eat in such conditions. In her case, even a common and loved by many event like barbeque out in the nature might cause her displeasure: "Smoke, dirt, peasant-like style! Yuck!" However, she has high demands not only to the outside world, but also to herself: she always strives to be the best, to know everything, to be able to do everything, to have time for everything. This woman strives for perfection. Using the language of psychology, she has a high motivation for achievement, seeks to reach the peak in everything that she engages in. In principle, she is not interested in all intermediate stages, in stages from zero to the last one. The main thing is to turn up at the top. At any cost...

DEMO 26

Description Of Women Born On March 20th Of Common Years From The Catalog Of Human Population

Presented demo is a very short description. A complete description consists of a very detailed description of functioning and qualities of personality: a general description and a description on 6 factors (intellectual, nutritional, physical, emotional, sexual, and environmental).

Considered person has a stable desire to have her own family. Whatever it takes. She seeks family life, family coziness. However, this woman wants to make a family not as some kind of formal or semi-formal union, but to create a union based on deep mutual understanding between spouses, who would be almost inseparable from each other. She wants this marriage to last a lifetime, according to the principle: "They lived happily ever after, and died on the same day."

Although this tendency, by and large, is only a manifestation of her basic motivation: to realize the principle of pairing, as the desire to have two copies of everything, to do everything in a pair with someone. Therefore, this tendency is traceable throughout her life. For example, in the physical factor, this woman seeks to have several interchangeable and sometimes even identical clothing items in her wardrobe. As far as selection of dresses, shoes, accessories, or any other elements of her appearance—she also uses the above principle, in the sense that her spouse, boyfriend, lover, the one who makes her pair must necessarily be involved in the search and the purchasing process. And, during this process, she usually acquires not one, but two pairs of shoes; the same applies to stockings, heels, dresses, and so on. The following peculiarity of her personality is closely related to the desire of this woman to always be in a pair with someone: she constantly tries to "tie" someone to herself, whether it is one of her friends, children, or a future husband.

This aspiration manifests in actions directed at connecting with a person whom she chose by creating a dependency on her. By doing this (that is—by tying and uniting with someone), this person organizes the process of their interaction in such a way that they can do the maximum number of things in this tandem: sets a common goal, assigns responsibilities to each, synchronizes actions of partners, and so on. These might be house chores, which are divided between spouses or a parent and a child, where one does laundry, irons, vacuums, cleans and washes the floors, and the other does grocery shopping, cooks, cleans the kitchen; or something else, for example, work related processes, common business, and so on.

This woman seeks to be always young, fresh, blooming, bright, flawless, and brilliant. The environment in which she resides and everything in that environment must correspond as well. The aspiration of this woman to adhere to such concept is expressed in her appearance (she is always well groomed, styles her hair and dresses according to the latest fashion trend) and in much more. For example, in her speech. She thinks that not only the form should be beautiful and graceful, but the content of her self-expression through speech must also be of high style. This is expressed not only in the beauty of syllable and elegance of verbal cobwebs, but also in that she actively declares ideals of goodness, beauty, humanism, world peace, and so on. In the intellectual factor, as well as in her general behavior, in any situation this person seeks to adhere to the style of women's salons of the century before last, in which enlightened ladies of noble blood played musical instruments, declared poetry, prose, displayed their own artwork. In short, the style of aristocracy is very close to her, and an aristocrat, as it is known, will be an aristocrat everywhere, always and in everything. Therefore, this woman's requirements, manners, behavior are similar in all other factors. For example, the nutritional factor. It can hardly be assumed that an aristocrat, or a person who aspires to be an aristocrat, would agree to have food in some cheap cafeteria, where the air is full of disgusting miasmas: sour cabbage soup, stale food or lumpens sitting at neighboring tables; or that she would dine at a table covered with a piece of paper with thick pieces of sausage served on it instead of a clean table with nicely served food. That is very unlikely. And, this is exactly what happens with this woman: situations mentioned above might result in loss of appetite or refusal to eat in such conditions. In her case, even a common and loved by many event like barbeque out in the nature might cause her displeasure: "Smoke, dirt, peasant-like style! Yuck!" However, she has high demands not only to the outside world, but also to herself: she always strives to be the best, to know everything, to be able to do everything, to have time for everything. This woman strives for perfection. Using the language of psychology, she has a high motivation for achievement, seeks to reach the peak in everything that she engages in. In principle, she is not interested in all intermediate stages, in stages from zero to the last one. The main thing is to turn up at the top. At any cost...

DEMO 27
Description Of Men Born On March 21ˢᵗ Of Leap Years From The Catalog Of Human Population

Presented demo is a very short description. A complete description consists of a very detailed description of functioning and qualities of personality: a general description and a description on 6 factors (intellectual, nutritional, physical, emotional, sexual, and environmental).

This individual has a strongly pronounced peculiarity, trait: he is all somehow bloodless, currentless, half-dead. Others might think that he does not live in the usual sense of the word, but rather exists based on the principle "neither dead nor alive." When looking at him, one begins to remember stories about zombies, people who died, but then some African sorcerer resurrected them and they came back to life. Similar characters are found in many ancient legends.

For example, it is told that the ancient Jewish rabbis could use any material or natural element (clay, sand, water, fire) to create an analogue of a human, a golem that was very similar to an alive, a real person. This human analog was able to walk, talk, and give responses adequate to situations. However, despite purely external similarity and resemblance, and seemingly complete identicality this was not a human. As far as the considered individual, in spite of all observable signs of life, his behavior reminds of that of a golem. He moves his arms and legs mechanically, says something and eats something, does something and communicates with someone, but he does all of this in such a way that it is as if in front of us is a resurrected deadman, just a body. It is as if this person's blood was drained and all of his life energy was sucked out of him. Remarkably, he is like this since birth, and so it is useless to try to attribute this fact to some external conditions, influence of other people, and events in his life. It is as if at the time of this person's birth, the invisible creator forgot to breathe the soul into him. For this reason, he is characterized by coldness, ice-like calmness, and everything that people call soulless. This specifically creates an impression of a corpse at a morgue, which has familiar external parameters and is still fresh, but is no longer alive. He is not involved; he is calm, silent, indifferent to everything and everyone, including himself. He is no longer in a hurry to go somewhere or do something, no longer wants anything in this life. This person's behavior and life philosophy somewhat reminds of famous characters from the well-known American movie called The Addams Family. They are all so cheerful and joyful, but when they put a bouquet of flowers in a vase, they cutoff the flower buds, and admire

beheaded sticks. This person sees himself and others as potential fertilizer, as that material, from which after death a burdock or some other plant will grow; it is as if while still alive he considers everyone, including his own self in terms of utilization mechanisms that exist in nature.

This person can be described as an apologist of death, who not only does not reject, but also defends and in fact praises this phenomenon. Like the great Plato, he is convinced that the body is the prison of the soul. He thinks that one can become immortal only by becoming free from the mortal flesh. He thinks that the soul should be free, and if this is so, then death of the body is a normal, even a positive phenomenon. This man is not afraid of death and it does not repel him; on the contrary, it raises his interest and even causes some enthusiasm. The theme of death (and everything connected with it) gets him hyped up, attracts, and draws his attention and thoughts like a magnet. This man is deeply concerned with the mystical process of transition from life to death, the process of transition from one state to a qualitatively different state, from one world to another; he is interested in questions that can be attributed to philosophy of death. In order to understand these questions, he reads a variety of materials on this subject—from obituaries and chronicles in low-grade tabloids, "yellow" press, to classical philosophical works. With a genuine interest, considered person also acquaints himself with various scientific research on this topic. In addition to scientific research, which highlights the theme of death from its own angle, this person might also be interested in mystical works, which open the curtain that conceals it from another angle. He might also be interested in how death is considered in various religious cults of antiquity and modernity. This person is interested in descriptions of battles with a great deal of bloodshed and battles from history, which were marked by a huge number of fatalities. In addition, in all of such type of historical descriptions of events related to wars and battles, this person is particularly attracted to descriptions of those historical figures (rulers, leaders, generals, etc.), who led a nation or part of a nation to a similar tragic and bloody outcome. He is extremely interested in stories about people who like kamikazes, samurais, and shahids go to their deaths. He might be interested in crime stories of bloody offenses, as well as main figures of these stories, the so-called "maniacs of the century" and "killers of the century." This person is interested in absolutely everything that leads to death of a person or historical events, material objects, natural phenomena, and so on related to it...

DEMO 28

Description Of Men Born On March 22nd Of Leap Years From The Catalog Of Human Population

Presented demo is a very short description. A complete description consists of a very detailed description of functioning and qualities of personality: a general description and a description on 6 factors (intellectual, nutritional, physical, emotional, sexual, and environmental).

This individual has a strongly pronounced peculiarity, trait: he is all somehow bloodless, currentless, half-dead. Others might think that he does not live in the usual sense of the word, but rather exists based on the principle "neither dead nor alive." When looking at him, one begins to remember stories about zombies, people who died, but then some African sorcerer resurrected them and they came back to life. Similar characters are found in many ancient legends.

For example, it is told that the ancient Jewish rabbis could use any material or natural element (clay, sand, water, fire) to create an analogue of a human, a golem that was very similar to an alive, a real person. This human analog was able to walk, talk, and give responses adequate to situations. However, despite purely external similarity and resemblance, and seemingly complete identicality this was not a human. As far as the considered individual, in spite of all observable signs of life, his behavior reminds of that of a golem. He moves his arms and legs mechanically, says something and eats something, does something and communicates with someone, but he does all of this in such a way that it is as if in front of us is a resurrected deadman, just a body. It is as if this person's blood was drained and all of his life energy was sucked out of him. Remarkably, he is like this since birth, and so it is useless to try to attribute this fact to some external conditions, influence of other people, and events in his life. It is as if at the time of this person's birth, the invisible creator forgot to breathe the soul into him. For this reason, he is characterized by coldness, ice-like calmness, and everything that people call soulless. This specifically creates an impression of a corpse at a morgue, which has familiar external parameters and is still fresh, but is no longer alive. He is not involved; he is calm, silent, indifferent to everything and everyone, including himself. He is no longer in a hurry to go somewhere or do something, no longer wants anything in this life. This person's behavior and life philosophy somewhat reminds of famous characters from the well-known American movie called The Addams Family. They are all so cheerful and joyful, but when they put a bouquet of flowers in a vase, they cutoff the flower buds, and admire

beheaded sticks. This person sees himself and others as potential fertilizer, as that material, from which after death a burdock or some other plant will grow; it is as if while still alive he considers everyone, including his own self in terms of utilization mechanisms that exist in nature.

This person can be described as an apologist of death, who not only does not reject, but also defends and in fact praises this phenomenon. Like the great Plato, he is convinced that the body is the prison of the soul. He thinks that one can become immortal only by becoming free from the mortal flesh. He thinks that the soul should be free, and if this is so, then death of the body is a normal, even a positive phenomenon. This man is not afraid of death and it does not repel him; on the contrary, it raises his interest and even causes some enthusiasm. The theme of death (and everything connected with it) gets him hyped up, attracts, and draws his attention and thoughts like a magnet. This man is deeply concerned with the mystical process of transition from life to death, the process of transition from one state to a qualitatively different state, from one world to another; he is interested in questions that can be attributed to philosophy of death. In order to understand these questions, he reads a variety of materials on this subject—from obituaries and chronicles in low-grade tabloids, "yellow" press, to classical philosophical works. With a genuine interest, considered person also acquaints himself with various scientific research on this topic. In addition to scientific research, which highlights the theme of death from its own angle, this person might also be interested in mystical works, which open the curtain that conceals it from another angle. He might also be interested in how death is considered in various religious cults of antiquity and modernity. This person is interested in descriptions of battles with a great deal of bloodshed and battles from history, which were marked by a huge number of fatalities. In addition, in all of such type of historical descriptions of events related to wars and battles, this person is particularly attracted to descriptions of those historical figures (rulers, leaders, generals, etc.), who led a nation or part of a nation to a similar tragic and bloody outcome. He is extremely interested in stories about people who like kamikazes, samurais, and shahids go to their deaths. He might be interested in crime stories of bloody offenses, as well as main figures of these stories, the so-called "maniacs of the century" and "killers of the century." This person is interested in absolutely everything that leads to death of a person or historical events, material objects, natural phenomena, and so on related to it...

DEMO 29

Description Of Men Born On March 22nd Of Common Years From The Catalog Of Human Population

Presented demo is a very short description. A complete description consists of a very detailed description of functioning and qualities of personality: a general description and a description on 6 factors (intellectual, nutritional, physical, emotional, sexual, and environmental).

This individual has a strongly pronounced peculiarity, trait: he is all somehow bloodless, currentless, half-dead. Others might think that he does not live in the usual sense of the word, but rather exists based on the principle "neither dead nor alive." When looking at him, one begins to remember stories about zombies, people who died, but then some African sorcerer resurrected them and they came back to life. Similar characters are found in many ancient legends.

For example, it is told that the ancient Jewish rabbis could use any material or natural element (clay, sand, water, fire) to create an analogue of a human, a golem that was very similar to an alive, a real person. This human analog was able to walk, talk, and give responses adequate to situations. However, despite purely external similarity and resemblance, and seemingly complete identicality this was not a human. As far as the considered individual, in spite of all observable signs of life, his behavior reminds of that of a golem. He moves his arms and legs mechanically, says something and eats something, does something and communicates with someone, but he does all of this in such a way that it is as if in front of us is a resurrected deadman, just a body. It is as if this person's blood was drained and all of his life energy was sucked out of him. Remarkably, he is like this since birth, and so it is useless to try to attribute this fact to some external conditions, influence of other people, and events in his life. It is as if at the time of this person's birth, the invisible creator forgot to breathe the soul into him. For this reason, he is characterized by coldness, ice-like calmness, and everything that people call soulless. This specifically creates an impression of a corpse at a morgue, which has familiar external parameters and is still fresh, but is no longer alive. He is not involved; he is calm, silent, indifferent to everything and everyone, including himself. He is no longer in a hurry to go somewhere or do something, no longer wants anything in this life. This person's behavior and life philosophy somewhat reminds of famous characters from the well-known American movie called The Addams Family. They are all so cheerful and joyful, but when they put a bouquet of flowers in a vase, they cutoff the flower buds, and admire

beheaded sticks. This person sees himself and others as potential fertilizer, as that material, from which after death a burdock or some other plant will grow; it is as if while still alive he considers everyone, including his own self in terms of utilization mechanisms that exist in nature.

This person can be described as an apologist of death, who not only does not reject, but also defends and in fact praises this phenomenon. Like the great Plato, he is convinced that the body is the prison of the soul. He thinks that one can become immortal only by becoming free from the mortal flesh. He thinks that the soul should be free, and if this is so, then death of the body is a normal, even a positive phenomenon. This man is not afraid of death and it does not repel him; on the contrary, it raises his interest and even causes some enthusiasm. The theme of death (and everything connected with it) gets him hyped up, attracts, and draws his attention and thoughts like a magnet. This man is deeply concerned with the mystical process of transition from life to death, the process of transition from one state to a qualitatively different state, from one world to another; he is interested in questions that can be attributed to philosophy of death. In order to understand these questions, he reads a variety of materials on this subject—from obituaries and chronicles in low-grade tabloids, "yellow" press, to classical philosophical works. With a genuine interest, considered person also acquaints himself with various scientific research on this topic. In addition to scientific research, which highlights the theme of death from its own angle, this person might also be interested in mystical works, which open the curtain that conceals it from another angle. He might also be interested in how death is considered in various religious cults of antiquity and modernity. This person is interested in descriptions of battles with a great deal of bloodshed and battles from history, which were marked by a huge number of fatalities. In addition, in all of such type of historical descriptions of events related to wars and battles, this person is particularly attracted to descriptions of those historical figures (rulers, leaders, generals, etc.), who led a nation or part of a nation to a similar tragic and bloody outcome. He is extremely interested in stories about people who like kamikazes, samurais, and shahids go to their deaths. He might be interested in crime stories of bloody offenses, as well as main figures of these stories, the so-called "maniacs of the century" and "killers of the century." This person is interested in absolutely everything that leads to death of a person or historical events, material objects, natural phenomena, and so on related to it...

DEMO 30

Description Of Men Born On March 23rd Of Common Years From The Catalog Of Human Population

Presented demo is a very short description. A complete description consists of a very detailed description of functioning and qualities of personality: a general description and a description on 6 factors (intellectual, nutritional, physical, emotional, sexual, and environmental).

This individual has a strongly pronounced peculiarity, trait: he is all somehow bloodless, currentless, half-dead. Others might think that he does not live in the usual sense of the word, but rather exists based on the principle "neither dead nor alive." When looking at him, one begins to remember stories about zombies, people who died, but then some African sorcerer resurrected them and they came back to life. Similar characters are found in many ancient legends.

For example, it is told that the ancient Jewish rabbis could use any material or natural element (clay, sand, water, fire) to create an analogue of a human, a golem that was very similar to an alive, a real person. This human analog was able to walk, talk, and give responses adequate to situations. However, despite purely external similarity and resemblance, and seemingly complete identicality this was not a human. As far as the considered individual, in spite of all observable signs of life, his behavior reminds of that of a golem. He moves his arms and legs mechanically, says something and eats something, does something and communicates with someone, but he does all of this in such a way that it is as if in front of us is a resurrected deadman, just a body. It is as if this person's blood was drained and all of his life energy was sucked out of him. Remarkably, he is like this since birth, and so it is useless to try to attribute this fact to some external conditions, influence of other people, and events in his life. It is as if at the time of this person's birth, the invisible creator forgot to breathe the soul into him. For this reason, he is characterized by coldness, ice-like calmness, and everything that people call soulless. This specifically creates an impression of a corpse at a morgue, which has familiar external parameters and is still fresh, but is no longer alive. He is not involved; he is calm, silent, indifferent to everything and everyone, including himself. He is no longer in a hurry to go somewhere or do something, no longer wants anything in this life. This person's behavior and life philosophy somewhat reminds of famous characters from the well-known American movie called The Addams Family. They are all so cheerful and joyful, but when they put a bouquet of flowers in a vase, they cutoff the flower buds, and admire

beheaded sticks. This person sees himself and others as potential fertilizer, as that material, from which after death a burdock or some other plant will grow; it is as if while still alive he considers everyone, including his own self in terms of utilization mechanisms that exist in nature.

This person can be described as an apologist of death, who not only does not reject, but also defends and in fact praises this phenomenon. Like the great Plato, he is convinced that the body is the prison of the soul. He thinks that one can become immortal only by becoming free from the mortal flesh. He thinks that the soul should be free, and if this is so, then death of the body is a normal, even a positive phenomenon. This man is not afraid of death and it does not repel him; on the contrary, it raises his interest and even causes some enthusiasm. The theme of death (and everything connected with it) gets him hyped up, attracts, and draws his attention and thoughts like a magnet. This man is deeply concerned with the mystical process of transition from life to death, the process of transition from one state to a qualitatively different state, from one world to another; he is interested in questions that can be attributed to philosophy of death. In order to understand these questions, he reads a variety of materials on this subject—from obituaries and chronicles in low-grade tabloids, "yellow" press, to classical philosophical works. With a genuine interest, considered person also acquaints himself with various scientific research on this topic. In addition to scientific research, which highlights the theme of death from its own angle, this person might also be interested in mystical works, which open the curtain that conceals it from another angle. He might also be interested in how death is considered in various religious cults of antiquity and modernity. This person is interested in descriptions of battles with a great deal of bloodshed and battles from history, which were marked by a huge number of fatalities. In addition, in all of such type of historical descriptions of events related to wars and battles, this person is particularly attracted to descriptions of those historical figures (rulers, leaders, generals, etc.), who led a nation or part of a nation to a similar tragic and bloody outcome. He is extremely interested in stories about people who like kamikazes, samurais, and shahids go to their deaths. He might be interested in crime stories of bloody offenses, as well as main figures of these stories, the so-called "maniacs of the century" and "killers of the century." This person is interested in absolutely everything that leads to death of a person or historical events, material objects, natural phenomena, and so on related to it...

DEMO 31

Description Of Men Born On April 3rd Of Leap Years From The Catalog Of Human Population

Presented demo is a very short description. A complete description consists of a very detailed description of functioning and qualities of personality: a general description and a description on 6 factors (intellectual, nutritional, physical, emotional, sexual, and environmental).

Considered man is a person who gains experience all his life. He bases his philosophy of life on experience. He appeals to his experience again and again, and one can often hear him say something like: "I tried this already", "I went through this and I know..." He considers examples from his personal life experiences as the best arguments to prove his claims, opinions, and attitudes. To him, experience is confirmation of his own professionalism, as well as an opportunity to stand out among, as he thinks, boneheads, and, of course, it helps him feel confident in any situation—"like fish in water." Therefore, this person shows admirable persistence in gaining life experience. In his youth, when, figuratively speaking, his "trunk" is still practically empty, he experiments actively and, it should be noted, quite freely. For example, in relationships with people he suddenly goes beyond the limits of normal, civilized relations, and he does this in order to see reactions of his opponent or opponents, to see what comes of it. Naturally, the risk is quite high in such a situation, and often reactions that he observes are rather harsh, rough, and sometimes cruel. However, this does not scare or repel him because this man learns rules in this way best of all. For example, the following rule: if you go beyond the limits of interpersonal relationships, you might get in serious trouble. And, once he experiences that firsthand—he learns it very well. Later on, he might use this experience as a tool to make someone lose their temper, provoke rage and as a guide on how to avoid trouble himself. He would, of course, benefit from meeting a good teacher, who would not only help him orient in life, but also would direct him by, for example, praising for good decisions and doing the right thing, and reproaching for actions that are too licentious, incongruous, and inappropriate. In his case, a well-known method of "a carrot and a stick" would give good results—it is more or less safe and does not stop from acquisition of new experiences! Moreover, by experimenting under the guidance of an experienced mentor, this man will be able to one day become a teacher for someone himself and will carefully foster his mentee or mentees. However, as it is known, not everyone is lucky when it comes to teachers. Without a stationary teacher (and, this a role can be fulfilled by parents or a school) this person risks to become a negligent, careless person, who thinks that "life will teach him." What it will teach him is a different question. However, if he is lucky and meets a caring mentor or teacher, then he might become a highly educated individual, capable of creating something worthwhile and maybe even outstanding like his own method, philosophy, doctrine concerning, for example, educational sphere, or something else... By the way, in the course of acquisition of yet another experience, the end to experimenting comes at that very moment when this person feels that he was able to separate all wheat from the chaff, was able to grasp the essence of this or that object or phenomenon. He has a particularity. If he thinks that he understood the root cause, the basis, the motive, then he immediately loses interest in the area of his study and proclaims that he already grasped everything, knows everything, and understands everything (even if this is far from reality). To this man, the surrounding world is as if divided into two halves: one where experience has already been acquired and that, which so far remains unlearned by him. He perceives the second part of the world—the unlearned—with directness of a child and it attracts him like a magnet, but only until he learns it and can say something like: "I know! Been there, done that!" By the way, in terms of information—there are no uninteresting details for this man: everything is important and everything is interesting. Even conversations that seem empty are part of invaluable experience that he does not forget. This individual is able to demonstrate a truly childlike directness and naivety through his words, voice, intonations and behavior. However, it is necessary to understand that this self-presentation is nothing more than a great tool for a certain kind of cannibalism. Behaving in this way, this man is counting on that people will be more willing to open up to him and be frank. As for cannibalism, in this case it has nothing to do with cannibalism in the literal sense of the word—his main "food" are thoughts of other people, other people's behavior, reactions, and so on. This man is interested in people in terms of borrowing their lifestyles. Since quite a large number of people exist—this person has no shortage of this kind of "food." His cannibalism consists of the following: by masterfully opening, figuratively speaking, "gates to another person's soul," he learns how and what they live by, slowly finds out the lowdown on them, learns what, so to speak, is in their soul, what they hide, the true motives that underlie their behavior...

DEMO 32
Description Of Men Born On April 4th Of Common Years From The Catalog Of Human Population

Presented demo is a very short description. A complete description consists of a very detailed description of functioning and qualities of personality: a general description and a description on 6 factors (intellectual, nutritional, physical, emotional, sexual, and environmental).

Considered man is a person who gains experience all his life. He bases his philosophy of life on experience. He appeals to his experience again and again, and one can often hear him say something like: "I tried this already", "I went through this and I know..." He considers examples from his personal life experiences as the best arguments to prove his claims, opinions, and attitudes. To him, experience is confirmation of his own professionalism, as well as an opportunity to stand out among, as he thinks, boneheads, and, of course, it helps him feel confident in any situation—"like fish in water." Therefore, this person shows admirable persistence in gaining life experience. In his youth, when, figuratively speaking, his "trunk" is still practically empty, he experiments actively and, it should be noted, quite freely. For example, in relationships with people he suddenly goes beyond the limits of normal, civilized relations, and he does this in order to see reactions of his opponent or opponents, to see what comes of it. Naturally, the risk is quite high in such a situation, and often reactions that he observes are rather harsh, rough, and sometimes cruel. However, this does not scare or repel him because this man learns rules in this way best of all. For example, the following rule: if you go beyond the limits of interpersonal relationships, you might get in serious trouble. And, once he experiences that firsthand—he learns it very well. Later on, he might use this experience as a tool to make someone lose their temper, provoke rage and as a guide on how to avoid trouble himself. He would, of course, benefit from meeting a good teacher, who would not only help him orient in life, but also would direct him by, for example, praising for good decisions and doing the right thing, and reproaching for actions that are too licentious, incongruous, and inappropriate. In his case, a well-known method of "a carrot and a stick" would give good results—it is more or less safe and does not stop from acquisition of new experiences! Moreover, by experimenting under the guidance of an experienced mentor, this man will be able to one day become a teacher for someone himself and will carefully foster his mentee or mentees. However, as it is known, not everyone is lucky when it comes to teachers. Without a stationary teacher (and, this a role can be fulfilled by parents or a school) this person risks to become a negligent, careless person, who thinks that "life will teach him." What it will teach him is a different question. However, if he is lucky and meets a caring mentor or teacher, then he might become a highly educated individual, capable of creating something worthwhile and maybe even outstanding like his own method, philosophy, doctrine concerning, for example, educational sphere, or something else... By the way, in the course of acquisition of yet another experience, the end to experimenting comes at that very moment when this person feels that he was able to separate all wheat from the chaff, was able to grasp the essence of this or that object or phenomenon. He has a particularity. If he thinks that he understood the root cause, the basis, the motive, then he immediately loses interest in the area of his study and proclaims that he already grasped everything, knows everything, and understands everything (even if this is far from reality). To this man, the surrounding world is as if divided into two halves: one where experience has already been acquired and that, which so far remains unlearned by him. He perceives the second part of the world—the unlearned—with directness of a child and it attracts him like a magnet, but only until he learns it and can say something like: "I know! Been there, done that!" By the way, in terms of information—there are no uninteresting details for this man: everything is important and everything is interesting. Even conversations that seem empty are part of invaluable experience that he does not forget. This individual is able to demonstrate a truly childlike directness and naivety through his words, voice, intonations and behavior. However, it is necessary to understand that this self-presentation is nothing more than a great tool for a certain kind of cannibalism. Behaving in this way, this man is counting on that people will be more willing to open up to him and be frank. As for cannibalism, in this case it has nothing to do with cannibalism in the literal sense of the word—his main "food" are thoughts of other people, other people's behavior, reactions, and so on. This man is interested in people in terms of borrowing their lifestyles. Since quite a large number of people exist—this person has no shortage of this kind of "food." His cannibalism consists of the following: by masterfully opening, figuratively speaking, "gates to another person's soul," he learns how and what they live by, slowly finds out the lowdown on them, learns what, so to speak, is in their soul, what they hide, the true motives that underlie their behavior...

DEMO 33

Description Of Women Born On April 5ᵗʰ Of Leap Years From The Catalog Of Human Population

Presented demo is a very short description. A complete description consists of a very detailed description of functioning and qualities of personality: a general description and a description on 6 factors (intellectual, nutritional, physical, emotional, sexual, and environmental).

One half of this woman's life consists of functioning like a powerful vacuum cleaner that sucks in everything indiscriminately, while lying on a couch, a bed, sitting in an armchair in front of a television, or with a book or an interlocutor, with a surprised expression on her face and stubbornly silent. If you want her to respond to your question, you can get a few interjections from her in response, but only after a long unintelligible mooing. Although sometimes she bursts and begins to speak, it would really be better if she did not speak...! The second period of her life is characterized by attempts to construct situational anomalies out of everything that she "sucked in"— that is, to get in trouble, have adventures by framing someone or acting meanly towards someone. Then, everyone will have something to do, there will be sorting out of relationships, while she will be in the center of circumstances, but innocent. It will be unclear how these circumstances developed, she will be the victim, and will keep a watchful eye on how things unfold in order to ensure that the spectacle continues (so that life is not boring) and will add oil to flames from time to time.

Considered person can be called a traveler—she is "here today and gone tomorrow." This woman has a steady and irresistible need to constantly change places. After lying down in complete idleness for a long time, the main thing for her is to always have a possibility to actively move and find a way or a path. This woman is a traveler, who is a big fan of maundering about aimlessly no matter where, no matter what for, and no matter with whom. She seeks not to be tied to anyone or anything, to be independent and not to have any obligations (especially necessities for goal-directed efforts, which any work activity requires).

The main direction of this individual is to lead a purely vacuous way of life, to indulge in a wide variety of pleasures, breaking almost all acceptable norms and common decencies. She is an inveterate tourist, who does not have time to work because she is "always on the go." Having the philosophy of tumbleweed and excellent acting skills coupled with a constant desire, so to speak, "to fall on someone's tail" or "to tag along," this woman would be happy to live on someone else's money (men's, women's, her own parents',

etc.). From her point of view, this approach provides her with the most valuable—a possibility to do nothing, not to work, to lounge about, to entertain, to muck and walk around, and to do this cheerfully, with impressions and preferably with adventures.

This woman is hungry for any kind of adventure, entertainment, including ones with a criminal bent. She likes and constantly looks for extreme situations, where she can get some bruises, break or shatter something, get or give a black eye... She wants extreme situations to always be present in her life. Therefore, once she finally finds "something interesting" from her point of view, then she gets involved in this situation without giving in much thought, "as if accidentally." If, from her point of view, there is nothing interesting expected "on the horizon," then this person will create an extreme situation with her own hands, so to speak. First of all, individual personality traits of this woman (such as an extremely quick temper, plain arrogance, haughtiness, pride and presumptuousness) allow her to quite easily create situations, in which she would have desired troubles. Secondly, she is a skillful provocateur: to irrelevantly fool about, to play a joke on someone supposedly not out of spite, to be rude with pleasure or to openly make fun of others—all this brings her joy (especially considering her highly pronounced sadistic tendencies). And thirdly, by nature this woman is a fighter, who always picks up a gauntlet thrown to her, will never miss a single provocation from the environment and will immediately and gladly respond to any one of them.

The range of possible troubles (extreme situations), which are consequences of actions of considered individual, can be quite wide: from a banal drunk-fight, a black eye and a knocked out tooth, to bloody knifing, holding by law enforcement officials, a night in jail and a criminal record. By the way, unlike other people it is not a problem for her, for example, to spend a night in such place. Moreover, attracting the attention of police officers in itself is often quite a permissible part of the overall "entertainment program" for her (and sometimes desirable), which can occur in the following way: she got drunk—got into a fight—served time. She can be held in jail or arrested as many times as necessary—this is just what she wants. This is her life; to her it is normal and is just another entertainment. From the point of view of this woman, this is the meaning of "cool," a good time, fun "to the max..."

DEMO 34
Description Of Men Born On April 5th Of Leap Years From The Catalog Of Human Population

Presented demo is a very short description. A complete description consists of a very detailed description of functioning and qualities of personality: a general description and a description on 6 factors (intellectual, nutritional, physical, emotional, sexual, and environmental).

It is possible to say that the considered person is "on tour" throughout his life, as he has a steady and irresistible need to constantly change places. Most important for him is to always have a possibility to actively move and constantly be "on the road." This man is a wonderer, who likes to maunder about somewhere endlessly and aimlessly: no matter where, no matter what for. He wants to travel, not to be tied to anyone or anything (for the most part, he is interested only in himself) and not to have any obligations (especially necessities for goal-directed efforts, which any work activity requires).

The main direction of this individual is to lead a purely vacuous way of life, to indulge in a wide variety of pleasures, breaking almost all acceptable norms and common decencies. He is an inveterate tourist, who does not have time to work because he is "always on the go." Having the philosophy of a gigolo and excellent acting skills coupled with a constant desire, so to speak, "to fall on someone's tail" or "to tag along," this person would be happy to live on someone else's money (woman's, his own parents', etc.). From his point of view, life of a gigolo provides him with the most valuable—a possibility to do nothing, not to work, to hang about, to entertain, to muck and walk around, and to do this cheerfully, with impressions and preferably with adventures.

This man is hungry for any kind of adventure, entertainment, including ones with a criminal bent. He likes and constantly looks for extreme situations and really needs them to always be present in his life. Therefore, once he finally finds "something interesting" from his point of view, then he gets involved in this situation without giving in much thought, "as if accidentally." If, from his point of view, there is nothing interesting expected "on the horizon," then this person will create an extreme situation with his own hands, so to speak. First of all, individual personality traits of this man (such as an extremely quick temper, plain arrogance, haughtiness, pride and presumptuousness) allow him to quite easily create situations, in which he would have desired troubles. Secondly, he is a skillful provocateur: to irrelevantly fool about, to play a joke on someone supposedly not out of

spite, to be rude with pleasure or to openly make fun of others—all this is not a problem for him and even brings him joy (especially considering his highly pronounced sadistic tendencies). And thirdly, by nature this person is a fighter, who always picks up a gauntlet thrown to him, will never miss a single provocation from the environment and will immediately and gladly respond to any one of them.

The range of possible troubles (extreme situations), which are consequences of actions of considered individual, can be quite wide: from a banal drunk-fight, a black eye and a knocked out tooth, to bloody knifing, holding by law enforcement officials, a night in jail and a criminal record. By the way, unlike other people it is not a problem for him, for example, to spend a night in such place. Moreover, attracting the attention of police officers in itself is often quite a permissible (and sometimes desirable) part of the overall "entertainment program" for him, which can occur in the following way: he got drunk—got into a fight—served time. He can be held in jail or arrested as many times as necessary—this is just what he wants. This is his life; to him it is normal and is just another entertainment. From the point of view of this person, this is the meaning of "cool," a good time, fun "to the max."

This man has pronounced criminal tendencies and a pronounced antisocial orientation. He is a reckless "highwayman," who is able to create "lawlessness" wherever he appears. He is a natural bandit with a knobstick under his jacket, and who is constantly in search of places and people that can be used for his gain. In other words, he actively looks for an opportunity to profit at the expense of others. Having absolutely no desire to work, to earn money "by the sweat of his brow," he is a big fan of taking what he needs from the environment "for free"—by deceit or force. If this individual chooses crime as his main way of life, then he will not care how, in what form and in what area to realize his criminal tendencies. He likes absolutely all types of criminal activities: stealing, various types of fraud, hooliganism, brigandage, murder, etc...

DEMO 35
Description Of Women Born On April 6th Of Leap Years From The Catalog Of Human Population

Presented demo is a very short description. A complete description consists of a very detailed description of functioning and qualities of personality: a general description and a description on 6 factors (intellectual, nutritional, physical, emotional, sexual, and environmental).

One half of this woman's life consists of functioning like a powerful vacuum cleaner that sucks in everything indiscriminately, while lying on a couch, a bed, sitting in an armchair in front of a television, or with a book or an interlocutor, with a surprised expression on her face and stubbornly silent. If you want her to respond to your question, you can get a few interjections from her in response, but only after a long unintelligible mooing. Although sometimes she bursts and begins to speak, it would really be better if she did not speak...! The second period of her life is characterized by attempts to construct situational anomalies out of everything that she "sucked in"— that is, to get in trouble, have adventures by framing someone or acting meanly towards someone. Then, everyone will have something to do, there will be sorting out of relationships, while she will be in the center of circumstances, but innocent. It will be unclear how these circumstances developed, she will be the victim, and will keep a watchful eye on how things unfold in order to ensure that the spectacle continues (so that life is not boring) and will add oil to flames from time to time.

Considered person can be called a traveler—she is "here today and gone tomorrow." This woman has a steady and irresistible need to constantly change places. After lying down in complete idleness for a long time, the main thing for her is to always have a possibility to actively move and find a way or a path. This woman is a traveler, who is a big fan of maundering about aimlessly no matter where, no matter what for, and no matter with whom. She seeks not to be tied to anyone or anything, to be independent and not to have any obligations (especially necessities for goal-directed efforts, which any work activity requires).

The main direction of this individual is to lead a purely vacuous way of life, to indulge in a wide variety of pleasures, breaking almost all acceptable norms and common decencies. She is an inveterate tourist, who does not have time to work because she is "always on the go." Having the philosophy of tumbleweed and excellent acting skills coupled with a constant desire, so to speak, "to fall on someone's tail" or "to tag along," this woman would be happy to live on someone else's money (men's, women's, her own parents',

etc.). From her point of view, this approach provides her with the most valuable—a possibility to do nothing, not to work, to lounge about, to entertain, to muck and walk around, and to do this cheerfully, with impressions and preferably with adventures.

This woman is hungry for any kind of adventure, entertainment, including ones with a criminal bent. She likes and constantly looks for extreme situations, where she can get some bruises, break or shatter something, get or give a black eye... She wants extreme situations to always be present in her life. Therefore, once she finally finds "something interesting" from her point of view, then she gets involved in this situation without giving in much thought, "as if accidentally." If, from her point of view, there is nothing interesting expected "on the horizon," then this person will create an extreme situation with her own hands, so to speak. First of all, individual personality traits of this woman (such as an extremely quick temper, plain arrogance, haughtiness, pride and presumptuousness) allow her to quite easily create situations, in which she would have desired troubles. Secondly, she is a skillful provocateur: to irrelevantly fool about, to play a joke on someone supposedly not out of spite, to be rude with pleasure or to openly make fun of others—all this brings her joy (especially considering her highly pronounced sadistic tendencies). And thirdly, by nature this woman is a fighter, who always picks up a gauntlet thrown to her, will never miss a single provocation from the environment and will immediately and gladly respond to any one of them.

The range of possible troubles (extreme situations), which are consequences of actions of considered individual, can be quite wide: from a banal drunk-fight, a black eye and a knocked out tooth, to bloody knifing, holding by law enforcement officials, a night in jail and a criminal record. By the way, unlike other people it is not a problem for her, for example, to spend a night in such place. Moreover, attracting the attention of police officers in itself is often quite a permissible part of the overall "entertainment program" for her (and sometimes desirable), which can occur in the following way: she got drunk—got into a fight—served time. She can be held in jail or arrested as many times as necessary—this is just what she wants. This is her life; to her it is normal and is just another entertainment. From the point of view of this woman, this is the meaning of "cool," a good time, fun "to the max..."

DEMO 36

Description Of Men Born On April 6th Of Leap Years From The Catalog Of Human Population

Presented demo is a very short description. A complete description consists of a very detailed description of functioning and qualities of personality: a general description and a description on 6 factors (intellectual, nutritional, physical, emotional, sexual, and environmental).

It is possible to say that the considered person is "on tour" throughout his life, as he has a steady and irresistible need to constantly change places. Most important for him is to always have a possibility to actively move and constantly be "on the road." This man is a wonderer, who likes to maunder about somewhere endlessly and aimlessly: no matter where, no matter what for. He wants to travel, not to be tied to anyone or anything (for the most part, he is interested only in himself) and not to have any obligations (especially necessities for goal-directed efforts, which any work activity requires).

The main direction of this individual is to lead a purely vacuous way of life, to indulge in a wide variety of pleasures, breaking almost all acceptable norms and common decencies. He is an inveterate tourist, who does not have time to work because he is "always on the go." Having the philosophy of a gigolo and excellent acting skills coupled with a constant desire, so to speak, "to fall on someone's tail" or "to tag along," this person would be happy to live on someone else's money (woman's, his own parents', etc.). From his point of view, life of a gigolo provides him with the most valuable—a possibility to do nothing, not to work, to hang about, to entertain, to muck and walk around, and to do this cheerfully, with impressions and preferably with adventures.

This man is hungry for any kind of adventure, entertainment, including ones with a criminal bent. He likes and constantly looks for extreme situations and really needs them to always be present in his life. Therefore, once he finally finds "something interesting" from his point of view, then he gets involved in this situation without giving in much thought, "as if accidentally." If, from his point of view, there is nothing interesting expected "on the horizon," then this person will create an extreme situation with his own hands, so to speak. First of all, individual personality traits of this man (such as an extremely quick temper, plain arrogance, haughtiness, pride and presumptuousness) allow him to quite easily create situations, in which he would have desired troubles. Secondly, he is a skillful provocateur: to irrelevantly fool about, to play a joke on someone supposedly not out of

spite, to be rude with pleasure or to openly make fun of others—all this is not a problem for him and even brings him joy (especially considering his highly pronounced sadistic tendencies). And thirdly, by nature this person is a fighter, who always picks up a gauntlet thrown to him, will never miss a single provocation from the environment and will immediately and gladly respond to any one of them.

The range of possible troubles (extreme situations), which are consequences of actions of considered individual, can be quite wide: from a banal drunk-fight, a black eye and a knocked out tooth, to bloody knifing, holding by law enforcement officials, a night in jail and a criminal record. By the way, unlike other people it is not a problem for him, for example, to spend a night in such place. Moreover, attracting the attention of police officers in itself is often quite a permissible (and sometimes desirable) part of the overall "entertainment program" for him, which can occur in the following way: he got drunk—got into a fight—served time. He can be held in jail or arrested as many times as necessary—this is just what he wants. This is his life; to him it is normal and is just another entertainment. From the point of view of this person, this is the meaning of "cool," a good time, fun "to the max."

This man has pronounced criminal tendencies and a pronounced antisocial orientation. He is a reckless "highwayman," who is able to create "lawlessness" wherever he appears. He is a natural bandit with a knobstick under his jacket, and who is constantly in search of places and people that can be used for his gain. In other words, he actively looks for an opportunity to profit at the expense of others. Having absolutely no desire to work, to earn money "by the sweat of his brow," he is a big fan of taking what he needs from the environment "for free"—by deceit or force. If this individual chooses crime as his main way of life, then he will not care how, in what form and in what area to realize his criminal tendencies. He likes absolutely all types of criminal activities: stealing, various types of fraud, hooliganism, brigandage, murder, etc...

DEMO 37
Description Of Women Born On April 6th Of Common Years From The Catalog Of Human Population

Presented demo is a very short description. A complete description consists of a very detailed description of functioning and qualities of personality: a general description and a description on 6 factors (intellectual, nutritional, physical, emotional, sexual, and environmental).

One half of this woman's life consists of functioning like a powerful vacuum cleaner that sucks in everything indiscriminately, while lying on a couch, a bed, sitting in an armchair in front of a television, or with a book or an interlocutor, with a surprised expression on her face and stubbornly silent. If you want her to respond to your question, you can get a few interjections from her in response, but only after a long unintelligible mooing. Although sometimes she bursts and begins to speak, it would really be better if she did not speak...! The second period of her life is characterized by attempts to construct situational anomalies out of everything that she "sucked in"— that is, to get in trouble, have adventures by framing someone or acting meanly towards someone. Then, everyone will have something to do, there will be sorting out of relationships, while she will be in the center of circumstances, but innocent. It will be unclear how these circumstances developed, she will be the victim, and will keep a watchful eye on how things unfold in order to ensure that the spectacle continues (so that life is not boring) and will add oil to flames from time to time.

Considered person can be called a traveler—she is "here today and gone tomorrow." This woman has a steady and irresistible need to constantly change places. After lying down in complete idleness for a long time, the main thing for her is to always have a possibility to actively move and find a way or a path. This woman is a traveler, who is a big fan of maundering about aimlessly no matter where, no matter what for, and no matter with whom. She seeks not to be tied to anyone or anything, to be independent and not to have any obligations (especially necessities for goal-directed efforts, which any work activity requires).

The main direction of this individual is to lead a purely vacuous way of life, to indulge in a wide variety of pleasures, breaking almost all acceptable norms and common decencies. She is an inveterate tourist, who does not have time to work because she is "always on the go." Having the philosophy of tumbleweed and excellent acting skills coupled with a constant desire, so to speak, "to fall on someone's tail" or "to tag along," this woman would be happy to live on someone else's money (men's, women's, her own parents',

etc.). From her point of view, this approach provides her with the most valuable—a possibility to do nothing, not to work, to lounge about, to entertain, to muck and walk around, and to do this cheerfully, with impressions and preferably with adventures.

This woman is hungry for any kind of adventure, entertainment, including ones with a criminal bent. She likes and constantly looks for extreme situations, where she can get some bruises, break or shatter something, get or give a black eye... She wants extreme situations to always be present in her life. Therefore, once she finally finds "something interesting" from her point of view, then she gets involved in this situation without giving in much thought, "as if accidentally." If, from her point of view, there is nothing interesting expected "on the horizon," then this person will create an extreme situation with her own hands, so to speak. First of all, individual personality traits of this woman (such as an extremely quick temper, plain arrogance, haughtiness, pride and presumptuousness) allow her to quite easily create situations, in which she would have desired troubles. Secondly, she is a skillful provocateur: to irrelevantly fool about, to play a joke on someone supposedly not out of spite, to be rude with pleasure or to openly make fun of others—all this brings her joy (especially considering her highly pronounced sadistic tendencies). And thirdly, by nature this woman is a fighter, who always picks up a gauntlet thrown to her, will never miss a single provocation from the environment and will immediately and gladly respond to any one of them.

The range of possible troubles (extreme situations), which are consequences of actions of considered individual, can be quite wide: from a banal drunk-fight, a black eye and a knocked out tooth, to bloody knifing, holding by law enforcement officials, a night in jail and a criminal record. By the way, unlike other people it is not a problem for her, for example, to spend a night in such place. Moreover, attracting the attention of police officers in itself is often quite a permissible part of the overall "entertainment program" for her (and sometimes desirable), which can occur in the following way: she got drunk—got into a fight—served time. She can be held in jail or arrested as many times as necessary—this is just what she wants. This is her life; to her it is normal and is just another entertainment. From the point of view of this woman, this is the meaning of "cool," a good time, fun "to the max..."

DEMO 38
Description Of Men Born On April 6ᵗʰ Of Common Years From The Catalog Of Human Population

Presented demo is a very short description. A complete description consists of a very detailed description of functioning and qualities of personality: a general description and a description on 6 factors (intellectual, nutritional, physical, emotional, sexual, and environmental).

It is possible to say that the considered person is "on tour" throughout his life, as he has a steady and irresistible need to constantly change places. Most important for him is to always have a possibility to actively move and constantly be "on the road." This man is a wonderer, who likes to maunder about somewhere endlessly and aimlessly: no matter where, no matter what for. He wants to travel, not to be tied to anyone or anything (for the most part, he is interested only in himself) and not to have any obligations (especially necessities for goal-directed efforts, which any work activity requires).

The main direction of this individual is to lead a purely vacuous way of life, to indulge in a wide variety of pleasures, breaking almost all acceptable norms and common decencies. He is an inveterate tourist, who does not have time to work because he is "always on the go." Having the philosophy of a gigolo and excellent acting skills coupled with a constant desire, so to speak, "to fall on someone's tail" or "to tag along," this person would be happy to live on someone else's money (woman's, his own parents', etc.). From his point of view, life of a gigolo provides him with the most valuable—a possibility to do nothing, not to work, to hang about, to entertain, to muck and walk around, and to do this cheerfully, with impressions and preferably with adventures.

This man is hungry for any kind of adventure, entertainment, including ones with a criminal bent. He likes and constantly looks for extreme situations and really needs them to always be present in his life. Therefore, once he finally finds "something interesting" from his point of view, then he gets involved in this situation without giving in much thought, "as if accidentally." If, from his point of view, there is nothing interesting expected "on the horizon," then this person will create an extreme situation with his own hands, so to speak. First of all, individual personality traits of this man (such as an extremely quick temper, plain arrogance, haughtiness, pride and presumptuousness) allow him to quite easily create situations, in which he would have desired troubles. Secondly, he is a skillful provocateur: to irrelevantly fool about, to play a joke on someone supposedly not out of

spite, to be rude with pleasure or to openly make fun of others—all this is not a problem for him and even brings him joy (especially considering his highly pronounced sadistic tendencies). And thirdly, by nature this person is a fighter, who always picks up a gauntlet thrown to him, will never miss a single provocation from the environment and will immediately and gladly respond to any one of them.

The range of possible troubles (extreme situations), which are consequences of actions of considered individual, can be quite wide: from a banal drunk-fight, a black eye and a knocked out tooth, to bloody knifing, holding by law enforcement officials, a night in jail and a criminal record. By the way, unlike other people it is not a problem for him, for example, to spend a night in such place. Moreover, attracting the attention of police officers in itself is often quite a permissible (and sometimes desirable) part of the overall "entertainment program" for him, which can occur in the following way: he got drunk—got into a fight—served time. He can be held in jail or arrested as many times as necessary—this is just what he wants. This is his life; to him it is normal and is just another entertainment. From the point of view of this person, this is the meaning of "cool," a good time, fun "to the max."

This man has pronounced criminal tendencies and a pronounced antisocial orientation. He is a reckless "highwayman," who is able to create "lawlessness" wherever he appears. He is a natural bandit with a knobstick under his jacket, and who is constantly in search of places and people that can be used for his gain. In other words, he actively looks for an opportunity to profit at the expense of others. Having absolutely no desire to work, to earn money "by the sweat of his brow," he is a big fan of taking what he needs from the environment "for free"—by deceit or force. If this individual chooses crime as his main way of life, then he will not care how, in what form and in what area to realize his criminal tendencies. He likes absolutely all types of criminal activities: stealing, various types of fraud, hooliganism, brigandage, murder, etc...

DEMO 39

Description Of Women Born On April 7th Of Leap Years From The Catalog Of Human Population

Presented demo is a very short description. A complete description consists of a very detailed description of functioning and qualities of personality: a general description and a description on 6 factors (intellectual, nutritional, physical, emotional, sexual, and environmental).

One half of this woman's life consists of functioning like a powerful vacuum cleaner that sucks in everything indiscriminately, while lying on a couch, a bed, sitting in an armchair in front of a television, or with a book or an interlocutor, with a surprised expression on her face and stubbornly silent. If you want her to respond to your question, you can get a few interjections from her in response, but only after a long unintelligible mooing. Although sometimes she bursts and begins to speak, it would really be better if she did not speak...! The second period of her life is characterized by attempts to construct situational anomalies out of everything that she "sucked in"— that is, to get in trouble, have adventures by framing someone or acting meanly towards someone. Then, everyone will have something to do, there will be sorting out of relationships, while she will be in the center of circumstances, but innocent. It will be unclear how these circumstances developed, she will be the victim, and will keep a watchful eye on how things unfold in order to ensure that the spectacle continues (so that life is not boring) and will add oil to flames from time to time.

Considered person can be called a traveler—she is "here today and gone tomorrow." This woman has a steady and irresistible need to constantly change places. After lying down in complete idleness for a long time, the main thing for her is to always have a possibility to actively move and find a way or a path. This woman is a traveler, who is a big fan of maundering about aimlessly no matter where, no matter what for, and no matter with whom. She seeks not to be tied to anyone or anything, to be independent and not to have any obligations (especially necessities for goal-directed efforts, which any work activity requires).

The main direction of this individual is to lead a purely vacuous way of life, to indulge in a wide variety of pleasures, breaking almost all acceptable norms and common decencies. She is an inveterate tourist, who does not have time to work because she is "always on the go." Having the philosophy of tumbleweed and excellent acting skills coupled with a constant desire, so to speak, "to fall on someone's tail" or "to tag along," this woman would be happy to live on someone else's money (men's, women's, her own parents',

etc.). From her point of view, this approach provides her with the most valuable—a possibility to do nothing, not to work, to lounge about, to entertain, to muck and walk around, and to do this cheerfully, with impressions and preferably with adventures.

This woman is hungry for any kind of adventure, entertainment, including ones with a criminal bent. She likes and constantly looks for extreme situations, where she can get some bruises, break or shatter something, get or give a black eye... She wants extreme situations to always be present in her life. Therefore, once she finally finds "something interesting" from her point of view, then she gets involved in this situation without giving in much thought, "as if accidentally." If, from her point of view, there is nothing interesting expected "on the horizon," then this person will create an extreme situation with her own hands, so to speak. First of all, individual personality traits of this woman (such as an extremely quick temper, plain arrogance, haughtiness, pride and presumptuousness) allow her to quite easily create situations, in which she would have desired troubles. Secondly, she is a skillful provocateur: to irrelevantly fool about, to play a joke on someone supposedly not out of spite, to be rude with pleasure or to openly make fun of others—all this brings her joy (especially considering her highly pronounced sadistic tendencies). And thirdly, by nature this woman is a fighter, who always picks up a gauntlet thrown to her, will never miss a single provocation from the environment and will immediately and gladly respond to any one of them.

The range of possible troubles (extreme situations), which are consequences of actions of considered individual, can be quite wide: from a banal drunk-fight, a black eye and a knocked out tooth, to bloody knifing, holding by law enforcement officials, a night in jail and a criminal record. By the way, unlike other people it is not a problem for her, for example, to spend a night in such place. Moreover, attracting the attention of police officers in itself is often quite a permissible part of the overall "entertainment program" for her (and sometimes desirable), which can occur in the following way: she got drunk—got into a fight—served time. She can be held in jail or arrested as many times as necessary—this is just what she wants. This is her life; to her it is normal and is just another entertainment. From the point of view of this woman, this is the meaning of "cool," a good time, fun "to the max..."

DEMO 40

Description Of Men Born On April 7ᵗʰ Of Leap Years From The Catalog Of Human Population

Presented demo is a very short description. A complete description consists of a very detailed description of functioning and qualities of personality: a general description and a description on 6 factors (intellectual, nutritional, physical, emotional, sexual, and environmental).

It is possible to say that the considered person is "on tour" throughout his life, as he has a steady and irresistible need to constantly change places. Most important for him is to always have a possibility to actively move and constantly be "on the road." This man is a wonderer, who likes to maunder about somewhere endlessly and aimlessly: no matter where, no matter what for. He wants to travel, not to be tied to anyone or anything (for the most part, he is interested only in himself) and not to have any obligations (especially necessities for goal-directed efforts, which any work activity requires).

The main direction of this individual is to lead a purely vacuous way of life, to indulge in a wide variety of pleasures, breaking almost all acceptable norms and common decencies. He is an inveterate tourist, who does not have time to work because he is "always on the go." Having the philosophy of a gigolo and excellent acting skills coupled with a constant desire, so to speak, "to fall on someone's tail" or "to tag along," this person would be happy to live on someone else's money (woman's, his own parents', etc.). From his point of view, life of a gigolo provides him with the most valuable—a possibility to do nothing, not to work, to hang about, to entertain, to muck and walk around, and to do this cheerfully, with impressions and preferably with adventures.

This man is hungry for any kind of adventure, entertainment, including ones with a criminal bent. He likes and constantly looks for extreme situations and really needs them to always be present in his life. Therefore, once he finally finds "something interesting" from his point of view, then he gets involved in this situation without giving in much thought, "as if accidentally." If, from his point of view, there is nothing interesting expected "on the horizon," then this person will create an extreme situation with his own hands, so to speak. First of all, individual personality traits of this man (such as an extremely quick temper, plain arrogance, haughtiness, pride and presumptuousness) allow him to quite easily create situations, in which he would have desired troubles. Secondly, he is a skillful provocateur: to irrelevantly fool about, to play a joke on someone supposedly not out of

spite, to be rude with pleasure or to openly make fun of others—all this is not a problem for him and even brings him joy (especially considering his highly pronounced sadistic tendencies). And thirdly, by nature this person is a fighter, who always picks up a gauntlet thrown to him, will never miss a single provocation from the environment and will immediately and gladly respond to any one of them.

The range of possible troubles (extreme situations), which are consequences of actions of considered individual, can be quite wide: from a banal drunk-fight, a black eye and a knocked out tooth, to bloody knifing, holding by law enforcement officials, a night in jail and a criminal record. By the way, unlike other people it is not a problem for him, for example, to spend a night in such place. Moreover, attracting the attention of police officers in itself is often quite a permissible (and sometimes desirable) part of the overall "entertainment program" for him, which can occur in the following way: he got drunk—got into a fight—served time. He can be held in jail or arrested as many times as necessary—this is just what he wants. This is his life; to him it is normal and is just another entertainment. From the point of view of this person, this is the meaning of "cool," a good time, fun "to the max."

This man has pronounced criminal tendencies and a pronounced antisocial orientation. He is a reckless "highwayman," who is able to create "lawlessness" wherever he appears. He is a natural bandit with a knobstick under his jacket, and who is constantly in search of places and people that can be used for his gain. In other words, he actively looks for an opportunity to profit at the expense of others. Having absolutely no desire to work, to earn money "by the sweat of his brow," he is a big fan of taking what he needs from the environment "for free"—by deceit or force. If this individual chooses crime as his main way of life, then he will not care how, in what form and in what area to realize his criminal tendencies. He likes absolutely all types of criminal activities: stealing, various types of fraud, hooliganism, brigandage, murder, etc...

DEMO 41

Description Of Women Born On April 7th Of Common Years From The Catalog Of Human Population

Presented demo is a very short description. A complete description consists of a very detailed description of functioning and qualities of personality: a general description and a description on 6 factors (intellectual, nutritional, physical, emotional, sexual, and environmental).

One half of this woman's life consists of functioning like a powerful vacuum cleaner that sucks in everything indiscriminately, while lying on a couch, a bed, sitting in an armchair in front of a television, or with a book or an interlocutor, with a surprised expression on her face and stubbornly silent. If you want her to respond to your question, you can get a few interjections from her in response, but only after a long unintelligible mooing. Although sometimes she bursts and begins to speak, it would really be better if she did not speak...! The second period of her life is characterized by attempts to construct situational anomalies out of everything that she "sucked in"— that is, to get in trouble, have adventures by framing someone or acting meanly towards someone. Then, everyone will have something to do, there will be sorting out of relationships, while she will be in the center of circumstances, but innocent. It will be unclear how these circumstances developed, she will be the victim, and will keep a watchful eye on how things unfold in order to ensure that the spectacle continues (so that life is not boring) and will add oil to flames from time to time.

Considered person can be called a traveler—she is "here today and gone tomorrow." This woman has a steady and irresistible need to constantly change places. After lying down in complete idleness for a long time, the main thing for her is to always have a possibility to actively move and find a way or a path. This woman is a traveler, who is a big fan of maundering about aimlessly no matter where, no matter what for, and no matter with whom. She seeks not to be tied to anyone or anything, to be independent and not to have any obligations (especially necessities for goal-directed efforts, which any work activity requires).

The main direction of this individual is to lead a purely vacuous way of life, to indulge in a wide variety of pleasures, breaking almost all acceptable norms and common decencies. She is an inveterate tourist, who does not have time to work because she is "always on the go." Having the philosophy of tumbleweed and excellent acting skills coupled with a constant desire, so to speak, "to fall on someone's tail" or "to tag along," this woman would be happy to live on someone else's money (men's, women's, her own parents',

etc.). From her point of view, this approach provides her with the most valuable—a possibility to do nothing, not to work, to lounge about, to entertain, to muck and walk around, and to do this cheerfully, with impressions and preferably with adventures.

This woman is hungry for any kind of adventure, entertainment, including ones with a criminal bent. She likes and constantly looks for extreme situations, where she can get some bruises, break or shatter something, get or give a black eye... She wants extreme situations to always be present in her life. Therefore, once she finally finds "something interesting" from her point of view, then she gets involved in this situation without giving in much thought, "as if accidentally." If, from her point of view, there is nothing interesting expected "on the horizon," then this person will create an extreme situation with her own hands, so to speak. First of all, individual personality traits of this woman (such as an extremely quick temper, plain arrogance, haughtiness, pride and presumptuousness) allow her to quite easily create situations, in which she would have desired troubles. Secondly, she is a skillful provocateur: to irrelevantly fool about, to play a joke on someone supposedly not out of spite, to be rude with pleasure or to openly make fun of others—all this brings her joy (especially considering her highly pronounced sadistic tendencies). And thirdly, by nature this woman is a fighter, who always picks up a gauntlet thrown to her, will never miss a single provocation from the environment and will immediately and gladly respond to any one of them.

The range of possible troubles (extreme situations), which are consequences of actions of considered individual, can be quite wide: from a banal drunk-fight, a black eye and a knocked out tooth, to bloody knifing, holding by law enforcement officials, a night in jail and a criminal record. By the way, unlike other people it is not a problem for her, for example, to spend a night in such place. Moreover, attracting the attention of police officers in itself is often quite a permissible part of the overall "entertainment program" for her (and sometimes desirable), which can occur in the following way: she got drunk—got into a fight—served time. She can be held in jail or arrested as many times as necessary—this is just what she wants. This is her life; to her it is normal and is just another entertainment. From the point of view of this woman, this is the meaning of "cool," a good time, fun "to the max..."

DEMO 42

Description Of Men Born On April 7ᵗʰ Of Common Years From The Catalog Of Human Population

Presented demo is a very short description. A complete description consists of a very detailed description of functioning and qualities of personality: a general description and a description on 6 factors (intellectual, nutritional, physical, emotional, sexual, and environmental).

It is possible to say that the considered person is "on tour" throughout his life, as he has a steady and irresistible need to constantly change places. Most important for him is to always have a possibility to actively move and constantly be "on the road." This man is a wonderer, who likes to maunder about somewhere endlessly and aimlessly: no matter where, no matter what for. He wants to travel, not to be tied to anyone or anything (for the most part, he is interested only in himself) and not to have any obligations (especially necessities for goal-directed efforts, which any work activity requires).

The main direction of this individual is to lead a purely vacuous way of life, to indulge in a wide variety of pleasures, breaking almost all acceptable norms and common decencies. He is an inveterate tourist, who does not have time to work because he is "always on the go." Having the philosophy of a gigolo and excellent acting skills coupled with a constant desire, so to speak, "to fall on someone's tail" or "to tag along," this person would be happy to live on someone else's money (woman's, his own parents', etc.). From his point of view, life of a gigolo provides him with the most valuable—a possibility to do nothing, not to work, to hang about, to entertain, to muck and walk around, and to do this cheerfully, with impressions and preferably with adventures.

This man is hungry for any kind of adventure, entertainment, including ones with a criminal bent. He likes and constantly looks for extreme situations and really needs them to always be present in his life. Therefore, once he finally finds "something interesting" from his point of view, then he gets involved in this situation without giving in much thought, "as if accidentally." If, from his point of view, there is nothing interesting expected "on the horizon," then this person will create an extreme situation with his own hands, so to speak. First of all, individual personality traits of this man (such as an extremely quick temper, plain arrogance, haughtiness, pride and presumptuousness) allow him to quite easily create situations, in which he would have desired troubles. Secondly, he is a skillful provocateur: to irrelevantly fool about, to play a joke on someone supposedly not out of

spite, to be rude with pleasure or to openly make fun of others—all this is not a problem for him and even brings him joy (especially considering his highly pronounced sadistic tendencies). And thirdly, by nature this person is a fighter, who always picks up a gauntlet thrown to him, will never miss a single provocation from the environment and will immediately and gladly respond to any one of them.

The range of possible troubles (extreme situations), which are consequences of actions of considered individual, can be quite wide: from a banal drunk-fight, a black eye and a knocked out tooth, to bloody knifing, holding by law enforcement officials, a night in jail and a criminal record. By the way, unlike other people it is not a problem for him, for example, to spend a night in such place. Moreover, attracting the attention of police officers in itself is often quite a permissible (and sometimes desirable) part of the overall "entertainment program" for him, which can occur in the following way: he got drunk—got into a fight—served time. He can be held in jail or arrested as many times as necessary—this is just what he wants. This is his life; to him it is normal and is just another entertainment. From the point of view of this person, this is the meaning of "cool," a good time, fun "to the max."

This man has pronounced criminal tendencies and a pronounced antisocial orientation. He is a reckless "highwayman," who is able to create "lawlessness" wherever he appears. He is a natural bandit with a knobstick under his jacket, and who is constantly in search of places and people that can be used for his gain. In other words, he actively looks for an opportunity to profit at the expense of others. Having absolutely no desire to work, to earn money "by the sweat of his brow," he is a big fan of taking what he needs from the environment "for free"—by deceit or force. If this individual chooses crime as his main way of life, then he will not care how, in what form and in what area to realize his criminal tendencies. He likes absolutely all types of criminal activities: stealing, various types of fraud, hooliganism, brigandage, murder, etc...

DEMO 43

Description Of Women Born On April 8ᵗʰ Of Leap Years From The Catalog Of Human Population

Presented demo is a very short description. A complete description consists of a very detailed description of functioning and qualities of personality: a general description and a description on 6 factors (intellectual, nutritional, physical, emotional, sexual, and environmental).

One half of this woman's life consists of functioning like a powerful vacuum cleaner that sucks in everything indiscriminately, while lying on a couch, a bed, sitting in an armchair in front of a television, or with a book or an interlocutor, with a surprised expression on her face and stubbornly silent. If you want her to respond to your question, you can get a few interjections from her in response, but only after a long unintelligible mooing. Although sometimes she bursts and begins to speak, it would really be better if she did not speak...! The second period of her life is characterized by attempts to construct situational anomalies out of everything that she "sucked in"— that is, to get in trouble, have adventures by framing someone or acting meanly towards someone. Then, everyone will have something to do, there will be sorting out of relationships, while she will be in the center of circumstances, but innocent. It will be unclear how these circumstances developed, she will be the victim, and will keep a watchful eye on how things unfold in order to ensure that the spectacle continues (so that life is not boring) and will add oil to flames from time to time.

Considered person can be called a traveler—she is "here today and gone tomorrow." This woman has a steady and irresistible need to constantly change places. After lying down in complete idleness for a long time, the main thing for her is to always have a possibility to actively move and find a way or a path. This woman is a traveler, who is a big fan of maundering about aimlessly no matter where, no matter what for, and no matter with whom. She seeks not to be tied to anyone or anything, to be independent and not to have any obligations (especially necessities for goal-directed efforts, which any work activity requires).

The main direction of this individual is to lead a purely vacuous way of life, to indulge in a wide variety of pleasures, breaking almost all acceptable norms and common decencies. She is an inveterate tourist, who does not have time to work because she is "always on the go." Having the philosophy of tumbleweed and excellent acting skills coupled with a constant desire, so to speak, "to fall on someone's tail" or "to tag along," this woman would be happy to live on someone else's money (men's, women's, her own parents',

etc.). From her point of view, this approach provides her with the most valuable—a possibility to do nothing, not to work, to lounge about, to entertain, to muck and walk around, and to do this cheerfully, with impressions and preferably with adventures.

This woman is hungry for any kind of adventure, entertainment, including ones with a criminal bent. She likes and constantly looks for extreme situations, where she can get some bruises, break or shatter something, get or give a black eye... She wants extreme situations to always be present in her life. Therefore, once she finally finds "something interesting" from her point of view, then she gets involved in this situation without giving in much thought, "as if accidentally." If, from her point of view, there is nothing interesting expected "on the horizon," then this person will create an extreme situation with her own hands, so to speak. First of all, individual personality traits of this woman (such as an extremely quick temper, plain arrogance, haughtiness, pride and presumptuousness) allow her to quite easily create situations, in which she would have desired troubles. Secondly, she is a skillful provocateur: to irrelevantly fool about, to play a joke on someone supposedly not out of spite, to be rude with pleasure or to openly make fun of others—all this brings her joy (especially considering her highly pronounced sadistic tendencies). And thirdly, by nature this woman is a fighter, who always picks up a gauntlet thrown to her, will never miss a single provocation from the environment and will immediately and gladly respond to any one of them.

The range of possible troubles (extreme situations), which are consequences of actions of considered individual, can be quite wide: from a banal drunk-fight, a black eye and a knocked out tooth, to bloody knifing, holding by law enforcement officials, a night in jail and a criminal record. By the way, unlike other people it is not a problem for her, for example, to spend a night in such place. Moreover, attracting the attention of police officers in itself is often quite a permissible part of the overall "entertainment program" for her (and sometimes desirable), which can occur in the following way: she got drunk—got into a fight—served time. She can be held in jail or arrested as many times as necessary—this is just what she wants. This is her life; to her it is normal and is just another entertainment. From the point of view of this woman, this is the meaning of "cool," a good time, fun "to the max..."

DEMO 44
Description Of Men Born On April 8th Of Leap Years From The Catalog Of Human Population

Presented demo is a very short description. A complete description consists of a very detailed description of functioning and qualities of personality: a general description and a description on 6 factors (intellectual, nutritional, physical, emotional, sexual, and environmental).

It is possible to say that the considered person is "on tour" throughout his life, as he has a steady and irresistible need to constantly change places. Most important for him is to always have a possibility to actively move and constantly be "on the road." This man is a wonderer, who likes to maunder about somewhere endlessly and aimlessly: no matter where, no matter what for. He wants to travel, not to be tied to anyone or anything (for the most part, he is interested only in himself) and not to have any obligations (especially necessities for goal-directed efforts, which any work activity requires).

The main direction of this individual is to lead a purely vacuous way of life, to indulge in a wide variety of pleasures, breaking almost all acceptable norms and common decencies. He is an inveterate tourist, who does not have time to work because he is "always on the go." Having the philosophy of a gigolo and excellent acting skills coupled with a constant desire, so to speak, "to fall on someone's tail" or "to tag along," this person would be happy to live on someone else's money (woman's, his own parents', etc.). From his point of view, life of a gigolo provides him with the most valuable—a possibility to do nothing, not to work, to hang about, to entertain, to muck and walk around, and to do this cheerfully, with impressions and preferably with adventures.

This man is hungry for any kind of adventure, entertainment, including ones with a criminal bent. He likes and constantly looks for extreme situations and really needs them to always be present in his life. Therefore, once he finally finds "something interesting" from his point of view, then he gets involved in this situation without giving in much thought, "as if accidentally." If, from his point of view, there is nothing interesting expected "on the horizon," then this person will create an extreme situation with his own hands, so to speak. First of all, individual personality traits of this man (such as an extremely quick temper, plain arrogance, haughtiness, pride and presumptuousness) allow him to quite easily create situations, in which he would have desired troubles. Secondly, he is a skillful provocateur: to irrelevantly fool about, to play a joke on someone supposedly not out of

spite, to be rude with pleasure or to openly make fun of others—all this is not a problem for him and even brings him joy (especially considering his highly pronounced sadistic tendencies). And thirdly, by nature this person is a fighter, who always picks up a gauntlet thrown to him, will never miss a single provocation from the environment and will immediately and gladly respond to any one of them.

The range of possible troubles (extreme situations), which are consequences of actions of considered individual, can be quite wide: from a banal drunk-fight, a black eye and a knocked out tooth, to bloody knifing, holding by law enforcement officials, a night in jail and a criminal record. By the way, unlike other people it is not a problem for him, for example, to spend a night in such place. Moreover, attracting the attention of police officers in itself is often quite a permissible (and sometimes desirable) part of the overall "entertainment program" for him, which can occur in the following way: he got drunk—got into a fight—served time. He can be held in jail or arrested as many times as necessary—this is just what he wants. This is his life; to him it is normal and is just another entertainment. From the point of view of this person, this is the meaning of "cool," a good time, fun "to the max."

This man has pronounced criminal tendencies and a pronounced antisocial orientation. He is a reckless "highwayman," who is able to create "lawlessness" wherever he appears. He is a natural bandit with a knobstick under his jacket, and who is constantly in search of places and people that can be used for his gain. In other words, he actively looks for an opportunity to profit at the expense of others. Having absolutely no desire to work, to earn money "by the sweat of his brow," he is a big fan of taking what he needs from the environment "for free"—by deceit or force. If this individual chooses crime as his main way of life, then he will not care how, in what form and in what area to realize his criminal tendencies. He likes absolutely all types of criminal activities: stealing, various types of fraud, hooliganism, brigandage, murder, etc...

DEMO 45

Description Of Women Born On April 8th Of Common Years From The Catalog Of Human Population

Presented demo is a very short description. A complete description consists of a very detailed description of functioning and qualities of personality: a general description and a description on 6 factors (intellectual, nutritional, physical, emotional, sexual, and environmental).

One half of this woman's life consists of functioning like a powerful vacuum cleaner that sucks in everything indiscriminately, while lying on a couch, a bed, sitting in an armchair in front of a television, or with a book or an interlocutor, with a surprised expression on her face and stubbornly silent. If you want her to respond to your question, you can get a few interjections from her in response, but only after a long unintelligible mooing. Although sometimes she bursts and begins to speak, it would really be better if she did not speak...! The second period of her life is characterized by attempts to construct situational anomalies out of everything that she "sucked in"— that is, to get in trouble, have adventures by framing someone or acting meanly towards someone. Then, everyone will have something to do, there will be sorting out of relationships, while she will be in the center of circumstances, but innocent. It will be unclear how these circumstances developed, she will be the victim, and will keep a watchful eye on how things unfold in order to ensure that the spectacle continues (so that life is not boring) and will add oil to flames from time to time.

Considered person can be called a traveler—she is "here today and gone tomorrow." This woman has a steady and irresistible need to constantly change places. After lying down in complete idleness for a long time, the main thing for her is to always have a possibility to actively move and find a way or a path. This woman is a traveler, who is a big fan of maundering about aimlessly no matter where, no matter what for, and no matter with whom. She seeks not to be tied to anyone or anything, to be independent and not to have any obligations (especially necessities for goal-directed efforts, which any work activity requires).

The main direction of this individual is to lead a purely vacuous way of life, to indulge in a wide variety of pleasures, breaking almost all acceptable norms and common decencies. She is an inveterate tourist, who does not have time to work because she is "always on the go." Having the philosophy of tumbleweed and excellent acting skills coupled with a constant desire, so to speak, "to fall on someone's tail" or "to tag along," this woman would be happy to live on someone else's money (men's, women's, her own parents',

etc.). From her point of view, this approach provides her with the most valuable—a possibility to do nothing, not to work, to lounge about, to entertain, to muck and walk around, and to do this cheerfully, with impressions and preferably with adventures.

This woman is hungry for any kind of adventure, entertainment, including ones with a criminal bent. She likes and constantly looks for extreme situations, where she can get some bruises, break or shatter something, get or give a black eye... She wants extreme situations to always be present in her life. Therefore, once she finally finds "something interesting" from her point of view, then she gets involved in this situation without giving in much thought, "as if accidentally." If, from her point of view, there is nothing interesting expected "on the horizon," then this person will create an extreme situation with her own hands, so to speak. First of all, individual personality traits of this woman (such as an extremely quick temper, plain arrogance, haughtiness, pride and presumptuousness) allow her to quite easily create situations, in which she would have desired troubles. Secondly, she is a skillful provocateur: to irrelevantly fool about, to play a joke on someone supposedly not out of spite, to be rude with pleasure or to openly make fun of others—all this brings her joy (especially considering her highly pronounced sadistic tendencies). And thirdly, by nature this woman is a fighter, who always picks up a gauntlet thrown to her, will never miss a single provocation from the environment and will immediately and gladly respond to any one of them.

The range of possible troubles (extreme situations), which are consequences of actions of considered individual, can be quite wide: from a banal drunk-fight, a black eye and a knocked out tooth, to bloody knifing, holding by law enforcement officials, a night in jail and a criminal record. By the way, unlike other people it is not a problem for her, for example, to spend a night in such place. Moreover, attracting the attention of police officers in itself is often quite a permissible part of the overall "entertainment program" for her (and sometimes desirable), which can occur in the following way: she got drunk—got into a fight—served time. She can be held in jail or arrested as many times as necessary—this is just what she wants. This is her life; to her it is normal and is just another entertainment. From the point of view of this woman, this is the meaning of "cool," a good time, fun "to the max..."

DEMO 46
Description Of Men Born On April 8th Of Common Years From The Catalog Of Human Population

Presented demo is a very short description. A complete description consists of a very detailed description of functioning and qualities of personality: a general description and a description on 6 factors (intellectual, nutritional, physical, emotional, sexual, and environmental).

It is possible to say that the considered person is "on tour" throughout his life, as he has a steady and irresistible need to constantly change places. Most important for him is to always have a possibility to actively move and constantly be "on the road." This man is a wonderer, who likes to maunder about somewhere endlessly and aimlessly: no matter where, no matter what for. He wants to travel, not to be tied to anyone or anything (for the most part, he is interested only in himself) and not to have any obligations (especially necessities for goal-directed efforts, which any work activity requires).

The main direction of this individual is to lead a purely vacuous way of life, to indulge in a wide variety of pleasures, breaking almost all acceptable norms and common decencies. He is an inveterate tourist, who does not have time to work because he is "always on the go." Having the philosophy of a gigolo and excellent acting skills coupled with a constant desire, so to speak, "to fall on someone's tail" or "to tag along," this person would be happy to live on someone else's money (woman's, his own parents', etc.). From his point of view, life of a gigolo provides him with the most valuable—a possibility to do nothing, not to work, to hang about, to entertain, to muck and walk around, and to do this cheerfully, with impressions and preferably with adventures.

This man is hungry for any kind of adventure, entertainment, including ones with a criminal bent. He likes and constantly looks for extreme situations and really needs them to always be present in his life. Therefore, once he finally finds "something interesting" from his point of view, then he gets involved in this situation without giving in much thought, "as if accidentally." If, from his point of view, there is nothing interesting expected "on the horizon," then this person will create an extreme situation with his own hands, so to speak. First of all, individual personality traits of this man (such as an extremely quick temper, plain arrogance, haughtiness, pride and presumptuousness) allow him to quite easily create situations, in which he would have desired troubles. Secondly, he is a skillful provocateur: to irrelevantly fool about, to play a joke on someone supposedly not out of

spite, to be rude with pleasure or to openly make fun of others—all this is not a problem for him and even brings him joy (especially considering his highly pronounced sadistic tendencies). And thirdly, by nature this person is a fighter, who always picks up a gauntlet thrown to him, will never miss a single provocation from the environment and will immediately and gladly respond to any one of them.

The range of possible troubles (extreme situations), which are consequences of actions of considered individual, can be quite wide: from a banal drunk-fight, a black eye and a knocked out tooth, to bloody knifing, holding by law enforcement officials, a night in jail and a criminal record. By the way, unlike other people it is not a problem for him, for example, to spend a night in such place. Moreover, attracting the attention of police officers in itself is often quite a permissible (and sometimes desirable) part of the overall "entertainment program" for him, which can occur in the following way: he got drunk—got into a fight—served time. He can be held in jail or arrested as many times as necessary—this is just what he wants. This is his life; to him it is normal and is just another entertainment. From the point of view of this person, this is the meaning of "cool," a good time, fun "to the max."

This man has pronounced criminal tendencies and a pronounced antisocial orientation. He is a reckless "highwayman," who is able to create "lawlessness" wherever he appears. He is a natural bandit with a knobstick under his jacket, and who is constantly in search of places and people that can be used for his gain. In other words, he actively looks for an opportunity to profit at the expense of others. Having absolutely no desire to work, to earn money "by the sweat of his brow," he is a big fan of taking what he needs from the environment "for free"—by deceit or force. If this individual chooses crime as his main way of life, then he will not care how, in what form and in what area to realize his criminal tendencies. He likes absolutely all types of criminal activities: stealing, various types of fraud, hooliganism, brigandage, murder, etc...

DEMO 47

Description Of Women Born On April 9th Of Leap Years From The Catalog Of Human Population

Presented demo is a very short description. A complete description consists of a very detailed description of functioning and qualities of personality: a general description and a description on 6 factors (intellectual, nutritional, physical, emotional, sexual, and environmental).

This person can be compared with the biblical Buridan's donkey, which could not choose between two haystacks one that could satisfy his hunger, and eventually died from hunger directly between them. This woman is in "the skin" of said character throughout her life. Moreover, the considered person is not so much a victim of some circumstances that involve a torturous choice—she regularly creates these circumstances in her life herself. For example, once she meets a man and marries him, she will surely find herself another man, as if "to have a set." This creates an impression that she does all this in order to be torn between them, to walk between them in a figure eight, or, as it is called, "to dance together" once she ensures that all three participants become personally acquainted.

Actually, this woman is inclined to organize dual situations around herself throughout her life in order to connect both "angles" with herself like a hypotenuse. This is exactly why someone or something equivalent in a single copy is not able to satisfy this woman. After all, what will she then tormentingly choose from? Who will she connect?! Being a great intrigante and conspirator, this woman literally knocks together heads of people, whom she wants to connect. This is exactly what will happen in every case with two men, as well as in all other situations. At the same time, it always seems to her that this happened as if by accident. In reality, it is simply her secret desire. And, this means that she will not be able to act in a different way. At work, with relatives, friends, business partners—she constantly "drains" them information about each other. This information is hard-hitting. Therefore, the finale is always the same.

Since this woman also secretly, but with enthusiasm constantly organizes tantamount polarities, selecting them in the form of two equal, equally important (needed, high-quality, loved, desired) magnitudes—there will always be not just single tandem "husband-lover" in her life, but also many other doublets. For example, she will create a doublet "apartment-country house" specifically in order to constantly ask herself questions, answer them, and, most importantly, to have the possibility for long and torturous rushing from one to another: "Where to make repairs first? For which place

should I buy furniture first? Where to spend the weekend?" This person might get two cars in order to think hard every morning, afternoon, evening and night: "Which car should I use? Which car to take to a car-wash first? On which car should I change tires first?" This woman will also be sure to duplicate clothes, in order to be able to "jump" out of one outfit into another before leaving home. She will buy two nearly identical dresses and will think for hours: "Should I wear this one or that one today? That one or this one?" It is important to understand that such "torments," which seem as such to an observer, are not at all torments for considered individual. This is a normal typical situation for this individual, which is necessary for her in order to let passions out. The thing is that presence of many doublets, as a reason for making a choice and connections, cause incredible passions in this person, and then they are let out. In the end, this leads her to a pleasant state of emptiness, satisfaction and great pleasure.

This woman is an eternal victim of constant languish, uncontrolled desires, which literally cause stagnation in her eyes. Since all this happens on a subconscious level, usually she does not at all realize what is actually happening. This person simply feels that she wants this and that equally. The only thing that she is able to pinpoint in her mind is a strong need: "I want very much!" In this sense, she reminds of a kettle with a whistle that is starting to boil, quietly at first, then begins to whistle, and at some point starts to jump up, splashing water in all directions and looks as if it is about to take off like a rocket. It is the same in her case. This woman tormentingly chooses, doubts for a while when trying to decide on something, infinitely reviews options, but then the boiling point becomes critical, and a toggle switch becomes activated in her mind: "That's it, I can't anymore!" In this state, she gets off the mark, ready to do anything in order to satisfy her need to urgently eat something, meet with someone, carry out a number of actions...

DEMO 48

Description Of Women Born On April 9th Of Common Years From The Catalog Of Human Population

Presented demo is a very short description. A complete description consists of a very detailed description of functioning and qualities of personality: a general description and a description on 6 factors (intellectual, nutritional, physical, emotional, sexual, and environmental).

One half of this woman's life consists of functioning like a powerful vacuum cleaner that sucks in everything indiscriminately, while lying on a couch, a bed, sitting in an armchair in front of a television, or with a book or an interlocutor, with a surprised expression on her face and stubbornly silent. If you want her to respond to your question, you can get a few interjections from her in response, but only after a long unintelligible mooing. Although sometimes she bursts and begins to speak, it would really be better if she did not speak...! The second period of her life is characterized by attempts to construct situational anomalies out of everything that she "sucked in"— that is, to get in trouble, have adventures by framing someone or acting meanly towards someone. Then, everyone will have something to do, there will be sorting out of relationships, while she will be in the center of circumstances, but innocent. It will be unclear how these circumstances developed, she will be the victim, and will keep a watchful eye on how things unfold in order to ensure that the spectacle continues (so that life is not boring) and will add oil to flames from time to time.

Considered person can be called a traveler—she is "here today and gone tomorrow." This woman has a steady and irresistible need to constantly change places. After lying down in complete idleness for a long time, the main thing for her is to always have a possibility to actively move and find a way or a path. This woman is a traveler, who is a big fan of maundering about aimlessly no matter where, no matter what for, and no matter with whom. She seeks not to be tied to anyone or anything, to be independent and not to have any obligations (especially necessities for goal-directed efforts, which any work activity requires).

The main direction of this individual is to lead a purely vacuous way of life, to indulge in a wide variety of pleasures, breaking almost all acceptable norms and common decencies. She is an inveterate tourist, who does not have time to work because she is "always on the go." Having the philosophy of tumbleweed and excellent acting skills coupled with a constant desire, so to speak, "to fall on someone's tail" or "to tag along," this woman would be happy to live on someone else's money (men's, women's, her own parents',

etc.). From her point of view, this approach provides her with the most valuable—a possibility to do nothing, not to work, to lounge about, to entertain, to muck and walk around, and to do this cheerfully, with impressions and preferably with adventures.

This woman is hungry for any kind of adventure, entertainment, including ones with a criminal bent. She likes and constantly looks for extreme situations, where she can get some bruises, break or shatter something, get or give a black eye... She wants extreme situations to always be present in her life. Therefore, once she finally finds "something interesting" from her point of view, then she gets involved in this situation without giving in much thought, "as if accidentally." If, from her point of view, there is nothing interesting expected "on the horizon," then this person will create an extreme situation with her own hands, so to speak. First of all, individual personality traits of this woman (such as an extremely quick temper, plain arrogance, haughtiness, pride and presumptuousness) allow her to quite easily create situations, in which she would have desired troubles. Secondly, she is a skillful provocateur: to irrelevantly fool about, to play a joke on someone supposedly not out of spite, to be rude with pleasure or to openly make fun of others—all this brings her joy (especially considering her highly pronounced sadistic tendencies). And thirdly, by nature this woman is a fighter, who always picks up a gauntlet thrown to her, will never miss a single provocation from the environment and will immediately and gladly respond to any one of them.

The range of possible troubles (extreme situations), which are consequences of actions of considered individual, can be quite wide: from a banal drunk-fight, a black eye and a knocked out tooth, to bloody knifing, holding by law enforcement officials, a night in jail and a criminal record. By the way, unlike other people it is not a problem for her, for example, to spend a night in such place. Moreover, attracting the attention of police officers in itself is often quite a permissible part of the overall "entertainment program" for her (and sometimes desirable), which can occur in the following way: she got drunk—got into a fight—served time. She can be held in jail or arrested as many times as necessary—this is just what she wants. This is her life; to her it is normal and is just another entertainment. From the point of view of this woman, this is the meaning of "cool," a good time, fun "to the max..."

DEMO 49
Description Of Men Born On April 9ᵗʰ Of Common Years From The Catalog Of Human Population

Presented demo is a very short description. A complete description consists of a very detailed description of functioning and qualities of personality: a general description and a description on 6 factors (intellectual, nutritional, physical, emotional, sexual, and environmental).

It is possible to say that the considered person is "on tour" throughout his life, as he has a steady and irresistible need to constantly change places. Most important for him is to always have a possibility to actively move and constantly be "on the road." This man is a wonderer, who likes to maunder about somewhere endlessly and aimlessly: no matter where, no matter what for. He wants to travel, not to be tied to anyone or anything (for the most part, he is interested only in himself) and not to have any obligations (especially necessities for goal-directed efforts, which any work activity requires).

The main direction of this individual is to lead a purely vacuous way of life, to indulge in a wide variety of pleasures, breaking almost all acceptable norms and common decencies. He is an inveterate tourist, who does not have time to work because he is "always on the go." Having the philosophy of a gigolo and excellent acting skills coupled with a constant desire, so to speak, "to fall on someone's tail" or "to tag along," this person would be happy to live on someone else's money (woman's, his own parents', etc.). From his point of view, life of a gigolo provides him with the most valuable—a possibility to do nothing, not to work, to hang about, to entertain, to muck and walk around, and to do this cheerfully, with impressions and preferably with adventures.

This man is hungry for any kind of adventure, entertainment, including ones with a criminal bent. He likes and constantly looks for extreme situations and really needs them to always be present in his life. Therefore, once he finally finds "something interesting" from his point of view, then he gets involved in this situation without giving in much thought, "as if accidentally." If, from his point of view, there is nothing interesting expected "on the horizon," then this person will create an extreme situation with his own hands, so to speak. First of all, individual personality traits of this man (such as an extremely quick temper, plain arrogance, haughtiness, pride and presumptuousness) allow him to quite easily create situations, in which he would have desired troubles. Secondly, he is a skillful provocateur: to irrelevantly fool about, to play a joke on someone supposedly not out of

spite, to be rude with pleasure or to openly make fun of others—all this is not a problem for him and even brings him joy (especially considering his highly pronounced sadistic tendencies). And thirdly, by nature this person is a fighter, who always picks up a gauntlet thrown to him, will never miss a single provocation from the environment and will immediately and gladly respond to any one of them.

The range of possible troubles (extreme situations), which are consequences of actions of considered individual, can be quite wide: from a banal drunk-fight, a black eye and a knocked out tooth, to bloody knifing, holding by law enforcement officials, a night in jail and a criminal record. By the way, unlike other people it is not a problem for him, for example, to spend a night in such place. Moreover, attracting the attention of police officers in itself is often quite a permissible (and sometimes desirable) part of the overall "entertainment program" for him, which can occur in the following way: he got drunk—got into a fight—served time. He can be held in jail or arrested as many times as necessary—this is just what he wants. This is his life; to him it is normal and is just another entertainment. From the point of view of this person, this is the meaning of "cool," a good time, fun "to the max."

This man has pronounced criminal tendencies and a pronounced antisocial orientation. He is a reckless "highwayman," who is able to create "lawlessness" wherever he appears. He is a natural bandit with a knobstick under his jacket, and who is constantly in search of places and people that can be used for his gain. In other words, he actively looks for an opportunity to profit at the expense of others. Having absolutely no desire to work, to earn money "by the sweat of his brow," he is a big fan of taking what he needs from the environment "for free"—by deceit or force. If this individual chooses crime as his main way of life, then he will not care how, in what form and in what area to realize his criminal tendencies. He likes absolutely all types of criminal activities: stealing, various types of fraud, hooliganism, brigandage, murder, etc...

DEMO 50
Description Of Women Born On April 10th Of Leap Years From The Catalog Of Human Population

Presented demo is a very short description. A complete description consists of a very detailed description of functioning and qualities of personality: a general description and a description on 6 factors (intellectual, nutritional, physical, emotional, sexual, and environmental).

This person can be compared with the biblical Buridan's donkey, which could not choose between two haystacks one that could satisfy his hunger, and eventually died from hunger directly between them. This woman is in "the skin" of said character throughout her life. Moreover, the considered person is not so much a victim of some circumstances that involve a torturous choice—she regularly creates these circumstances in her life herself. For example, once she meets a man and marries him, she will surely find herself another man, as if "to have a set." This creates an impression that she does all this in order to be torn between them, to walk between them in a figure eight, or, as it is called, "to dance together" once she ensures that all three participants become personally acquainted.

Actually, this woman is inclined to organize dual situations around herself throughout her life in order to connect both "angles" with herself like a hypotenuse. This is exactly why someone or something equivalent in a single copy is not able to satisfy this woman. After all, what will she then tormentingly choose from? Who will she connect?! Being a great intrigante and conspirator, this woman literally knocks together heads of people, whom she wants to connect. This is exactly what will happen in every case with two men, as well as in all other situations. At the same time, it always seems to her that this happened as if by accident. In reality, it is simply her secret desire. And, this means that she will not be able to act in a different way. At work, with relatives, friends, business partners—she constantly "drains" them information about each other. This information is hard-hitting. Therefore, the finale is always the same.

Since this woman also secretly, but with enthusiasm constantly organizes tantamount polarities, selecting them in the form of two equal, equally important (needed, high-quality, loved, desired) magnitudes—there will always be not just single tandem "husband-lover" in her life, but also many other doublets. For example, she will create a doublet "apartment-country house" specifically in order to constantly ask herself questions, answer them, and, most importantly, to have the possibility for long and torturous rushing from one to another: "Where to make repairs first? For which place

should I buy furniture first? Where to spend the weekend?" This person might get two cars in order to think hard every morning, afternoon, evening and night: "Which car should I use? Which car to take to a car-wash first? On which car should I change tires first?" This woman will also be sure to duplicate clothes, in order to be able to "jump" out of one outfit into another before leaving home. She will buy two nearly identical dresses and will think for hours: "Should I wear this one or that one today? That one or this one?" It is important to understand that such "torments," which seem as such to an observer, are not at all torments for considered individual. This is a normal typical situation for this individual, which is necessary for her in order to let passions out. The thing is that presence of many doublets, as a reason for making a choice and connections, cause incredible passions in this person, and then they are let out. In the end, this leads her to a pleasant state of emptiness, satisfaction and great pleasure.

This woman is an eternal victim of constant languish, uncontrolled desires, which literally cause stagnation in her eyes. Since all this happens on a subconscious level, usually she does not at all realize what is actually happening. This person simply feels that she wants this and that equally. The only thing that she is able to pinpoint in her mind is a strong need: "I want very much!" In this sense, she reminds of a kettle with a whistle that is starting to boil, quietly at first, then begins to whistle, and at some point starts to jump up, splashing water in all directions and looks as if it is about to take off like a rocket. It is the same in her case. This woman tormentingly chooses, doubts for a while when trying to decide on something, infinitely reviews options, but then the boiling point becomes critical, and a toggle switch becomes activated in her mind: "That's it, I can't anymore!" In this state, she gets off the mark, ready to do anything in order to satisfy her need to urgently eat something, meet with someone, carry out a number of actions...

DEMO 51

Description Of Women Born On April 10ᵗʰ Of Common Years From The Catalog Of Human Population

Presented demo is a very short description. A complete description consists of a very detailed description of functioning and qualities of personality: a general description and a description on 6 factors (intellectual, nutritional, physical, emotional, sexual, and environmental).

This person can be compared with the biblical Buridan's donkey, which could not choose between two haystacks one that could satisfy his hunger, and eventually died from hunger directly between them. This woman is in "the skin" of said character throughout her life. Moreover, the considered person is not so much a victim of some circumstances that involve a torturous choice—she regularly creates these circumstances in her life herself. For example, once she meets a man and marries him, she will surely find herself another man, as if "to have a set." This creates an impression that she does all this in order to be torn between them, to walk between them in a figure eight, or, as it is called, "to dance together" once she ensures that all three participants become personally acquainted.

Actually, this woman is inclined to organize dual situations around herself throughout her life in order to connect both "angles" with herself like a hypotenuse. This is exactly why someone or something equivalent in a single copy is not able to satisfy this woman. After all, what will she then tormentingly choose from? Who will she connect?! Being a great intrigante and conspirator, this woman literally knocks together heads of people, whom she wants to connect. This is exactly what will happen in every case with two men, as well as in all other situations. At the same time, it always seems to her that this happened as if by accident. In reality, it is simply her secret desire. And, this means that she will not be able to act in a different way. At work, with relatives, friends, business partners—she constantly "drains" them information about each other. This information is hard-hitting. Therefore, the finale is always the same.

Since this woman also secretly, but with enthusiasm constantly organizes tantamount polarities, selecting them in the form of two equal, equally important (needed, high-quality, loved, desired) magnitudes—there will always be not just single tandem "husband-lover" in her life, but also many other doublets. For example, she will create a doublet "apartment-country house" specifically in order to constantly ask herself questions, answer them, and, most importantly, to have the possibility for long and torturous rushing from one to another: "Where to make repairs first? For which place

should I buy furniture first? Where to spend the weekend?" This person might get two cars in order to think hard every morning, afternoon, evening and night: "Which car should I use? Which car to take to a car-wash first? On which car should I change tires first?" This woman will also be sure to duplicate clothes, in order to be able to "jump" out of one outfit into another before leaving home. She will buy two nearly identical dresses and will think for hours: "Should I wear this one or that one today? That one or this one?" It is important to understand that such "torments," which seem as such to an observer, are not at all torments for considered individual. This is a normal typical situation for this individual, which is necessary for her in order to let passions out. The thing is that presence of many doublets, as a reason for making a choice and connections, cause incredible passions in this person, and then they are let out. In the end, this leads her to a pleasant state of emptiness, satisfaction and great pleasure.

This woman is an eternal victim of constant languish, uncontrolled desires, which literally cause stagnation in her eyes. Since all this happens on a subconscious level, usually she does not at all realize what is actually happening. This person simply feels that she wants this and that equally. The only thing that she is able to pinpoint in her mind is a strong need: "I want very much!" In this sense, she reminds of a kettle with a whistle that is starting to boil, quietly at first, then begins to whistle, and at some point starts to jump up, splashing water in all directions and looks as if it is about to take off like a rocket. It is the same in her case. This woman tormentingly chooses, doubts for a while when trying to decide on something, infinitely reviews options, but then the boiling point becomes critical, and a toggle switch becomes activated in her mind: "That's it, I can't anymore!" In this state, she gets off the mark, ready to do anything in order to satisfy her need to urgently eat something, meet with someone, carry out a number of actions...

DEMO 52

Description Of Women Born On April 11ᵗʰ Of Leap Years From The Catalog Of Human Population

Presented demo is a very short description. A complete description consists of a very detailed description of functioning and qualities of personality: a general description and a description on 6 factors (intellectual, nutritional, physical, emotional, sexual, and environmental).

Until a certain age, considered person lives in the mode of gathering of various experiences based on the principle "life teaches;" and, this age is not 20 or even 30, but rather a time when it is said that a person is going through the so-called "midlife crisis"—sometime between 33 and 40 years of age. Therefore, this woman's life is clearly divided into two periods. The first one is when she constantly, greedily, without getting tired, absorbs fantastic amounts of information, life experiences on all factors like a sponge, and the second comes when she is already weathered and well-seen—she becomes like Captain Vrungel (a cartoon character from Soviet times), who responded to any question with: "We know, been there!" Up to this point, that is—until she becomes a person of many experiences, she can be compared to an empty container, which must regularly get filled-up with something. Like the aforementioned Captain, this woman must travel through more than one sea prior to allowing herself to be in the position of a know-it-all. Therefore, this woman will go to many lengths in order to know, to try, to see with her own eyes, to touch, to ferret out and clarify everything possible. Her whole life turns into one continuous experiment. In order to achieve the goal in the form of understanding of some phenomenon or object of the surrounding world, this individual as if tries each one of them on like dresses in a store: first, second, third. This is her method for getting an opportunity to construct her opinion, impression about something in order to say later on: "Oh, I've already come across this! I know this, I've tried it!" And, in this process she is fearless, tireless, and open to dangerous and plainly ridiculous variants. For example, in order to understand what "tortures of hell" are, she is ready to descend to hell-fire of truly unbearable sufferings; and, in order to learn everything about gonorrhea, she is ready to go to all lengths in the sexual factor. Sometimes this seems absurd to an observer, but she is ready to test on herself, for example, what it means to get soaked under cold rain and end up with pneumonia, or why one should not stick two knitting needles into an electrical outlet. However, in spite of everything, absolutely any one of her actions works towards realization of her main goal, which is gathering

enough experiences in her savings box. She uses any situation for learning. In this sense, her own life reminds of a river channel, into which flow a huge number of small streams, or an apartment of a traveler, who traveled all his life and brought home a small memorable thing from every trip. The following mechanism exists as one effective ways to become familiar with something new during the period of gathering of experience: when it is necessary for her to do something, the principle of "I want/I do not want" turns on. For example, when learning the system of intake of raw foods, she will not have the desire to violate it, while explaining this to herself and to others as: "I like to eat everything raw." This woman really stops wanting, adjusts, subordinates her psychophysiology to that action, which she was going to take for the sake of getting the next portion of experience. Thus, lifestyle, behavior, even needs of this woman fully submit to laws of actions of an area, learning of which she is engaged in. At the end of the period of gathering of experience, she becomes a truly unsinkable amphibian, who feels like a fish in water in any society and any situation, a person about whom it is said that she went through fire, water, copper pipes, and now neither sinks in water nor burns in fire, and can tell a lot about life.

The algorithm of gaining experience works in all areas, but it is important to her to find answers to the following questions: what is the true picture of the world? What is the real picture of human relationships, situations? Cumulatively, there is a presence of an attempt to divide society into pieces, like a pie, and then sort people, their lives, their situation, and then learn piece by piece. It is as if this person was tasked with compiling a cadaster of people, destinies, which itself would present an attempt to account, classify, catalog in order to answer questions: who, what is he/she like and what for exists on earth. Moreover, one of her functions is the ability to sort out any type of grading of anything and anyone very well. Therefore, this woman is not interested in characters of the same type and usually she says about such people: "Well, I have already encountered this type of people!" (In general, she does not spend any time of her life on studying something that she has already come across before.) In order to understand another person's life, ways of existence in the world, motivations, she uses the method, which actors use in order to understand characters, which they should play: getting into their image, getting into someone else's skin. This individual uses specifically Stanislavsky's acting method in order to understand the great variety of human worlds. It should be noted that this woman is extremely inquisitive and sly in the process of learning of motives that govern both individuals and social groups. She is interested in a variety of questions and, as a result, learns an infinite number of strategies and tactics of people's lives...

DEMO 53
Description Of Women Born On April 11ᵗʰ Of Common Years From The Catalog Of Human Population

Presented demo is a very short description. A complete description consists of a very detailed description of functioning and qualities of personality: a general description and a description on 6 factors (intellectual, nutritional, physical, emotional, sexual, and environmental).

This person can be compared with the biblical Buridan's donkey, which could not choose between two haystacks one that could satisfy his hunger, and eventually died from hunger directly between them. This woman is in "the skin" of said character throughout her life. Moreover, the considered person is not so much a victim of some circumstances that involve a torturous choice—she regularly creates these circumstances in her life herself. For example, once she meets a man and marries him, she will surely find herself another man, as if "to have a set." This creates an impression that she does all this in order to be torn between them, to walk between them in a figure eight, or, as it is called, "to dance together" once she ensures that all three participants become personally acquainted.

Actually, this woman is inclined to organize dual situations around herself throughout her life in order to connect both "angles" with herself like a hypotenuse. This is exactly why someone or something equivalent in a single copy is not able to satisfy this woman. After all, what will she then tormentingly choose from? Who will she connect?! Being a great intrigante and conspirator, this woman literally knocks together heads of people, whom she wants to connect. This is exactly what will happen in every case with two men, as well as in all other situations. At the same time, it always seems to her that this happened as if by accident. In reality, it is simply her secret desire. And, this means that she will not be able to act in a different way. At work, with relatives, friends, business partners—she constantly "drains" them information about each other. This information is hard-hitting. Therefore, the finale is always the same.

Since this woman also secretly, but with enthusiasm constantly organizes tantamount polarities, selecting them in the form of two equal, equally important (needed, high-quality, loved, desired) magnitudes—there will always be not just single tandem "husband-lover" in her life, but also many other doublets. For example, she will create a doublet "apartment-country house" specifically in order to constantly ask herself questions, answer them, and, most importantly, to have the possibility for long and torturous rushing from one to another: "Where to make repairs first? For which place

should I buy furniture first? Where to spend the weekend?" This person might get two cars in order to think hard every morning, afternoon, evening and night: "Which car should I use? Which car to take to a car-wash first? On which car should I change tires first?" This woman will also be sure to duplicate clothes, in order to be able to "jump" out of one outfit into another before leaving home. She will buy two nearly identical dresses and will think for hours: "Should I wear this one or that one today? That one or this one?" It is important to understand that such "torments," which seem as such to an observer, are not at all torments for considered individual. This is a normal typical situation for this individual, which is necessary for her in order to let passions out. The thing is that presence of many doublets, as a reason for making a choice and connections, cause incredible passions in this person, and then they are let out. In the end, this leads her to a pleasant state of emptiness, satisfaction and great pleasure.

This woman is an eternal victim of constant languish, uncontrolled desires, which literally cause stagnation in her eyes. Since all this happens on a subconscious level, usually she does not at all realize what is actually happening. This person simply feels that she wants this and that equally. The only thing that she is able to pinpoint in her mind is a strong need: "I want very much!" In this sense, she reminds of a kettle with a whistle that is starting to boil, quietly at first, then begins to whistle, and at some point starts to jump up, splashing water in all directions and looks as if it is about to take off like a rocket. It is the same in her case. This woman tormentingly chooses, doubts for a while when trying to decide on something, infinitely reviews options, but then the boiling point becomes critical, and a toggle switch becomes activated in her mind: "That's it, I can't anymore!" In this state, she gets off the mark, ready to do anything in order to satisfy her need to urgently eat something, meet with someone, carry out a number of actions...

DEMO 54

Description Of Women Born On April 12ᵗʰ Of Leap Years From The Catalog Of Human Population

Presented demo is a very short description. A complete description consists of a very detailed description of functioning and qualities of personality: a general description and a description on 6 factors (intellectual, nutritional, physical, emotional, sexual, and environmental).

Until a certain age, considered person lives in the mode of gathering of various experiences based on the principle "life teaches;" and, this age is not 20 or even 30, but rather a time when it is said that a person is going through the so-called "midlife crisis"—sometime between 33 and 40 years of age. Therefore, this woman's life is clearly divided into two periods. The first one is when she constantly, greedily, without getting tired, absorbs fantastic amounts of information, life experiences on all factors like a sponge, and the second comes when she is already weathered and well-seen—she becomes like Captain Vrungel (a cartoon character from Soviet times), who responded to any question with: "We know, been there!" Up to this point, that is—until she becomes a person of many experiences, she can be compared to an empty container, which must regularly get filled-up with something. Like the aforementioned Captain, this woman must travel through more than one sea prior to allowing herself to be in the position of a know-it-all. Therefore, this woman will go to many lengths in order to know, to try, to see with her own eyes, to touch, to ferret out and clarify everything possible. Her whole life turns into one continuous experiment. In order to achieve the goal in the form of understanding of some phenomenon or object of the surrounding world, this individual as if tries each one of them on like dresses in a store: first, second, third. This is her method for getting an opportunity to construct her opinion, impression about something in order to say later on: "Oh, I've already come across this! I know this, I've tried it!" And, in this process she is fearless, tireless, and open to dangerous and plainly ridiculous variants. For example, in order to understand what "tortures of hell" are, she is ready to descend to hell-fire of truly unbearable sufferings; and, in order to learn everything about gonorrhea, she is ready to go to all lengths in the sexual factor. Sometimes this seems absurd to an observer, but she is ready to test on herself, for example, what it means to get soaked under cold rain and end up with pneumonia, or why one should not stick two knitting needles into an electrical outlet. However, in spite of everything, absolutely any one of her actions works towards realization of her main goal, which is gathering

enough experiences in her savings box. She uses any situation for learning. In this sense, her own life reminds of a river channel, into which flow a huge number of small streams, or an apartment of a traveler, who traveled all his life and brought home a small memorable thing from every trip. The following mechanism exists as one effective ways to become familiar with something new during the period of gathering of experience: when it is necessary for her to do something, the principle of "I want/I do not want" turns on. For example, when learning the system of intake of raw foods, she will not have the desire to violate it, while explaining this to herself and to others as: "I like to eat everything raw." This woman really stops wanting, adjusts, subordinates her psychophysiology to that action, which she was going to take for the sake of getting the next portion of experience. Thus, lifestyle, behavior, even needs of this woman fully submit to laws of actions of an area, learning of which she is engaged in. At the end of the period of gathering of experience, she becomes a truly unsinkable amphibian, who feels like a fish in water in any society and any situation, a person about whom it is said that she went through fire, water, copper pipes, and now neither sinks in water nor burns in fire, and can tell a lot about life.

The algorithm of gaining experience works in all areas, but it is important to her to find answers to the following questions: what is the true picture of the world? What is the real picture of human relationships, situations? Cumulatively, there is a presence of an attempt to divide society into pieces, like a pie, and then sort people, their lives, their situation, and then learn piece by piece. It is as if this person was tasked with compiling a cadaster of people, destinies, which itself would present an attempt to account, classify, catalog in order to answer questions: who, what is he/she like and what for exists on earth. Moreover, one of her functions is the ability to sort out any type of grading of anything and anyone very well. Therefore, this woman is not interested in characters of the same type and usually she says about such people: "Well, I have already encountered this type of people!" (In general, she does not spend any time of her life on studying something that she has already come across before.) In order to understand another person's life, ways of existence in the world, motivations, she uses the method, which actors use in order to understand characters, which they should play: getting into their image, getting into someone else's skin. This individual uses specifically Stanislavsky's acting method in order to understand the great variety of human worlds. It should be noted that this woman is extremely inquisitive and sly in the process of learning of motives that govern both individuals and social groups. She is interested in a variety of questions and, as a result, learns an infinite number of strategies and tactics of people's lives...

DEMO 55
Description Of Women Born On April 12ᵗʰ Of Common Years From The Catalog Of Human Population

Presented demo is a very short description. A complete description consists of a very detailed description of functioning and qualities of personality: a general description and a description on 6 factors (intellectual, nutritional, physical, emotional, sexual, and environmental).

Until a certain age, considered person lives in the mode of gathering of various experiences based on the principle "life teaches;" and, this age is not 20 or even 30, but rather a time when it is said that a person is going through the so-called "midlife crisis"—sometime between 33 and 40 years of age. Therefore, this woman's life is clearly divided into two periods. The first one is when she constantly, greedily, without getting tired, absorbs fantastic amounts of information, life experiences on all factors like a sponge, and the second comes when she is already weathered and well-seen—she becomes like Captain Vrungel (a cartoon character from Soviet times), who responded to any question with: "We know, been there!" Up to this point, that is—until she becomes a person of many experiences, she can be compared to an empty container, which must regularly get filled-up with something. Like the aforementioned Captain, this woman must travel through more than one sea prior to allowing herself to be in the position of a know-it-all. Therefore, this woman will go to many lengths in order to know, to try, to see with her own eyes, to touch, to ferret out and clarify everything possible. Her whole life turns into one continuous experiment. In order to achieve the goal in the form of understanding of some phenomenon or object of the surrounding world, this individual as if tries each one of them on like dresses in a store: first, second, third. This is her method for getting an opportunity to construct her opinion, impression about something in order to say later on: "Oh, I've already come across this! I know this, I've tried it!" And, in this process she is fearless, tireless, and open to dangerous and plainly ridiculous variants. For example, in order to understand what "tortures of hell" are, she is ready to descend to hell-fire of truly unbearable sufferings; and, in order to learn everything about gonorrhea, she is ready to go to all lengths in the sexual factor. Sometimes this seems absurd to an observer, but she is ready to test on herself, for example, what it means to get soaked under cold rain and end up with pneumonia, or why one should not stick two knitting needles into an electrical outlet. However, in spite of everything, absolutely any one of her actions works towards realization of her main goal, which is gathering

enough experiences in her savings box. She uses any situation for learning. In this sense, her own life reminds of a river channel, into which flow a huge number of small streams, or an apartment of a traveler, who traveled all his life and brought home a small memorable thing from every trip. The following mechanism exists as one effective ways to become familiar with something new during the period of gathering of experience: when it is necessary for her to do something, the principle of "I want/I do not want" turns on. For example, when learning the system of intake of raw foods, she will not have the desire to violate it, while explaining this to herself and to others as: "I like to eat everything raw." This woman really stops wanting, adjusts, subordinates her psychophysiology to that action, which she was going to take for the sake of getting the next portion of experience. Thus, lifestyle, behavior, even needs of this woman fully submit to laws of actions of an area, learning of which she is engaged in. At the end of the period of gathering of experience, she becomes a truly unsinkable amphibian, who feels like a fish in water in any society and any situation, a person about whom it is said that she went through fire, water, copper pipes, and now neither sinks in water nor burns in fire, and can tell a lot about life.

The algorithm of gaining experience works in all areas, but it is important to her to find answers to the following questions: what is the true picture of the world? What is the real picture of human relationships, situations? Cumulatively, there is a presence of an attempt to divide society into pieces, like a pie, and then sort people, their lives, their situation, and then learn piece by piece. It is as if this person was tasked with compiling a cadaster of people, destinies, which itself would present an attempt to account, classify, catalog in order to answer questions: who, what is he/she like and what for exists on earth. Moreover, one of her functions is the ability to sort out any type of grading of anything and anyone very well. Therefore, this woman is not interested in characters of the same type and usually she says about such people: "Well, I have already encountered this type of people!" (In general, she does not spend any time of her life on studying something that she has already come across before.) In order to understand another person's life, ways of existence in the world, motivations, she uses the method, which actors use in order to understand characters, which they should play: getting into their image, getting into someone else's skin. This individual uses specifically Stanislavsky's acting method in order to understand the great variety of human worlds. It should be noted that this woman is extremely inquisitive and sly in the process of learning of motives that govern both individuals and social groups. She is interested in a variety of questions and, as a result, learns an infinite number of strategies and tactics of people's lives...

DEMO 56

Description Of Women Born On April 13ᵗʰ Of Common Years From The Catalog Of Human Population

Presented demo is a very short description. A complete description consists of a very detailed description of functioning and qualities of personality: a general description and a description on 6 factors (intellectual, nutritional, physical, emotional, sexual, and environmental).

Until a certain age, considered person lives in the mode of gathering of various experiences based on the principle "life teaches;" and, this age is not 20 or even 30, but rather a time when it is said that a person is going through the so-called "midlife crisis"—sometime between 33 and 40 years of age. Therefore, this woman's life is clearly divided into two periods. The first one is when she constantly, greedily, without getting tired, absorbs fantastic amounts of information, life experiences on all factors like a sponge, and the second comes when she is already weathered and well-seen—she becomes like Captain Vrungel (a cartoon character from Soviet times), who responded to any question with: "We know, been there!" Up to this point, that is—until she becomes a person of many experiences, she can be compared to an empty container, which must regularly get filled-up with something. Like the aforementioned Captain, this woman must travel through more than one sea prior to allowing herself to be in the position of a know-it-all. Therefore, this woman will go to many lengths in order to know, to try, to see with her own eyes, to touch, to ferret out and clarify everything possible. Her whole life turns into one continuous experiment. In order to achieve the goal in the form of understanding of some phenomenon or object of the surrounding world, this individual as if tries each one of them on like dresses in a store: first, second, third. This is her method for getting an opportunity to construct her opinion, impression about something in order to say later on: "Oh, I've already come across this! I know this, I've tried it!" And, in this process she is fearless, tireless, and open to dangerous and plainly ridiculous variants. For example, in order to understand what "tortures of hell" are, she is ready to descend to hell-fire of truly unbearable sufferings; and, in order to learn everything about gonorrhea, she is ready to go to all lengths in the sexual factor. Sometimes this seems absurd to an observer, but she is ready to test on herself, for example, what it means to get soaked under cold rain and end up with pneumonia, or why one should not stick two knitting needles into an electrical outlet. However, in spite of everything, absolutely any one of her actions works towards realization of her main goal, which is gathering

enough experiences in her savings box. She uses any situation for learning. In this sense, her own life reminds of a river channel, into which flow a huge number of small streams, or an apartment of a traveler, who traveled all his life and brought home a small memorable thing from every trip. The following mechanism exists as one effective ways to become familiar with something new during the period of gathering of experience: when it is necessary for her to do something, the principle of "I want/I do not want" turns on. For example, when learning the system of intake of raw foods, she will not have the desire to violate it, while explaining this to herself and to others as: "I like to eat everything raw." This woman really stops wanting, adjusts, subordinates her psychophysiology to that action, which she was going to take for the sake of getting the next portion of experience. Thus, lifestyle, behavior, even needs of this woman fully submit to laws of actions of an area, learning of which she is engaged in. At the end of the period of gathering of experience, she becomes a truly unsinkable amphibian, who feels like a fish in water in any society and any situation, a person about whom it is said that she went through fire, water, copper pipes, and now neither sinks in water nor burns in fire, and can tell a lot about life.

The algorithm of gaining experience works in all areas, but it is important to her to find answers to the following questions: what is the true picture of the world? What is the real picture of human relationships, situations? Cumulatively, there is a presence of an attempt to divide society into pieces, like a pie, and then sort people, their lives, their situation, and then learn piece by piece. It is as if this person was tasked with compiling a cadaster of people, destinies, which itself would present an attempt to account, classify, catalog in order to answer questions: who, what is he/she like and what for exists on earth. Moreover, one of her functions is the ability to sort out any type of grading of anything and anyone very well. Therefore, this woman is not interested in characters of the same type and usually she says about such people: "Well, I have already encountered this type of people!" (In general, she does not spend any time of her life on studying something that she has already come across before.) In order to understand another person's life, ways of existence in the world, motivations, she uses the method, which actors use in order to understand characters, which they should play: getting into their image, getting into someone else's skin. This individual uses specifically Stanislavsky's acting method in order to understand the great variety of human worlds. It should be noted that this woman is extremely inquisitive and sly in the process of learning of motives that govern both individuals and social groups. She is interested in a variety of questions and, as a result, learns an infinite number of strategies and tactics of people's lives...

DEMO 57

Description Of Women Born On April 17ᵗʰ Of Leap Years From The Catalog Of Human Population

Presented demo is a very short description. A complete description consists of a very detailed description of functioning and qualities of personality: a general description and a description on 6 factors (intellectual, nutritional, physical, emotional, sexual, and environmental).

This person can be characterized as highly experienced, or what is called "age-old," a woman who has gone through many different situations during the course of her life, "has been through fire, water and copper pipes" and now "knows everything, knows how to do anything, experienced it all." She perceives herself as sort of "an old lady" at any age and with any number of life experiences. And, this inner feeling of hers immediately transfers to a person with whom she comes into contact: he immediately feels that in front of him is a person wise from experience. It is also possible to say the following about this woman: "old and young alike," meaning that, when in such a "deeply wise" state—an elderly person becomes like a child, again begins to perceive this world in a very child-like way: without show, bustle, etc. This does not at all imply any kind of senile dementia, which is commonly called "falling into second childhood." No, on the contrary: the consciousness of such person is so clear and sharp that specifically this quality makes the impression that she is an absolutely wise woman, who gained knowledge of everything a long time ago and is now contemplating the world and events in it as they are, a woman who knows the true value of things and phenomena of this world. This woman looks at the world around her with clear eyes, simply fixating everything that happens in it, and as if mirroring it. All of her reactions to events are, on the one hand, child-like natural, and, on the other hand, wise and calm.

Naturally, being so "wise," this woman is an instructress in everything and for everyone. Who if not she knows better what action someone must take, what he or she should do or say and when... In essence, the considered person is a general manager, who single-handedly superintends, guides, plans, and controls everything. She can be compared with an administrator at a hotel: on the one hand, it is immediately obvious who is behind the wheel here, and, on the other hand, it seems unclear for what purpose because each person who lives or works in a hotel is his own master and seeks to do as he sees fit. However, when such an administrator suddenly disappears somewhere, then at once it becomes clear to everyone who was the one who held everything together because without his managing-

directing force everything starts to go down, and chaos and confusion begin at that hotel.

This person manages quite measuredly, without a hurry, she is not rushing anywhere, does not "create tension" by her dictate, does not yell and stomp her feet: she leads a person to wherever she sees fit quietly, calmly and gently. Even if she is not in the best physical shape, old, weak and sick—even then her management style is always quite firm. Sometimes it is said about such people: "one surprisingly cannot sleep upon your downy cot," that is—she takes the governing into her hands, while she wears "flannel gloves." She does not need to prove anything to anyone, she already knows that everything will be as she wants and that is it. This woman intuitively knows what needs to be done, where and when to be, and she organizes the space around her in such a way that she can always keep up without having to rush. In principle, she has no strategy or tactics for actions—she herself is strategy, as well as tactics. She simply makes a decision, acts and gets a result—quietly and peacefully. She is a commander, who confidently leads an army.

This woman knows how to firmly express her thoughts. However, in spite of her firmness, she always considers her opponent, treats him with respect and uses only civilized forms of communication. She is always ready to consider circumstances of another person, ready to listen to them and take them into account.

This woman constantly puts herself in someone else's shows, showing compassion and care. She is able to caringly go into all the details that relate to another person: "How did you sleep, on which side?", "What did you have for lunch today after salad, and was your drink with or without caffeine?" She is very attentive to other people, shows them compassion and limitless participation in their affairs, in their lives.

A characteristic peculiarity of this individual is that she always seeks to make people with whom she communicates trust her greatly, and she is willing to behave in a way that sooner or later will cause their trust. In general, she believes that full-value communication between people cannot occur without trust.

This person is convinced that caring for another person significantly develops all kinds of interpersonal relationships: helps them develop, enriches and bonds them, and this specifically strengthens all kinds of kinship and friendship ties. She is a very observant person in relation to other people, as well as to the world around her. This woman is ready to sacrifice her personal interests, preferences, time, and energy in order to arrange or organize something for others...

DEMO 58

Description Of Women Born On April 18th Of Leap Years From The Catalog Of Human Population

Presented demo is a very short description. A complete description consists of a very detailed description of functioning and qualities of personality: a general description and a description on 6 factors (intellectual, nutritional, physical, emotional, sexual, and environmental).

This person can be characterized as highly experienced, or what is called "age-old," a woman who has gone through many different situations during the course of her life, "has been through fire, water and copper pipes" and now "knows everything, knows how to do anything, experienced it all." She perceives herself as sort of "an old lady" at any age and with any number of life experiences. And, this inner feeling of hers immediately transfers to a person with whom she comes into contact: he immediately feels that in front of him is a person wise from experience. It is also possible to say the following about this woman: "old and young alike," meaning that, when in such a "deeply wise" state—an elderly person becomes like a child, again begins to perceive this world in a very child-like way: without show, bustle, etc. This does not at all imply any kind of senile dementia, which is commonly called "falling into second childhood." No, on the contrary: the consciousness of such person is so clear and sharp that specifically this quality makes the impression that she is an absolutely wise woman, who gained knowledge of everything a long time ago and is now contemplating the world and events in it as they are, a woman who knows the true value of things and phenomena of this world. This woman looks at the world around her with clear eyes, simply fixating everything that happens in it, and as if mirroring it. All of her reactions to events are, on the one hand, child-like natural, and, on the other hand, wise and calm.

Naturally, being so "wise," this woman is an instructress in everything and for everyone. Who if not she knows better what action someone must take, what he or she should do or say and when... In essence, the considered person is a general manager, who single-handedly superintends, guides, plans, and controls everything. She can be compared with an administrator at a hotel: on the one hand, it is immediately obvious who is behind the wheel here, and, on the other hand, it seems unclear for what purpose because each person who lives or works in a hotel is his own master and seeks to do as he sees fit. However, when such an administrator suddenly disappears somewhere, then at once it becomes clear to everyone who was the one who held everything together because without his managing-

directing force everything starts to go down, and chaos and confusion begin at that hotel.

This person manages quite measuredly, without a hurry, she is not rushing anywhere, does not "create tension" by her dictate, does not yell and stomp her feet: she leads a person to wherever she sees fit quietly, calmly and gently. Even if she is not in the best physical shape, old, weak and sick—even then her management style is always quite firm. Sometimes it is said about such people: "one surprisingly cannot sleep upon your downy cot," that is—she takes the governing into her hands, while she wears "flannel gloves." She does not need to prove anything to anyone, she already knows that everything will be as she wants and that is it. This woman intuitively knows what needs to be done, where and when to be, and she organizes the space around her in such a way that she can always keep up without having to rush. In principle, she has no strategy or tactics for actions—she herself is strategy, as well as tactics. She simply makes a decision, acts and gets a result—quietly and peacefully. She is a commander, who confidently leads an army.

This woman knows how to firmly express her thoughts. However, in spite of her firmness, she always considers her opponent, treats him with respect and uses only civilized forms of communication. She is always ready to consider circumstances of another person, ready to listen to them and take them into account.

This woman constantly puts herself in someone else's shows, showing compassion and care. She is able to caringly go into all the details that relate to another person: "How did you sleep, on which side?", "What did you have for lunch today after salad, and was your drink with or without caffeine?" She is very attentive to other people, shows them compassion and limitless participation in their affairs, in their lives.

A characteristic peculiarity of this individual is that she always seeks to make people with whom she communicates trust her greatly, and she is willing to behave in a way that sooner or later will cause their trust. In general, she believes that full-value communication between people cannot occur without trust.

This person is convinced that caring for another person significantly develops all kinds of interpersonal relationships: helps them develop, enriches and bonds them, and this specifically strengthens all kinds of kinship and friendship ties. She is a very observant person in relation to other people, as well as to the world around her. This woman is ready to sacrifice her personal interests, preferences, time, and energy in order to arrange or organize something for others...

DEMO 59
Description Of Women Born On April 18th Of Common Years From The Catalog Of Human Population

Presented demo is a very short description. A complete description consists of a very detailed description of functioning and qualities of personality: a general description and a description on 6 factors (intellectual, nutritional, physical, emotional, sexual, and environmental).

This person can be characterized as highly experienced, or what is called "age-old," a woman who has gone through many different situations during the course of her life, "has been through fire, water and copper pipes" and now "knows everything, knows how to do anything, experienced it all." She perceives herself as sort of "an old lady" at any age and with any number of life experiences. And, this inner feeling of hers immediately transfers to a person with whom she comes into contact: he immediately feels that in front of him is a person wise from experience. It is also possible to say the following about this woman: "old and young alike," meaning that, when in such a "deeply wise" state—an elderly person becomes like a child, again begins to perceive this world in a very child-like way: without show, bustle, etc. This does not at all imply any kind of senile dementia, which is commonly called "falling into second childhood." No, on the contrary: the consciousness of such person is so clear and sharp that specifically this quality makes the impression that she is an absolutely wise woman, who gained knowledge of everything a long time ago and is now contemplating the world and events in it as they are, a woman who knows the true value of things and phenomena of this world. This woman looks at the world around her with clear eyes, simply fixating everything that happens in it, and as if mirroring it. All of her reactions to events are, on the one hand, child-like natural, and, on the other hand, wise and calm.

Naturally, being so "wise," this woman is an instructress in everything and for everyone. Who if not she knows better what action someone must take, what he or she should do or say and when... In essence, the considered person is a general manager, who single-handedly superintends, guides, plans, and controls everything. She can be compared with an administrator at a hotel: on the one hand, it is immediately obvious who is behind the wheel here, and, on the other hand, it seems unclear for what purpose because each person who lives or works in a hotel is his own master and seeks to do as he sees fit. However, when such an administrator suddenly disappears somewhere, then at once it becomes clear to everyone who was the one who held everything together because without his managing-

directing force everything starts to go down, and chaos and confusion begin at that hotel.

This person manages quite measuredly, without a hurry, she is not rushing anywhere, does not "create tension" by her dictate, does not yell and stomp her feet: she leads a person to wherever she sees fit quietly, calmly and gently. Even if she is not in the best physical shape, old, weak and sick—even then her management style is always quite firm. Sometimes it is said about such people: "one surprisingly cannot sleep upon your downy cot," that is—she takes the governing into her hands, while she wears "flannel gloves." She does not need to prove anything to anyone, she already knows that everything will be as she wants and that is it. This woman intuitively knows what needs to be done, where and when to be, and she organizes the space around her in such a way that she can always keep up without having to rush. In principle, she has no strategy or tactics for actions—she herself is strategy, as well as tactics. She simply makes a decision, acts and gets a result—quietly and peacefully. She is a commander, who confidently leads an army.

This woman knows how to firmly express her thoughts. However, in spite of her firmness, she always considers her opponent, treats him with respect and uses only civilized forms of communication. She is always ready to consider circumstances of another person, ready to listen to them and take them into account.

This woman constantly puts herself in someone else's shows, showing compassion and care. She is able to caringly go into all the details that relate to another person: "How did you sleep, on which side?", "What did you have for lunch today after salad, and was your drink with or without caffeine?" She is very attentive to other people, shows them compassion and limitless participation in their affairs, in their lives.

A characteristic peculiarity of this individual is that she always seeks to make people with whom she communicates trust her greatly, and she is willing to behave in a way that sooner or later will cause their trust. In general, she believes that full-value communication between people cannot occur without trust.

This person is convinced that caring for another person significantly develops all kinds of interpersonal relationships: helps them develop, enriches and bonds them, and this specifically strengthens all kinds of kinship and friendship ties. She is a very observant person in relation to other people, as well as to the world around her. This woman is ready to sacrifice her personal interests, preferences, time, and energy in order to arrange or organize something for others...

DEMO 60

Description Of Women Born On April 19ᵗʰ Of Common Years From The Catalog Of Human Population

Presented demo is a very short description. A complete description consists of a very detailed description of functioning and qualities of personality: a general description and a description on 6 factors (intellectual, nutritional, physical, emotional, sexual, and environmental).

This person can be characterized as highly experienced, or what is called "age-old," a woman who has gone through many different situations during the course of her life, "has been through fire, water and copper pipes" and now "knows everything, knows how to do anything, experienced it all." She perceives herself as sort of "an old lady" at any age and with any number of life experiences. And, this inner feeling of hers immediately transfers to a person with whom she comes into contact: he immediately feels that in front of him is a person wise from experience. It is also possible to say the following about this woman: "old and young alike," meaning that, when in such a "deeply wise" state—an elderly person becomes like a child, again begins to perceive this world in a very child-like way: without show, bustle, etc. This does not at all imply any kind of senile dementia, which is commonly called "falling into second childhood." No, on the contrary: the consciousness of such person is so clear and sharp that specifically this quality makes the impression that she is an absolutely wise woman, who gained knowledge of everything a long time ago and is now contemplating the world and events in it as they are, a woman who knows the true value of things and phenomena of this world. This woman looks at the world around her with clear eyes, simply fixating everything that happens in it, and as if mirroring it. All of her reactions to events are, on the one hand, child-like natural, and, on the other hand, wise and calm.

Naturally, being so "wise," this woman is an instructress in everything and for everyone. Who if not she knows better what action someone must take, what he or she should do or say and when... In essence, the considered person is a general manager, who single-handedly superintends, guides, plans, and controls everything. She can be compared with an administrator at a hotel: on the one hand, it is immediately obvious who is behind the wheel here, and, on the other hand, it seems unclear for what purpose because each person who lives or works in a hotel is his own master and seeks to do as he sees fit. However, when such an administrator suddenly disappears somewhere, then at once it becomes clear to everyone who was the one who held everything together because without his managing-

directing force everything starts to go down, and chaos and confusion begin at that hotel.

This person manages quite measuredly, without a hurry, she is not rushing anywhere, does not "create tension" by her dictate, does not yell and stomp her feet: she leads a person to wherever she sees fit quietly, calmly and gently. Even if she is not in the best physical shape, old, weak and sick— even then her management style is always quite firm. Sometimes it is said about such people: "one surprisingly cannot sleep upon your downy cot," that is—she takes the governing into her hands, while she wears "flannel gloves." She does not need to prove anything to anyone, she already knows that everything will be as she wants and that is it. This woman intuitively knows what needs to be done, where and when to be, and she organizes the space around her in such a way that she can always keep up without having to rush. In principle, she has no strategy or tactics for actions—she herself is strategy, as well as tactics. She simply makes a decision, acts and gets a result—quietly and peacefully. She is a commander, who confidently leads an army.

This woman knows how to firmly express her thoughts. However, in spite of her firmness, she always considers her opponent, treats him with respect and uses only civilized forms of communication. She is always ready to consider circumstances of another person, ready to listen to them and take them into account.

This woman constantly puts herself in someone else's shows, showing compassion and care. She is able to caringly go into all the details that relate to another person: "How did you sleep, on which side?", "What did you have for lunch today after salad, and was your drink with or without caffeine?" She is very attentive to other people, shows them compassion and limitless participation in their affairs, in their lives.

A characteristic peculiarity of this individual is that she always seeks to make people with whom she communicates trust her greatly, and she is willing to behave in a way that sooner or later will cause their trust. In general, she believes that full-value communication between people cannot occur without trust.

This person is convinced that caring for another person significantly develops all kinds of interpersonal relationships: helps them develop, enriches and bonds them, and this specifically strengthens all kinds of kinship and friendship ties. She is a very observant person in relation to other people, as well as to the world around her. This woman is ready to sacrifice her personal interests, preferences, time, and energy in order to arrange or organize something for others...

DEMO 61

Description Of Women Born On April 23ᵗʰ Of Leap Years From The Catalog Of Human Population

Presented demo is a very short description. A complete description consists of a very detailed description of functioning and qualities of personality: a general description and a description on 6 factors (intellectual, nutritional, physical, emotional, sexual, and environmental).

One of the characteristic traits of considered individual is that her qualities coincide with the traditional understanding of the word "woman": soft, flexible, weak, defenseless. That is—at least, if you look at her, so to speak, "from the facade." She is ready to be a woman always, everywhere and in everything: to engage in traditional female tasks (she makes a clear distinction between female and male tasks), to get married as it is prescribed to a woman, to become a mother and a homemaker, and to do needlework. Housework, upbringing of children, traditional female roles, typical female chatter with girlfriends until late night and similar things—all this is about her. However, this woman also has well defined specific characteristics. One of them is the use of clichés, as peculiar pouring of her true essence into some form with transitions from one cliché to another. In this sense, this woman is a multi-tasking operator: first she is a maid, then a servant, then a homemaker, then a wife faithfully looking into her spouse's mouth, then a strict, decisive, stern businesswoman, then a gentle lover, and then a philandering hetaera. Her guises change depending on a situation and goals: a shaman, a lady, a matchmaker, a priestess, a goddess, a queen, a schoolgirl, a clown, a nun, an actress, an amazon, a commander, a beggar, a tradeswoman, a spy... In short, the range is great, and she is a wonderful simulator!

By nature, she has a talent for transformations and has a huge number of roles that she can use. And, every time she is different in each new role. Is it necessary to appear poor and unfortunate? No problem! Is there a need to appear as innocent as a lamb? There is nothing easier! For example, she can masterfully play a role of an unpretentious, simple woman with wild flowers in her hair, who, while floating down a river on a row boat with a suitor, tells him about the beauty of simple country life. Or, she can act as a religious person, who broadcasts with a trembling voice about holiness, hermits, coziness and calmness of the soul, and a silent, peaceful, and calm life. However, all this will be simply discourses in order to please someone. Since, for example, to this most "simple, country" woman a straw mattress, hens in the yard, a husband-farmer, cheap necklace made of glass beads as

a wedding present, a countryside log-house smelling of strange medicinal herbs that are hanging in the corners—are actually completely unacceptable. Despite all of her declarations about simplicity, she does not like any simple, cheap, poor quality products—they repel her. Insects (an inevitable part of country life) alone are enough! And, what about simple countryside log-houses with carved architraves? What about a greasy suitor, who goes on date with her in a dirty jacket smeared with oil and brings a bottle of vodka instead of flowers? What about mooing, with which simple semiliterate villagers replace speech? And, what about conversations that are catastrophically primitive? From the point of view of the considered person, all of the above can be summed up in one word—a nightmare. If she is not lucky in life, and will be forced to live or even spend her whole life in such conditions, then this can easily cause her to have a serious conflict with reality to the point of illnesses. Since, in a similar environment she feels that she is becoming dull slowly, but inevitably, and, in her opinion, that is unhealthy. So, "a woman with wild flowers in her hair" is just one of many examples of those uncountable roles, which she can impersonate, but no more than that.

It is necessary to note that behind a weak, fragile, graceful lady hides a solid, goal-oriented individual with a firm intent to achieve her goals. In the process of movement toward realization of the conceived, this woman tends to use all chances, and if there are none, then she will create them. She is capable of, so to speak, passing through closed doors and involving anyone, who can somehow help her. This penetrative ability especially manifests when her goals are glory and fame (even though she is inclined to declare that she does not need fame). She is a very pushy woman, and, with all of her femininity, she knows how to insist on her own way gently, but persistently.

Especially during the first half of her life, in her youth, this woman differs in that she thinks that everything that she does is in the name of a good cause. As she thinks, her actions are always motivated by kindest intentions. However, the kindness of this woman is peculiar. For example, in a conversation with someone she shares information that she considered necessary for her interlocutor, and, as a result, he gets a strong psychological trauma, curses everything in this world and says: "It would be better if I didn't know all this!" Or, an opposite situation: someone urgently needs information that this woman has, but she thinks that it is better not to say anything, allegedly this way will be better for this person. The result is that that person remained without information that is important to him. Or, she might "kindly" suggest to a very heavy-set girlfriend to take up running with the goal of becoming healthy. The girlfriend follows the advice, goes jogging and gets a heart attack! Or, out of "best intentions," this woman might organize a cheerful party for the elderly with alcohol and dancing...

DEMO 62

Description Of Women Born On April 24ᵗʰ Of Leap Years From The Catalog Of Human Population

Presented demo is a very short description. A complete description consists of a very detailed description of functioning and qualities of personality: a general description and a description on 6 factors (intellectual, nutritional, physical, emotional, sexual, and environmental).

One of the characteristic traits of considered individual is that her qualities coincide with the traditional understanding of the word "woman": soft, flexible, weak, defenseless. That is—at least, if you look at her, so to speak, "from the facade." She is ready to be a woman always, everywhere and in everything: to engage in traditional female tasks (she makes a clear distinction between female and male tasks), to get married as it is prescribed to a woman, to become a mother and a homemaker, and to do needlework. Housework, upbringing of children, traditional female roles, typical female chatter with girlfriends until late night and similar things—all this is about her. However, this woman also has well defined specific characteristics. One of them is the use of clichés, as peculiar pouring of her true essence into some form with transitions from one cliché to another. In this sense, this woman is a multi-tasking operator: first she is a maid, then a servant, then a homemaker, then a wife faithfully looking into her spouse's mouth, then a strict, decisive, stern businesswoman, then a gentle lover, and then a philandering hetaera. Her guises change depending on a situation and goals: a shaman, a lady, a matchmaker, a priestess, a goddess, a queen, a schoolgirl, a clown, a nun, an actress, an amazon, a commander, a beggar, a tradeswoman, a spy... In short, the range is great, and she is a wonderful simulator!

By nature, she has a talent for transformations and has a huge number of roles that she can use. And, every time she is different in each new role. Is it necessary to appear poor and unfortunate? No problem! Is there a need to appear as innocent as a lamb? There is nothing easier! For example, she can masterfully play a role of an unpretentious, simple woman with wild flowers in her hair, who, while floating down a river on a row boat with a suitor, tells him about the beauty of simple country life. Or, she can act as a religious person, who broadcasts with a trembling voice about holiness, hermits, coziness and calmness of the soul, and a silent, peaceful, and calm life. However, all this will be simply discourses in order to please someone. Since, for example, to this most "simple, country" woman a straw mattress, hens in the yard, a husband-farmer, cheap necklace made of glass beads as

a wedding present, a countryside log-house smelling of strange medicinal herbs that are hanging in the corners—are actually completely unacceptable. Despite all of her declarations about simplicity, she does not like any simple, cheap, poor quality products—they repel her. Insects (an inevitable part of country life) alone are enough! And, what about simple countryside log-houses with carved architraves? What about a greasy suitor, who goes on date with her in a dirty jacket smeared with oil and brings a bottle of vodka instead of flowers? What about mooing, with which simple semiliterate villagers replace speech? And, what about conversations that are catastrophically primitive? From the point of view of the considered person, all of the above can be summed up in one word—a nightmare. If she is not lucky in life, and will be forced to live or even spend her whole life in such conditions, then this can easily cause her to have a serious conflict with reality to the point of illnesses. Since, in a similar environment she feels that she is becoming dull slowly, but inevitably, and, in her opinion, that is unhealthy. So, "a woman with wild flowers in her hair" is just one of many examples of those uncountable roles, which she can impersonate, but no more than that.

It is necessary to note that behind a weak, fragile, graceful lady hides a solid, goal-oriented individual with a firm intent to achieve her goals. In the process of movement toward realization of the conceived, this woman tends to use all chances, and if there are none, then she will create them. She is capable of, so to speak, passing through closed doors and involving anyone, who can somehow help her. This penetrative ability especially manifests when her goals are glory and fame (even though she is inclined to declare that she does not need fame). She is a very pushy woman, and, with all of her femininity, she knows how to insist on her own way gently, but persistently.

Especially during the first half of her life, in her youth, this woman differs in that she thinks that everything that she does is in the name of a good cause. As she thinks, her actions are always motivated by kindest intentions. However, the kindness of this woman is peculiar. For example, in a conversation with someone she shares information that she considered necessary for her interlocutor, and, as a result, he gets a strong psychological trauma, curses everything in this world and says: "It would be better if I didn't know all this!" Or, an opposite situation: someone urgently needs information that this woman has, but she thinks that it is better not to say anything, allegedly this way will be better for this person. The result is that that person remained without information that is important to him. Or, she might "kindly" suggest to a very heavy-set girlfriend to take up running with the goal of becoming healthy. The girlfriend follows the advice, goes jogging and gets a heart attack! Or, out of "best intentions," this woman might organize a cheerful party for the elderly with alcohol and dancing...

DEMO 63
Description Of Women Born On April 24ᵗʰ Of Common Years From The Catalog Of Human Population

Presented demo is a very short description. A complete description consists of a very detailed description of functioning and qualities of personality: a general description and a description on 6 factors (intellectual, nutritional, physical, emotional, sexual, and environmental).

One of the characteristic traits of considered individual is that her qualities coincide with the traditional understanding of the word "woman": soft, flexible, weak, defenseless. That is—at least, if you look at her, so to speak, "from the facade." She is ready to be a woman always, everywhere and in everything: to engage in traditional female tasks (she makes a clear distinction between female and male tasks), to get married as it is prescribed to a woman, to become a mother and a homemaker, and to do needlework. Housework, upbringing of children, traditional female roles, typical female chatter with girlfriends until late night and similar things—all this is about her. However, this woman also has well defined specific characteristics. One of them is the use of clichés, as peculiar pouring of her true essence into some form with transitions from one cliché to another. In this sense, this woman is a multi-tasking operator: first she is a maid, then a servant, then a homemaker, then a wife faithfully looking into her spouse's mouth, then a strict, decisive, stern businesswoman, then a gentle lover, and then a philandering hetaera. Her guises change depending on a situation and goals: a shaman, a lady, a matchmaker, a priestess, a goddess, a queen, a schoolgirl, a clown, a nun, an actress, an amazon, a commander, a beggar, a tradeswoman, a spy... In short, the range is great, and she is a wonderful simulator!

By nature, she has a talent for transformations and has a huge number of roles that she can use. And, every time she is different in each new role. Is it necessary to appear poor and unfortunate? No problem! Is there a need to appear as innocent as a lamb? There is nothing easier! For example, she can masterfully play a role of an unpretentious, simple woman with wild flowers in her hair, who, while floating down a river on a row boat with a suitor, tells him about the beauty of simple country life. Or, she can act as a religious person, who broadcasts with a trembling voice about holiness, hermits, coziness and calmness of the soul, and a silent, peaceful, and calm life. However, all this will be simply discourses in order to please someone. Since, for example, to this most "simple, country" woman a straw mattress, hens in the yard, a husband-farmer, cheap necklace made of glass beads as

a wedding present, a countryside log-house smelling of strange medicinal herbs that are hanging in the corners—are actually completely unacceptable. Despite all of her declarations about simplicity, she does not like any simple, cheap, poor quality products—they repel her. Insects (an inevitable part of country life) alone are enough! And, what about simple countryside log-houses with carved architraves? What about a greasy suitor, who goes on date with her in a dirty jacket smeared with oil and brings a bottle of vodka instead of flowers? What about mooing, with which simple semiliterate villagers replace speech? And, what about conversations that are catastrophically primitive? From the point of view of the considered person, all of the above can be summed up in one word—a nightmare. If she is not lucky in life, and will be forced to live or even spend her whole life in such conditions, then this can easily cause her to have a serious conflict with reality to the point of illnesses. Since, in a similar environment she feels that she is becoming dull slowly, but inevitably, and, in her opinion, that is unhealthy. So, "a woman with wild flowers in her hair" is just one of many examples of those uncountable roles, which she can impersonate, but no more than that.

It is necessary to note that behind a weak, fragile, graceful lady hides a solid, goal-oriented individual with a firm intent to achieve her goals. In the process of movement toward realization of the conceived, this woman tends to use all chances, and if there are none, then she will create them. She is capable of, so to speak, passing through closed doors and involving anyone, who can somehow help her. This penetrative ability especially manifests when her goals are glory and fame (even though she is inclined to declare that she does not need fame). She is a very pushy woman, and, with all of her femininity, she knows how to insist on her own way gently, but persistently.

Especially during the first half of her life, in her youth, this woman differs in that she thinks that everything that she does is in the name of a good cause. As she thinks, her actions are always motivated by kindest intentions. However, the kindness of this woman is peculiar. For example, in a conversation with someone she shares information that she considered necessary for her interlocutor, and, as a result, he gets a strong psychological trauma, curses everything in this world and says: "It would be better if I didn't know all this!" Or, an opposite situation: someone urgently needs information that this woman has, but she thinks that it is better not to say anything, allegedly this way will be better for this person. The result is that that person remained without information that is important to him. Or, she might "kindly" suggest to a very heavy-set girlfriend to take up running with the goal of becoming healthy. The girlfriend follows the advice, goes jogging and gets a heart attack! Or, out of "best intentions," this woman might organize a cheerful party for the elderly with alcohol and dancing...

DEMO 64
Description Of Men Born On April 25ᵗʰ Of Leap Years From The Catalog Of Human Population

Presented demo is a very short description. A complete description consists of a very detailed description of functioning and qualities of personality: a general description and a description on 6 factors (intellectual, nutritional, physical, emotional, sexual, and environmental).

Characteristic traits of this person are aristocratism, politeness and extreme deference. He regards himself, as well as the surrounding world with awe, reverence (it is even possible to say—with admiration). This deference takes many different forms, sometimes a bit hypertrophied and therefore amusing. His demeanor reminds of rulers quite a lot: emperors, kings, mahatmas, in other words— governors, leaders, masters, prophets, major and authoritative politicians. He can also be compared with a diplomat, who was assigned quite a difficult task, or with a person, who works for a very influential official. In principle, it is enough to look closely at the behavior of vice-presidents and assistants to presidents of countries, and then it will become more or less clear how this man behaves.

This person is marked by intelligence, nobleness, correctness and ability to behave in a civilized manner in society. In the sphere of interrelations, this man is cautious and extremely tolerant: he has quite a lenient approach to imprecisions, violations, misconducts of others, to human weaknesses, passions. (Of course, since he himself is a person, who is quite flexible, pleasant in communication—he is not a fan of stubborn, dumb and ignorant people.) If necessary, he is even capable of taking the blame, mistakes of another person upon himself. In general, he has a tendency to take, so to speak, "all the sorrows of the world" upon himself.

Unlike people, who imagine themselves as great and strike an attitude on this account, this man is not in favor of posing himself as an authority or bearer of the truth of all times. He does not seek to stand out, to become an outstanding, unique individual, to mark his name in the history of humanity and in the centuries. He will never, so to speak, overwhelm his opponent or opponents with weighty arguments, proofs of his rightness in order to humiliate them—he does not seek to make public laughing-stocks out of his interlocutors in order to appear as a literate, educated, erudite person against their background.

This person does not need another's humiliation in order to have a sense of his own self-worth and value. Noble modesty and self-collectedness are also

expressed in his speech: for example, it is not characteristic of this man to speak sharply, with disrespect or to use slang. While observing this intellectual, one might think that he is so timid, bashful, and shy that it will not be difficult to offend him. However, it is not so. Behavior specified above (for him it is quite a normal, usual state) does not in any way mean that he is unable to stand up for himself. For example, despite all of his aristocratic luster, he is capable of yelling and cussing so loudly (what is called "yelling at the top of one's voice") during the moments of stress that only, so to speak, penguins at the South Pole will not hear him.

Yes, this person is extremely benevolent towards other people, but, of course, only to those, who are not trying to offend, terrorize him. Those who behave in a civilized, benevolent and proper manner—this person also treats very nicely: he is always ready to respond to their requests, always ready to help. He has a great sense of justness. Also, he is convinced that it is necessary to live correctly, honestly.

This person is a peculiar exemplar of steadfastness, courage, bravery, justice. And, he thinks that it is necessary to fight for these values! Fight anywhere and everywhere! These values specifically must be stood up for. He thinks it is necessary to insist specifically on this model of behavior, and to make such an exemplar out of himself! He thinks that if this gets achieved—happiness, simple human happiness will come, and he will be happy and all those around him will be happy too. Then, people will help each other; for example, help those, who got in trouble. In other words— "kindness and beauty will save the world..." However, this person thinks that in order for this to be the epitome of beauty, ethics, morals, culture— you yourself must be an exemplar of all this.

However, the noble nature of this individual, his deference towards others do not prevent this person from having any less of a deference towards money, gold, treasures, precious stones, or, in other words—wealth. No matter how he hides his avid character, it is very difficult to do, especially at times when he is literally entirely enveloped in the "gold rush..."

DEMO 65

Description Of Women Born On April 25ᵗʰ Of Common Years From The Catalog Of Human Population

Presented demo is a very short description. A complete description consists of a very detailed description of functioning and qualities of personality: a general description and a description on 6 factors (intellectual, nutritional, physical, emotional, sexual, and environmental).

One of the characteristic traits of considered individual is that her qualities coincide with the traditional understanding of the word "woman": soft, flexible, weak, defenseless. That is—at least, if you look at her, so to speak, "from the facade." She is ready to be a woman always, everywhere and in everything: to engage in traditional female tasks (she makes a clear distinction between female and male tasks), to get married as it is prescribed to a woman, to become a mother and a homemaker, and to do needlework. Housework, upbringing of children, traditional female roles, typical female chatter with girlfriends until late night and similar things—all this is about her. However, this woman also has well defined specific characteristics. One of them is the use of clichés, as peculiar pouring of her true essence into some form with transitions from one cliché to another. In this sense, this woman is a multi-tasking operator: first she is a maid, then a servant, then a homemaker, then a wife faithfully looking into her spouse's mouth, then a strict, decisive, stern businesswoman, then a gentle lover, and then a philandering hetaera. Her guises change depending on a situation and goals: a shaman, a lady, a matchmaker, a priestess, a goddess, a queen, a schoolgirl, a clown, a nun, an actress, an amazon, a commander, a beggar, a tradeswoman, a spy... In short, the range is great, and she is a wonderful simulator!

By nature, she has a talent for transformations and has a huge number of roles that she can use. And, every time she is different in each new role. Is it necessary to appear poor and unfortunate? No problem! Is there a need to appear as innocent as a lamb? There is nothing easier! For example, she can masterfully play a role of an unpretentious, simple woman with wild flowers in her hair, who, while floating down a river on a row boat with a suitor, tells him about the beauty of simple country life. Or, she can act as a religious person, who broadcasts with a trembling voice about holiness, hermits, coziness and calmness of the soul, and a silent, peaceful, and calm life. However, all this will be simply discourses in order to please someone. Since, for example, to this most "simple, country" woman a straw mattress, hens in the yard, a husband-farmer, cheap necklace made of glass beads as

a wedding present, a countryside log-house smelling of strange medicinal herbs that are hanging in the corners—are actually completely unacceptable. Despite all of her declarations about simplicity, she does not like any simple, cheap, poor quality products—they repel her. Insects (an inevitable part of country life) alone are enough! And, what about simple countryside log-houses with carved architraves? What about a greasy suitor, who goes on date with her in a dirty jacket smeared with oil and brings a bottle of vodka instead of flowers? What about mooing, with which simple semiliterate villagers replace speech? And, what about conversations that are catastrophically primitive? From the point of view of the considered person, all of the above can be summed up in one word—a nightmare. If she is not lucky in life, and will be forced to live or even spend her whole life in such conditions, then this can easily cause her to have a serious conflict with reality to the point of illnesses. Since, in a similar environment she feels that she is becoming dull slowly, but inevitably, and, in her opinion, that is unhealthy. So, "a woman with wild flowers in her hair" is just one of many examples of those uncountable roles, which she can impersonate, but no more than that.

It is necessary to note that behind a weak, fragile, graceful lady hides a solid, goal-oriented individual with a firm intent to achieve her goals. In the process of movement toward realization of the conceived, this woman tends to use all chances, and if there are none, then she will create them. She is capable of, so to speak, passing through closed doors and involving anyone, who can somehow help her. This penetrative ability especially manifests when her goals are glory and fame (even though she is inclined to declare that she does not need fame). She is a very pushy woman, and, with all of her femininity, she knows how to insist on her own way gently, but persistently.

Especially during the first half of her life, in her youth, this woman differs in that she thinks that everything that she does is in the name of a good cause. As she thinks, her actions are always motivated by kindest intentions. However, the kindness of this woman is peculiar. For example, in a conversation with someone she shares information that she considered necessary for her interlocutor, and, as a result, he gets a strong psychological trauma, curses everything in this world and says: "It would be better if I didn't know all this!" Or, an opposite situation: someone urgently needs information that this woman has, but she thinks that it is better not to say anything, allegedly this way will be better for this person. The result is that that person remained without information that is important to him. Or, she might "kindly" suggest to a very heavy-set girlfriend to take up running with the goal of becoming healthy. The girlfriend follows the advice, goes jogging and gets a heart attack! Or, out of "best intentions," this woman might organize a cheerful party for the elderly with alcohol and dancing...

DEMO 66

Description Of Men Born On April 26ᵗʰ Of Leap Years From The Catalog Of Human Population

Presented demo is a very short description. A complete description consists of a very detailed description of functioning and qualities of personality: a general description and a description on 6 factors (intellectual, nutritional, physical, emotional, sexual, and environmental).

Characteristic traits of this person are aristocratism, politeness and extreme deference. He regards himself, as well as the surrounding world with awe, reverence (it is even possible to say—with admiration). This deference takes many different forms, sometimes a bit hypertrophied and therefore amusing. His demeanor reminds of rulers quite a lot: emperors, kings, mahatmas, in other words— governors, leaders, masters, prophets, major and authoritative politicians. He can also be compared with a diplomat, who was assigned quite a difficult task, or with a person, who works for a very influential official. In principle, it is enough to look closely at the behavior of vice-presidents and assistants to presidents of countries, and then it will become more or less clear how this man behaves.

This person is marked by intelligence, nobleness, correctness and ability to behave in a civilized manner in society. In the sphere of interrelations, this man is cautious and extremely tolerant: he has quite a lenient approach to imprecisions, violations, misconducts of others, to human weaknesses, passions. (Of course, since he himself is a person, who is quite flexible, pleasant in communication—he is not a fan of stubborn, dumb and ignorant people.) If necessary, he is even capable of taking the blame, mistakes of another person upon himself. In general, he has a tendency to take, so to speak, "all the sorrows of the world" upon himself.

Unlike people, who imagine themselves as great and strike an attitude on this account, this man is not in favor of posing himself as an authority or bearer of the truth of all times. He does not seek to stand out, to become an outstanding, unique individual, to mark his name in the history of humanity and in the centuries. He will never, so to speak, overwhelm his opponent or opponents with weighty arguments, proofs of his rightness in order to humiliate them—he does not seek to make public laughing-stocks out of his interlocutors in order to appear as a literate, educated, erudite person against their background.

This person does not need another's humiliation in order to have a sense of his own self-worth and value. Noble modesty and self-collectedness are also

expressed in his speech: for example, it is not characteristic of this man to speak sharply, with disrespect or to use slang. While observing this intellectual, one might think that he is so timid, bashful, and shy that it will not be difficult to offend him. However, it is not so. Behavior specified above (for him it is quite a normal, usual state) does not in any way mean that he is unable to stand up for himself. For example, despite all of his aristocratic luster, he is capable of yelling and cussing so loudly (what is called "yelling at the top of one's voice") during the moments of stress that only, so to speak, penguins at the South Pole will not hear him.

Yes, this person is extremely benevolent towards other people, but, of course, only to those, who are not trying to offend, terrorize him. Those who behave in a civilized, benevolent and proper manner—this person also treats very nicely: he is always ready to respond to their requests, always ready to help. He has a great sense of justness. Also, he is convinced that it is necessary to live correctly, honestly.

This person is a peculiar exemplar of steadfastness, courage, bravery, justice. And, he thinks that it is necessary to fight for these values! Fight anywhere and everywhere! These values specifically must be stood up for. He thinks it is necessary to insist specifically on this model of behavior, and to make such an exemplar out of himself! He thinks that if this gets achieved—happiness, simple human happiness will come, and he will be happy and all those around him will be happy too. Then, people will help each other; for example, help those, who got in trouble. In other words— "kindness and beauty will save the world..." However, this person thinks that in order for this to be the epitome of beauty, ethics, morals, culture— you yourself must be an exemplar of all this.

However, the noble nature of this individual, his deference towards others do not prevent this person from having any less of a deference towards money, gold, treasures, precious stones, or, in other words—wealth. No matter how he hides his avid character, it is very difficult to do, especially at times when he is literally entirely enveloped in the "gold rush..."

DEMO 67
Description Of Men Born On April 26ᵗʰ Of Common Years From The Catalog Of Human Population

Presented demo is a very short description. A complete description consists of a very detailed description of functioning and qualities of personality: a general description and a description on 6 factors (intellectual, nutritional, physical, emotional, sexual, and environmental).

Characteristic traits of this person are aristocratism, politeness and extreme deference. He regards himself, as well as the surrounding world with awe, reverence (it is even possible to say—with admiration). This deference takes many different forms, sometimes a bit hypertrophied and therefore amusing. His demeanor reminds of rulers quite a lot: emperors, kings, mahatmas, in other words— governors, leaders, masters, prophets, major and authoritative politicians. He can also be compared with a diplomat, who was assigned quite a difficult task, or with a person, who works for a very influential official. In principle, it is enough to look closely at the behavior of vice-presidents and assistants to presidents of countries, and then it will become more or less clear how this man behaves.

This person is marked by intelligence, nobleness, correctness and ability to behave in a civilized manner in society. In the sphere of interrelations, this man is cautious and extremely tolerant: he has quite a lenient approach to imprecisions, violations, misconducts of others, to human weaknesses, passions. (Of course, since he himself is a person, who is quite flexible, pleasant in communication—he is not a fan of stubborn, dumb and ignorant people.) If necessary, he is even capable of taking the blame, mistakes of another person upon himself. In general, he has a tendency to take, so to speak, "all the sorrows of the world" upon himself.

Unlike people, who imagine themselves as great and strike an attitude on this account, this man is not in favor of posing himself as an authority or bearer of the truth of all times. He does not seek to stand out, to become an outstanding, unique individual, to mark his name in the history of humanity and in the centuries. He will never, so to speak, overwhelm his opponent or opponents with weighty arguments, proofs of his rightness in order to humiliate them—he does not seek to make public laughing-stocks out of his interlocutors in order to appear as a literate, educated, erudite person against their background.

This person does not need another's humiliation in order to have a sense of his own self-worth and value. Noble modesty and self-collectedness are also

expressed in his speech: for example, it is not characteristic of this man to speak sharply, with disrespect or to use slang. While observing this intellectual, one might think that he is so timid, bashful, and shy that it will not be difficult to offend him. However, it is not so. Behavior specified above (for him it is quite a normal, usual state) does not in any way mean that he is unable to stand up for himself. For example, despite all of his aristocratic luster, he is capable of yelling and cussing so loudly (what is called "yelling at the top of one's voice") during the moments of stress that only, so to speak, penguins at the South Pole will not hear him.

Yes, this person is extremely benevolent towards other people, but, of course, only to those, who are not trying to offend, terrorize him. Those who behave in a civilized, benevolent and proper manner—this person also treats very nicely: he is always ready to respond to their requests, always ready to help. He has a great sense of justness. Also, he is convinced that it is necessary to live correctly, honestly.

This person is a peculiar exemplar of steadfastness, courage, bravery, justice. And, he thinks that it is necessary to fight for these values! Fight anywhere and everywhere! These values specifically must be stood up for. He thinks it is necessary to insist specifically on this model of behavior, and to make such an exemplar out of himself! He thinks that if this gets achieved—happiness, simple human happiness will come, and he will be happy and all those around him will be happy too. Then, people will help each other; for example, help those, who got in trouble. In other words— "kindness and beauty will save the world..." However, this person thinks that in order for this to be the epitome of beauty, ethics, morals, culture— you yourself must be an exemplar of all this.

However, the noble nature of this individual, his deference towards others do not prevent this person from having any less of a deference towards money, gold, treasures, precious stones, or, in other words—wealth. No matter how he hides his avid character, it is very difficult to do, especially at times when he is literally entirely enveloped in the "gold rush..."

DEMO 68

Description Of Men Born On April 27th Of Leap Years From The Catalog Of Human Population

Presented demo is a very short description. A complete description consists of a very detailed description of functioning and qualities of personality: a general description and a description on 6 factors (intellectual, nutritional, physical, emotional, sexual, and environmental).

Characteristic traits of this person are aristocratism, politeness and extreme deference. He regards himself, as well as the surrounding world with awe, reverence (it is even possible to say—with admiration). This deference takes many different forms, sometimes a bit hypertrophied and therefore amusing. His demeanor reminds of rulers quite a lot: emperors, kings, mahatmas, in other words— governors, leaders, masters, prophets, major and authoritative politicians. He can also be compared with a diplomat, who was assigned quite a difficult task, or with a person, who works for a very influential official. In principle, it is enough to look closely at the behavior of vice-presidents and assistants to presidents of countries, and then it will become more or less clear how this man behaves.

This person is marked by intelligence, nobleness, correctness and ability to behave in a civilized manner in society. In the sphere of interrelations, this man is cautious and extremely tolerant: he has quite a lenient approach to imprecisions, violations, misconducts of others, to human weaknesses, passions. (Of course, since he himself is a person, who is quite flexible, pleasant in communication—he is not a fan of stubborn, dumb and ignorant people.) If necessary, he is even capable of taking the blame, mistakes of another person upon himself. In general, he has a tendency to take, so to speak, "all the sorrows of the world" upon himself.

Unlike people, who imagine themselves as great and strike an attitude on this account, this man is not in favor of posing himself as an authority or bearer of the truth of all times. He does not seek to stand out, to become an outstanding, unique individual, to mark his name in the history of humanity and in the centuries. He will never, so to speak, overwhelm his opponent or opponents with weighty arguments, proofs of his rightness in order to humiliate them—he does not seek to make public laughing-stocks out of his interlocutors in order to appear as a literate, educated, erudite person against their background.

This person does not need another's humiliation in order to have a sense of his own self-worth and value. Noble modesty and self-collectedness are also

expressed in his speech: for example, it is not characteristic of this man to speak sharply, with disrespect or to use slang. While observing this intellectual, one might think that he is so timid, bashful, and shy that it will not be difficult to offend him. However, it is not so. Behavior specified above (for him it is quite a normal, usual state) does not in any way mean that he is unable to stand up for himself. For example, despite all of his aristocratic luster, he is capable of yelling and cussing so loudly (what is called "yelling at the top of one's voice") during the moments of stress that only, so to speak, penguins at the South Pole will not hear him.

Yes, this person is extremely benevolent towards other people, but, of course, only to those, who are not trying to offend, terrorize him. Those who behave in a civilized, benevolent and proper manner—this person also treats very nicely: he is always ready to respond to their requests, always ready to help. He has a great sense of justness. Also, he is convinced that it is necessary to live correctly, honestly.

This person is a peculiar exemplar of steadfastness, courage, bravery, justice. And, he thinks that it is necessary to fight for these values! Fight anywhere and everywhere! These values specifically must be stood up for. He thinks it is necessary to insist specifically on this model of behavior, and to make such an exemplar out of himself! He thinks that if this gets achieved—happiness, simple human happiness will come, and he will be happy and all those around him will be happy too. Then, people will help each other; for example, help those, who got in trouble. In other words— "kindness and beauty will save the world..." However, this person thinks that in order for this to be the epitome of beauty, ethics, morals, culture— you yourself must be an exemplar of all this.

However, the noble nature of this individual, his deference towards others do not prevent this person from having any less of a deference towards money, gold, treasures, precious stones, or, in other words—wealth. No matter how he hides his avid character, it is very difficult to do, especially at times when he is literally entirely enveloped in the "gold rush..."

DEMO 69

Description Of Men Born On April 27ᵗʰ Of Common Years From The Catalog Of Human Population

Presented demo is a very short description. A complete description consists of a very detailed description of functioning and qualities of personality: a general description and a description on 6 factors (intellectual, nutritional, physical, emotional, sexual, and environmental).

Characteristic traits of this person are aristocratism, politeness and extreme deference. He regards himself, as well as the surrounding world with awe, reverence (it is even possible to say—with admiration). This deference takes many different forms, sometimes a bit hypertrophied and therefore amusing. His demeanor reminds of rulers quite a lot: emperors, kings, mahatmas, in other words— governors, leaders, masters, prophets, major and authoritative politicians. He can also be compared with a diplomat, who was assigned quite a difficult task, or with a person, who works for a very influential official. In principle, it is enough to look closely at the behavior of vice-presidents and assistants to presidents of countries, and then it will become more or less clear how this man behaves.

This person is marked by intelligence, nobleness, correctness and ability to behave in a civilized manner in society. In the sphere of interrelations, this man is cautious and extremely tolerant: he has quite a lenient approach to imprecisions, violations, misconducts of others, to human weaknesses, passions. (Of course, since he himself is a person, who is quite flexible, pleasant in communication—he is not a fan of stubborn, dumb and ignorant people.) If necessary, he is even capable of taking the blame, mistakes of another person upon himself. In general, he has a tendency to take, so to speak, "all the sorrows of the world" upon himself.

Unlike people, who imagine themselves as great and strike an attitude on this account, this man is not in favor of posing himself as an authority or bearer of the truth of all times. He does not seek to stand out, to become an outstanding, unique individual, to mark his name in the history of humanity and in the centuries. He will never, so to speak, overwhelm his opponent or opponents with weighty arguments, proofs of his rightness in order to humiliate them—he does not seek to make public laughing-stocks out of his interlocutors in order to appear as a literate, educated, erudite person against their background.

This person does not need another's humiliation in order to have a sense of his own self-worth and value. Noble modesty and self-collectedness are also

expressed in his speech: for example, it is not characteristic of this man to speak sharply, with disrespect or to use slang. While observing this intellectual, one might think that he is so timid, bashful, and shy that it will not be difficult to offend him. However, it is not so. Behavior specified above (for him it is quite a normal, usual state) does not in any way mean that he is unable to stand up for himself. For example, despite all of his aristocratic luster, he is capable of yelling and cussing so loudly (what is called "yelling at the top of one's voice") during the moments of stress that only, so to speak, penguins at the South Pole will not hear him.

Yes, this person is extremely benevolent towards other people, but, of course, only to those, who are not trying to offend, terrorize him. Those who behave in a civilized, benevolent and proper manner—this person also treats very nicely: he is always ready to respond to their requests, always ready to help. He has a great sense of justness. Also, he is convinced that it is necessary to live correctly, honestly.

This person is a peculiar exemplar of steadfastness, courage, bravery, justice. And, he thinks that it is necessary to fight for these values! Fight anywhere and everywhere! These values specifically must be stood up for. He thinks it is necessary to insist specifically on this model of behavior, and to make such an exemplar out of himself! He thinks that if this gets achieved—happiness, simple human happiness will come, and he will be happy and all those around him will be happy too. Then, people will help each other; for example, help those, who got in trouble. In other words— "kindness and beauty will save the world..." However, this person thinks that in order for this to be the epitome of beauty, ethics, morals, culture— you yourself must be an exemplar of all this.

However, the noble nature of this individual, his deference towards others do not prevent this person from having any less of a deference towards money, gold, treasures, precious stones, or, in other words—wealth. No matter how he hides his avid character, it is very difficult to do, especially at times when he is literally entirely enveloped in the "gold rush..."

DEMO 70
Description Of Men Born On April 28ᵗʰ Of Common Years From The Catalog Of Human Population

Presented demo is a very short description. A complete description consists of a very detailed description of functioning and qualities of personality: a general description and a description on 6 factors (intellectual, nutritional, physical, emotional, sexual, and environmental).

Characteristic traits of this person are aristocratism, politeness and extreme deference. He regards himself, as well as the surrounding world with awe, reverence (it is even possible to say—with admiration). This deference takes many different forms, sometimes a bit hypertrophied and therefore amusing. His demeanor reminds of rulers quite a lot: emperors, kings, mahatmas, in other words— governors, leaders, masters, prophets, major and authoritative politicians. He can also be compared with a diplomat, who was assigned quite a difficult task, or with a person, who works for a very influential official. In principle, it is enough to look closely at the behavior of vice-presidents and assistants to presidents of countries, and then it will become more or less clear how this man behaves.

This person is marked by intelligence, nobleness, correctness and ability to behave in a civilized manner in society. In the sphere of interrelations, this man is cautious and extremely tolerant: he has quite a lenient approach to imprecisions, violations, misconducts of others, to human weaknesses, passions. (Of course, since he himself is a person, who is quite flexible, pleasant in communication—he is not a fan of stubborn, dumb and ignorant people.) If necessary, he is even capable of taking the blame, mistakes of another person upon himself. In general, he has a tendency to take, so to speak, "all the sorrows of the world" upon himself.

Unlike people, who imagine themselves as great and strike an attitude on this account, this man is not in favor of posing himself as an authority or bearer of the truth of all times. He does not seek to stand out, to become an outstanding, unique individual, to mark his name in the history of humanity and in the centuries. He will never, so to speak, overwhelm his opponent or opponents with weighty arguments, proofs of his rightness in order to humiliate them—he does not seek to make public laughing-stocks out of his interlocutors in order to appear as a literate, educated, erudite person against their background.

This person does not need another's humiliation in order to have a sense of his own self-worth and value. Noble modesty and self-collectedness are also

expressed in his speech: for example, it is not characteristic of this man to speak sharply, with disrespect or to use slang. While observing this intellectual, one might think that he is so timid, bashful, and shy that it will not be difficult to offend him. However, it is not so. Behavior specified above (for him it is quite a normal, usual state) does not in any way mean that he is unable to stand up for himself. For example, despite all of his aristocratic luster, he is capable of yelling and cussing so loudly (what is called "yelling at the top of one's voice") during the moments of stress that only, so to speak, penguins at the South Pole will not hear him.

Yes, this person is extremely benevolent towards other people, but, of course, only to those, who are not trying to offend, terrorize him. Those who behave in a civilized, benevolent and proper manner—this person also treats very nicely: he is always ready to respond to their requests, always ready to help. He has a great sense of justness. Also, he is convinced that it is necessary to live correctly, honestly.

This person is a peculiar exemplar of steadfastness, courage, bravery, justice. And, he thinks that it is necessary to fight for these values! Fight anywhere and everywhere! These values specifically must be stood up for. He thinks it is necessary to insist specifically on this model of behavior, and to make such an exemplar out of himself! He thinks that if this gets achieved—happiness, simple human happiness will come, and he will be happy and all those around him will be happy too. Then, people will help each other; for example, help those, who got in trouble. In other words— "kindness and beauty will save the world..." However, this person thinks that in order for this to be the epitome of beauty, ethics, morals, culture— you yourself must be an exemplar of all this.

However, the noble nature of this individual, his deference towards others do not prevent this person from having any less of a deference towards money, gold, treasures, precious stones, or, in other words—wealth. No matter how he hides his avid character, it is very difficult to do, especially at times when he is literally entirely enveloped in the "gold rush..."

DEMO 71

Description Of Women Born On May 9th Of Leap Years From The Catalog Of Human Population

Presented demo is a very short description. A complete description consists of a very detailed description of functioning and qualities of personality: a general description and a description on 6 factors (intellectual, nutritional, physical, emotional, sexual, and environmental).

In the intellectual sphere, the considered person is always concerned about something, all sort of strangely mixed-up, all in a continuous fluster. She is all trembling, anxious, worried about others, herself, anything and everything. This woman never feels calm, safe and considers actions of people around her as constant attacks on her, accusations, aggressive pretensions. She feels that she is "a scapegoat," a target for ridicule and that all people who simply feel like it—maltreat her due to her feminine weakness. As it seems to her, she is always the one at fault, every person tries to offend, to humiliate her, and therefore she is always playing the role of "I'm a poor, miserable!" Although she herself loves and knows how to offend, mock, and especially tease. Rather, all above-mentioned actions of others that are directed at her—she provokes herself. First of all, she does this in order to complain plenty after and say: "Here we go again, I'm being blamed!" and to accuse everyone around that they are offending her, and are not only tying her to the house, family and children, but also are making a laughing-stock out of her. This woman does this because she loves to present herself as an unskilled, awkward person, who acts irrelevantly, constantly makes mistakes, etc.

This individual often considers herself "a blowball"—blow on it and it will disperse. She regularly demonstrates her helplessness, defenselessness, ineptitude and keeps saying that she feels that she is in danger, that "the world is so cruel." Actually, such behavior on her part is used to show others and, first of all, to show a man, her husband that she needs support, guarding, protection, and, of course, financial support; and, in the end, under the slogan "Let's do everything all together, as a family"—to get him to actually work for her. Especially while children are small, she thinks that their father and/or her husband is simply obligated not only to participate in joint nurturing and upbringing, but also to create the most favorable material conditions for her and the children. Anxiety and bustling are also connected with a huge number of things to do, which she herself arranges for herself in her life.

Her life can be compared to a crossword puzzle in a newspaper, which contains an unthinkable number of words, but instead of words she has things to do... And, this crossword puzzle has no end. A characteristic peculiarity of this individual is that she always finds a huge pile of things to do, concerns and problems, from which she literally bursts at the seams. On the outside, in some sense she is very similar to an ordinary-looking small gray sparrow, which constantly rushes about and fusses, while flying from one place to another: pecks a worm here, a grain there and flies on... This woman is like a sparrow: from morning until night she travels short (duration and distance wise), absorbed in affairs and concerns, and she does all this with a fuss, faster and faster, jumps from one thing to another. "An early bird gets the god's hand," she thinks, and that is why from early morning she is on her feet. And, it all begins: she fusses and bustles about, runs around, appears here and there, makes phone calls, wipes one child's nose, puts something into another child's mouth, stirs something that is cooking on the stove during the breaks, irons her husband's shirt at the last moment just before he needs to leave. An observer might get dizzy from her fussing around. And, in the end she says: "Oh, I don't even have time to drink coffee..." or "Oops, somehow I forgot to wash my face..." This happens because she likes to complain, to whine that she is locked at home, all the housework falls on her, and in addition everything is bad, everything hurts—it is a nightmare! This woman "lives through her eyes": she sees something and then flies there with all her might. The bustling of this woman also consists in that it is necessary for her to go away somewhere constantly. However, these must be nearby, short distances from her home. To rush to the other end of not only the world, but even town or neighborhood in which she lives, to travel, to fly, to sail somewhere far—all this is uncomfortable for her. Going to the other side of town or traveling to another country—these actions are equally problematic for this women. All long-distance flights are not for her. Therefore, she does not travel for prolonged periods of time or far from where her nest, her home, her favorite nestlings are.

However, love and attachment of this woman to her "nest" do not lead to cleanliness and order in her house: there is trash everywhere, things are scattered all over the place. It feels like she was just about to clean everything up, but something interrupted the process. Actually, for this woman the state "it is necessary to clean up" never ends or rather it never becomes a real action. She is not a very good homemaker: she is unable to not only clean up, but even to prepare a delicious meal...

DEMO 72

Description Of Women Born On May 10ᵗʰ Of Leap Years From The Catalog Of Human Population

Presented demo is a very short description. A complete description consists of a very detailed description of functioning and qualities of personality: a general description and a description on 6 factors (intellectual, nutritional, physical, emotional, sexual, and environmental).

In the intellectual sphere, the considered person is always concerned about something, all sort of strangely mixed-up, all in a continuous fluster. She is all trembling, anxious, worried about others, herself, anything and everything. This woman never feels calm, safe and considers actions of people around her as constant attacks on her, accusations, aggressive pretensions. She feels that she is "a scapegoat," a target for ridicule and that all people who simply feel like it—maltreat her due to her feminine weakness. As it seems to her, she is always the one at fault, every person tries to offend, to humiliate her, and therefore she is always playing the role of "I'm a poor, miserable!" Although she herself loves and knows how to offend, mock, and especially tease. Rather, all above-mentioned actions of others that are directed at her—she provokes herself. First of all, she does this in order to complain plenty after and say: "Here we go again, I'm being blamed!" and to accuse everyone around that they are offending her, and are not only tying her to the house, family and children, but also are making a laughing-stock out of her. This woman does this because she loves to present herself as an unskilled, awkward person, who acts irrelevantly, constantly makes mistakes, etc.

This individual often considers herself "a blowball"—blow on it and it will disperse. She regularly demonstrates her helplessness, defenselessness, ineptitude and keeps saying that she feels that she is in danger, that "the world is so cruel." Actually, such behavior on her part is used to show others and, first of all, to show a man, her husband that she needs support, guarding, protection, and, of course, financial support; and, in the end, under the slogan "Let's do everything all together, as a family"—to get him to actually work for her. Especially while children are small, she thinks that their father and/or her husband is simply obligated not only to participate in joint nurturing and upbringing, but also to create the most favorable material conditions for her and the children. Anxiety and bustling are also connected with a huge number of things to do, which she herself arranges for herself in her life.

Her life can be compared to a crossword puzzle in a newspaper, which contains an unthinkable number of words, but instead of words she has things to do... And, this crossword puzzle has no end. A characteristic peculiarity of this individual is that she always finds a huge pile of things to do, concerns and problems, from which she literally bursts at the seams. On the outside, in some sense she is very similar to an ordinary-looking small gray sparrow, which constantly rushes about and fusses, while flying from one place to another: pecks a worm here, a grain there and flies on... This woman is like a sparrow: from morning until night she travels short (duration and distance wise), absorbed in affairs and concerns, and she does all this with a fuss, faster and faster, jumps from one thing to another. "An early bird gets the god's hand," she thinks, and that is why from early morning she is on her feet. And, it all begins: she fusses and bustles about, runs around, appears here and there, makes phone calls, wipes one child's nose, puts something into another child's mouth, stirs something that is cooking on the stove during the breaks, irons her husband's shirt at the last moment just before he needs to leave. An observer might get dizzy from her fussing around. And, in the end she says: "Oh, I don't even have time to drink coffee..." or "Oops, somehow I forgot to wash my face..." This happens because she likes to complain, to whine that she is locked at home, all the housework falls on her, and in addition everything is bad, everything hurts—it is a nightmare! This woman "lives through her eyes": she sees something and then flies there with all her might. The bustling of this woman also consists in that it is necessary for her to go away somewhere constantly. However, these must be nearby, short distances from her home. To rush to the other end of not only the world, but even town or neighborhood in which she lives, to travel, to fly, to sail somewhere far—all this is uncomfortable for her. Going to the other side of town or traveling to another country—these actions are equally problematic for this women. All long-distance flights are not for her. Therefore, she does not travel for prolonged periods of time or far from where her nest, her home, her favorite nestlings are.

However, love and attachment of this woman to her "nest" do not lead to cleanliness and order in her house: there is trash everywhere, things are scattered all over the place. It feels like she was just about to clean everything up, but something interrupted the process. Actually, for this woman the state "it is necessary to clean up" never ends or rather it never becomes a real action. She is not a very good homemaker: she is unable to not only clean up, but even to prepare a delicious meal...

DEMO 73

Description Of Women Born On May 10th Of Common Years From The Catalog Of Human Population

Presented demo is a very short description. A complete description consists of a very detailed description of functioning and qualities of personality: a general description and a description on 6 factors (intellectual, nutritional, physical, emotional, sexual, and environmental).

In the intellectual sphere, the considered person is always concerned about something, all sort of strangely mixed-up, all in a continuous fluster. She is all trembling, anxious, worried about others, herself, anything and everything. This woman never feels calm, safe and considers actions of people around her as constant attacks on her, accusations, aggressive pretensions. She feels that she is "a scapegoat," a target for ridicule and that all people who simply feel like it—maltreat her due to her feminine weakness. As it seems to her, she is always the one at fault, every person tries to offend, to humiliate her, and therefore she is always playing the role of "I'm a poor, miserable!" Although she herself loves and knows how to offend, mock, and especially tease. Rather, all above-mentioned actions of others that are directed at her—she provokes herself. First of all, she does this in order to complain plenty after and say: "Here we go again, I'm being blamed!" and to accuse everyone around that they are offending her, and are not only tying her to the house, family and children, but also are making a laughing-stock out of her. This woman does this because she loves to present herself as an unskilled, awkward person, who acts irrelevantly, constantly makes mistakes, etc.

This individual often considers herself "a blowball"—blow on it and it will disperse. She regularly demonstrates her helplessness, defenselessness, ineptitude and keeps saying that she feels that she is in danger, that "the world is so cruel." Actually, such behavior on her part is used to show others and, first of all, to show a man, her husband that she needs support, guarding, protection, and, of course, financial support; and, in the end, under the slogan "Let's do everything all together, as a family"—to get him to actually work for her. Especially while children are small, she thinks that their father and/or her husband is simply obligated not only to participate in joint nurturing and upbringing, but also to create the most favorable material conditions for her and the children. Anxiety and bustling are also connected with a huge number of things to do, which she herself arranges for herself in her life.

Her life can be compared to a crossword puzzle in a newspaper, which contains an unthinkable number of words, but instead of words she has things to do... And, this crossword puzzle has no end. A characteristic peculiarity of this individual is that she always finds a huge pile of things to do, concerns and problems, from which she literally bursts at the seams. On the outside, in some sense she is very similar to an ordinary-looking small gray sparrow, which constantly rushes about and fusses, while flying from one place to another: pecks a worm here, a grain there and flies on... This woman is like a sparrow: from morning until night she travels short (duration and distance wise), absorbed in affairs and concerns, and she does all this with a fuss, faster and faster, jumps from one thing to another. "An early bird gets the god's hand," she thinks, and that is why from early morning she is on her feet. And, it all begins: she fusses and bustles about, runs around, appears here and there, makes phone calls, wipes one child's nose, puts something into another child's mouth, stirs something that is cooking on the stove during the breaks, irons her husband's shirt at the last moment just before he needs to leave. An observer might get dizzy from her fussing around. And, in the end she says: "Oh, I don't even have time to drink coffee..." or "Oops, somehow I forgot to wash my face..." This happens because she likes to complain, to whine that she is locked at home, all the housework falls on her, and in addition everything is bad, everything hurts—it is a nightmare! This woman "lives through her eyes": she sees something and then flies there with all her might. The bustling of this woman also consists in that it is necessary for her to go away somewhere constantly. However, these must be nearby, short distances from her home. To rush to the other end of not only the world, but even town or neighborhood in which she lives, to travel, to fly, to sail somewhere far—all this is uncomfortable for her. Going to the other side of town or traveling to another country—these actions are equally problematic for this women. All long-distance flights are not for her. Therefore, she does not travel for prolonged periods of time or far from where her nest, her home, her favorite nestlings are.

However, love and attachment of this woman to her "nest" do not lead to cleanliness and order in her house: there is trash everywhere, things are scattered all over the place. It feels like she was just about to clean everything up, but something interrupted the process. Actually, for this woman the state "it is necessary to clean up" never ends or rather it never becomes a real action. She is not a very good homemaker: she is unable to not only clean up, but even to prepare a delicious meal...

DEMO 74

Description Of Women Born On May 11ᵗʰ Of Common Years From The Catalog Of Human Population

Presented demo is a very short description. A complete description consists of a very detailed description of functioning and qualities of personality: a general description and a description on 6 factors (intellectual, nutritional, physical, emotional, sexual, and environmental).

In the intellectual sphere, the considered person is always concerned about something, all sort of strangely mixed-up, all in a continuous fluster. She is all trembling, anxious, worried about others, herself, anything and everything. This woman never feels calm, safe and considers actions of people around her as constant attacks on her, accusations, aggressive pretensions. She feels that she is "a scapegoat," a target for ridicule and that all people who simply feel like it—maltreat her due to her feminine weakness. As it seems to her, she is always the one at fault, every person tries to offend, to humiliate her, and therefore she is always playing the role of "I'm a poor, miserable!" Although she herself loves and knows how to offend, mock, and especially tease. Rather, all above-mentioned actions of others that are directed at her—she provokes herself. First of all, she does this in order to complain plenty after and say: "Here we go again, I'm being blamed!" and to accuse everyone around that they are offending her, and are not only tying her to the house, family and children, but also are making a laughing-stock out of her. This woman does this because she loves to present herself as an unskilled, awkward person, who acts irrelevantly, constantly makes mistakes, etc.

This individual often considers herself "a blowball"—blow on it and it will disperse. She regularly demonstrates her helplessness, defenselessness, ineptitude and keeps saying that she feels that she is in danger, that "the world is so cruel." Actually, such behavior on her part is used to show others and, first of all, to show a man, her husband that she needs support, guarding, protection, and, of course, financial support; and, in the end, under the slogan "Let's do everything all together, as a family"—to get him to actually work for her. Especially while children are small, she thinks that their father and/or her husband is simply obligated not only to participate in joint nurturing and upbringing, but also to create the most favorable material conditions for her and the children. Anxiety and bustling are also connected with a huge number of things to do, which she herself arranges for herself in her life.

Her life can be compared to a crossword puzzle in a newspaper, which contains an unthinkable number of words, but instead of words she has things to do... And, this crossword puzzle has no end. A characteristic peculiarity of this individual is that she always finds a huge pile of things to do, concerns and problems, from which she literally bursts at the seams. On the outside, in some sense she is very similar to an ordinary-looking small gray sparrow, which constantly rushes about and fusses, while flying from one place to another: pecks a worm here, a grain there and flies on... This woman is like a sparrow: from morning until night she travels short (duration and distance wise), absorbed in affairs and concerns, and she does all this with a fuss, faster and faster, jumps from one thing to another. "An early bird gets the god's hand," she thinks, and that is why from early morning she is on her feet. And, it all begins: she fusses and bustles about, runs around, appears here and there, makes phone calls, wipes one child's nose, puts something into another child's mouth, stirs something that is cooking on the stove during the breaks, irons her husband's shirt at the last moment just before he needs to leave. An observer might get dizzy from her fussing around. And, in the end she says: "Oh, I don't even have time to drink coffee..." or "Oops, somehow I forgot to wash my face..." This happens because she likes to complain, to whine that she is locked at home, all the housework falls on her, and in addition everything is bad, everything hurts—it is a nightmare! This woman "lives through her eyes": she sees something and then flies there with all her might. The bustling of this woman also consists in that it is necessary for her to go away somewhere constantly. However, these must be nearby, short distances from her home. To rush to the other end of not only the world, but even town or neighborhood in which she lives, to travel, to fly, to sail somewhere far—all this is uncomfortable for her. Going to the other side of town or traveling to another country—these actions are equally problematic for this women. All long-distance flights are not for her. Therefore, she does not travel for prolonged periods of time or far from where her nest, her home, her favorite nestlings are.

However, love and attachment of this woman to her "nest" do not lead to cleanliness and order in her house: there is trash everywhere, things are scattered all over the place. It feels like she was just about to clean everything up, but something interrupted the process. Actually, for this woman the state "it is necessary to clean up" never ends or rather it never becomes a real action. She is not a very good homemaker: she is unable to not only clean up, but even to prepare a delicious meal...

DEMO 75
Description Of Women Born On May 19th Of Leap Years From The Catalog Of Human Population

Presented demo is a very short description. A complete description consists of a very detailed description of functioning and qualities of personality: a general description and a description on 6 factors (intellectual, nutritional, physical, emotional, sexual, and environmental).

This person presents herself as a deity in a luxurious radiance: warm, sunny, ideal. This woman has a royal attitude and psychology of an empress. Striving for power is a natural state for her because, as she believes, power is money, and all this combined is the basis, the essence of her life space. Her life goal is to make everyone and everything submit to her. It is desirable for power to be total, so that it would be possible to control not only people's actions, but also their thoughts and desires.

Naturally, she considers herself an ideal ruler (wise, kind, just, one who makes only the right decisions, etc.). However, this does not mean that she sits around in idleness because she thinks that she is "the best." Having imperialistic ambitions, she knows how to defend them in competitive fighting. She must get the first place always and everywhere. In such "races," this woman will make every effort to prove that she is the best. In order to be number one, in addition to "races" in the environment, she takes cares of making the needed impression—this makes her way to power easier, which in its turn allows her to maintain any image that she likes.

This woman is seriously preoccupied with creating a "bright image," a kind of mirage. She thoroughly makes sure that others perceive her as kind, beautiful, impeccable, and noble. She seeks to look straightforward, openhearted, frank, and open like a flower during the flowering period. A huge amount of energy is spent to ensure that secret sides of her nature never surface and become known to someone. She prefers the image of a holy righteous woman.

On the outside she is smiling, optimistic, well-groomed and tidy, well-brought-up, it is even possible to say that she is tenderly well-meaning and easy in communication. Her voice is usually very pleasant, quiet, and polite. She looks delicate and pampered, but it is not recommended to anyone to mistake her for a soft, comfortable pillow. Quiet voice and angelic appearance, the mask of a polished aristocrat—all this is a beautiful cover and her conscious attempts to appear irresistibly attractive in all respects.

And, there are always plenty of lovers of the beautiful. This woman sets the price herself and it is quite high.

She always clearly knows what she wants and calculates the variants of getting it quite well. This woman is a realist and she firmly stands on the ground with both feet. She is a woman of business—firm and pragmatic. Therefore, at any moment her angelic voice can change to a confident voice, which makes clear, short statements, as if giving orders, and a delicate violet turns into a judgmatic and insidious intriguer or an imperious, fierce fury with eyes glistening of wrath. Multi-faced metamorphoses (pretending) are usual and natural for her because she was born with an amazing gift of transformations. For example, she is able to play a role of a beautiful, submissive lady absolutely accurately. However, this does not mean that in this role she supports or is satisfied by other people's ideas, desires, and decisions. On the contrary, she alone always sets the rules of the game!

This person not only considers herself the head, the leader, but also actively insists on it, while turning into a dictator. She thinks that she knows everything and always. She often assumes the role of a judge, who evaluates someone or something, judges, determines and issues a verdict. As a result of being fully convinced that she is always right, she tries to impose her views on others, edify, moralize and tell them how to live. She intervenes in the lives of others and explains this by that she wants to safeguard from evil, to protect, to make sure that nothing bad happens, and seeks to aid, support someone. She shows that she cares about someone, helps someone, cherishes, fosters, and provides patronage. However, sometimes all this occurs in the form of a dictate, with a stern, imposing look, and a clear and conscious goal—to subjugate everyone.

This woman is a careerist. Career is a mandatory element in her life. And, if there is at least a minimal possibility to make it—she will work on it. She needs a career in order to realize her aptitudes, to get money, fame, and, most importantly, power. A career not only helps her self-realize in some activity, but also to obtain all possible ranks, awards, medals, titles, prestigious prizes, which she finds very attractive, as well as to receive material resources to satisfy all of her pretensions that are very far from modest. Having an immeasurable passion for luxury, this woman serves "the golden calf" with pleasure and sometimes reaches near orgasmic pleasure from possession of material wealth...

DEMO 76

Description Of Men Born On May 19th Of Leap Years From The Catalog Of Human Population

Presented demo is a very short description. A complete description consists of a very detailed description of functioning and qualities of personality: a general description and a description on 6 factors (intellectual, nutritional, physical, emotional, sexual, and environmental).

Considered person presents himself as a deity in a luxurious radiance: warm, sunny, ideal. However, this does not mean that he sits around in idleness because he thinks that he is "the best." Having imperialistic ambitions, he knows how to defend them in competitive fighting—there is nothing he enjoys more than competing with someone who is smarter (more handsome, rich, professional, etc.). He must get the first place always and everywhere. In such "races," he will make every effort to prove that he is the best. In order to be number one, in addition to "races" in the environment, he also takes cares of making the needed impression. This man is seriously preoccupied with creating a "bright image," a mirage. He seeks to ensure that others perceive him as kind, impeccable, noble, straightforward, frank, openhearted...

A huge amount of energy is spent to ensure that secret sides of his nature (passion for intriguery, insidiousness, malignity, extreme greediness, dissoluteness, etc.) never surface and become known to someone. He prefers the image of a holy righteous man, a monk, immaculate as Jesus or any other analogous prophet. On the outside, he is smiling, optimistic, well-groomed, well-brought-up (it is even possible to say that he is tender in communication), well-meaning. In short, he is light and pleasant. Usually, his voice is also very pleasant: quiet, polite. Although he might look delicate and pampered, it is not recommended to anyone to mistake him for a soft and comfortable pillow; especially because he is really not like that at all. Quiet voice, angelic appearance, the mask of a simpleton, a well-meaning jollier—all this is for the poor. These are his conscious attempts to seem better, a tool for getting what he wants. And, he always clearly knows what he wants and knows how to calculate the variants of getting the desired. This is a realist, who firmly stands on the ground with both feet: business-minded, firm, and pragmatic. That is why one should not be surprised if at any moment his well-meaning, quiet voice suddenly changes to a confident, imperious voice, which makes clear, short statements, as if giving orders and a "soft pillow" turns into a judgmatic, insidious intriguer with a fierce face and eyes glistening of wrath.

This person thinks of himself as an ideal ruler: wise, kind, just, one who makes only the right decisions. This person not only considers himself the head, the leader, but also actively insists on it ("Come on, everyone listen here!") and sometimes turns into a dictator. Thinking that he has the correct perception of everything, knows everything and always, he assumes the role of a judge, who evaluates, judges, determines and issues a verdict. In general, he takes on too much, thinking that he has the right not only to spread, but also to impose his personal views on others by edifying, moralizing and telling people how they should live. Without any embarrassment, he can intervene in the life of another, allegedly driven by an aspiration to safeguard from the evil, "to put down something soft to fall on," to protect, to aid, to support someone. It might seem that he simply wants to care, cherish, foster, provide patronage, guard, but in reality all this occurs only with one goal—to subjugate everyone. Even his help, even his support can often take place in the form of a dictate. Besides, by nature he is not a bad jailer, and therefore he will easily make a golden cage for anyone, and all this will be done quietly, peacefully, unnoticeably.

With all his might, this man seeks to ensure that life would constantly surprise him, would be supernatural, eccentric, strange and incredible, would amaze him by originality of the occurring and would be similar to a world of wonders. He is persistently drawn to the world of bright shows, outlandish illusions, lies and masks, to the world of great fraudsters, where the hero is the one who deludes masterfully and brilliantly plays a trick on all the rest. He is also drawn to the world of casinos and good fortune, the world of exciting thrillers, mysticism, the world of the eccentric, the world of unusual, weird forms. First of all, a world of show-business (theater, film, television, circus) can become such a world; a world of tricks, strange and absurd escapades; or science, with its unsolvable puzzles and insane theories; or the world of aristocracy and nobility, where every day there are dazzling receptions in various places with people of all sorts and kinds. Or jurisprudence—since that is also nothing but a show, lies, masks. He is also interested in the world of paranormal phenomena: extrasensory experts, magicians, werewolves, mages, evil spirits, nightmares and secrets. He is attracted by any unorthodox, outlandish, fantastic, original teachings. And, it does not matter if they have neither meaning, nor a word of truth because that is exactly what attracts him—lies and trumpery...

DEMO 77

Description Of Women Born On May 20ᵗʰ Of Leap Years From The Catalog Of Human Population

Presented demo is a very short description. A complete description consists of a very detailed description of functioning and qualities of personality: a general description and a description on 6 factors (intellectual, nutritional, physical, emotional, sexual, and environmental).

This person presents herself as a deity in a luxurious radiance: warm, sunny, ideal. This woman has a royal attitude and psychology of an empress. Striving for power is a natural state for her because, as she believes, power is money, and all this combined is the basis, the essence of her life space. Her life goal is to make everyone and everything submit to her. It is desirable for power to be total, so that it would be possible to control not only people's actions, but also their thoughts and desires.

Naturally, she considers herself an ideal ruler (wise, kind, just, one who makes only the right decisions, etc.). However, this does not mean that she sits around in idleness because she thinks that she is "the best." Having imperialistic ambitions, she knows how to defend them in competitive fighting. She must get the first place always and everywhere. In such "races," this woman will make every effort to prove that she is the best. In order to be number one, in addition to "races" in the environment, she takes cares of making the needed impression—this makes her way to power easier, which in its turn allows her to maintain any image that she likes.

This woman is seriously preoccupied with creating a "bright image," a kind of mirage. She thoroughly makes sure that others perceive her as kind, beautiful, impeccable, and noble. She seeks to look straightforward, openhearted, frank, and open like a flower during the flowering period. A huge amount of energy is spent to ensure that secret sides of her nature never surface and become known to someone. She prefers the image of a holy righteous woman.

On the outside she is smiling, optimistic, well-groomed and tidy, well-brought-up, it is even possible to say that she is tenderly well-meaning and easy in communication. Her voice is usually very pleasant, quiet, and polite. She looks delicate and pampered, but it is not recommended to anyone to mistake her for a soft, comfortable pillow. Quiet voice and angelic appearance, the mask of a polished aristocrat—all this is a beautiful cover and her conscious attempts to appear irresistibly attractive in all respects.

And, there are always plenty of lovers of the beautiful. This woman sets the price herself and it is quite high.

She always clearly knows what she wants and calculates the variants of getting it quite well. This woman is a realist and she firmly stands on the ground with both feet. She is a woman of business—firm and pragmatic. Therefore, at any moment her angelic voice can change to a confident voice, which makes clear, short statements, as if giving orders, and a delicate violet turns into a judgmatic and insidious intriguer or an imperious, fierce fury with eyes glistening of wrath. Multi-faced metamorphoses (pretending) are usual and natural for her because she was born with an amazing gift of transformations. For example, she is able to play a role of a beautiful, submissive lady absolutely accurately. However, this does not mean that in this role she supports or is satisfied by other people's ideas, desires, and decisions. On the contrary, she alone always sets the rules of the game!

This person not only considers herself the head, the leader, but also actively insists on it, while turning into a dictator. She thinks that she knows everything and always. She often assumes the role of a judge, who evaluates someone or something, judges, determines and issues a verdict. As a result of being fully convinced that she is always right, she tries to impose her views on others, edify, moralize and tell them how to live. She intervenes in the lives of others and explains this by that she wants to safeguard from evil, to protect, to make sure that nothing bad happens, and seeks to aid, support someone. She shows that she cares about someone, helps someone, cherishes, fosters, and provides patronage. However, sometimes all this occurs in the form of a dictate, with a stern, imposing look, and a clear and conscious goal—to subjugate everyone.

This woman is a careerist. Career is a mandatory element in her life. And, if there is at least a minimal possibility to make it—she will work on it. She needs a career in order to realize her aptitudes, to get money, fame, and, most importantly, power. A career not only helps her self-realize in some activity, but also to obtain all possible ranks, awards, medals, titles, prestigious prizes, which she finds very attractive, as well as to receive material resources to satisfy all of her pretensions that are very far from modest. Having an immeasurable passion for luxury, this woman serves "the golden calf" with pleasure and sometimes reaches near orgasmic pleasure from possession of material wealth...

DEMO 78

Description Of Men Born On May 20ᵗʰ Of Leap Years From The Catalog Of Human Population

Presented demo is a very short description. A complete description consists of a very detailed description of functioning and qualities of personality: a general description and a description on 6 factors (intellectual, nutritional, physical, emotional, sexual, and environmental).

Considered person presents himself as a deity in a luxurious radiance: warm, sunny, ideal. However, this does not mean that he sits around in idleness because he thinks that he is "the best." Having imperialistic ambitions, he knows how to defend them in competitive fighting—there is nothing he enjoys more than competing with someone who is smarter (more handsome, rich, professional, etc.). He must get the first place always and everywhere. In such "races," he will make every effort to prove that he is the best. In order to be number one, in addition to "races" in the environment, he also takes cares of making the needed impression. This man is seriously preoccupied with creating a "bright image," a mirage. He seeks to ensure that others perceive him as kind, impeccable, noble, straightforward, frank, openhearted...

A huge amount of energy is spent to ensure that secret sides of his nature (passion for intriguery, insidiousness, malignity, extreme greediness, dissoluteness, etc.) never surface and become known to someone. He prefers the image of a holy righteous man, a monk, immaculate as Jesus or any other analogous prophet. On the outside, he is smiling, optimistic, well-groomed, well-brought-up (it is even possible to say that he is tender in communication), well-meaning. In short, he is light and pleasant. Usually, his voice is also very pleasant: quiet, polite. Although he might look delicate and pampered, it is not recommended to anyone to mistake him for a soft and comfortable pillow; especially because he is really not like that at all. Quiet voice, angelic appearance, the mask of a simpleton, a well-meaning jollier—all this is for the poor. These are his conscious attempts to seem better, a tool for getting what he wants. And, he always clearly knows what he wants and knows how to calculate the variants of getting the desired. This is a realist, who firmly stands on the ground with both feet: business-minded, firm, and pragmatic. That is why one should not be surprised if at any moment his well-meaning, quiet voice suddenly changes to a confident, imperious voice, which makes clear, short statements, as if giving orders and a "soft pillow" turns into a judgmatic, insidious intriguer with a fierce face and eyes glistening of wrath.

This person thinks of himself as an ideal ruler: wise, kind, just, one who makes only the right decisions. This person not only considers himself the head, the leader, but also actively insists on it ("Come on, everyone listen here!") and sometimes turns into a dictator. Thinking that he has the correct perception of everything, knows everything and always, he assumes the role of a judge, who evaluates, judges, determines and issues a verdict. In general, he takes on too much, thinking that he has the right not only to spread, but also to impose his personal views on others by edifying, moralizing and telling people how they should live. Without any embarrassment, he can intervene in the life of another, allegedly driven by an aspiration to safeguard from the evil, "to put down something soft to fall on," to protect, to aid, to support someone. It might seem that he simply wants to care, cherish, foster, provide patronage, guard, but in reality all this occurs only with one goal—to subjugate everyone. Even his help, even his support can often take place in the form of a dictate. Besides, by nature he is not a bad jailer, and therefore he will easily make a golden cage for anyone, and all this will be done quietly, peacefully, unnoticeably.

With all his might, this man seeks to ensure that life would constantly surprise him, would be supernatural, eccentric, strange and incredible, would amaze him by originality of the occurring and would be similar to a world of wonders. He is persistently drawn to the world of bright shows, outlandish illusions, lies and masks, to the world of great fraudsters, where the hero is the one who deludes masterfully and brilliantly plays a trick on all the rest. He is also drawn to the world of casinos and good fortune, the world of exciting thrillers, mysticism, the world of the eccentric, the world of unusual, weird forms. First of all, a world of show-business (theater, film, television, circus) can become such a world; a world of tricks, strange and absurd escapades; or science, with its unsolvable puzzles and insane theories; or the world of aristocracy and nobility, where every day there are dazzling receptions in various places with people of all sorts and kinds. Or jurisprudence—since that is also nothing but a show, lies, masks. He is also interested in the world of paranormal phenomena: extrasensory experts, magicians, werewolves, mages, evil spirits, nightmares and secrets. He is attracted by any unorthodox, outlandish, fantastic, original teachings. And, it does not matter if they have neither meaning, nor a word of truth because that is exactly what attracts him—lies and trumpery...

DEMO 79
Description Of Women Born On May 20th Of Common Years From The Catalog Of Human Population

Presented demo is a very short description. A complete description consists of a very detailed description of functioning and qualities of personality: a general description and a description on 6 factors (intellectual, nutritional, physical, emotional, sexual, and environmental).

This person presents herself as a deity in a luxurious radiance: warm, sunny, ideal. This woman has a royal attitude and psychology of an empress. Striving for power is a natural state for her because, as she believes, power is money, and all this combined is the basis, the essence of her life space. Her life goal is to make everyone and everything submit to her. It is desirable for power to be total, so that it would be possible to control not only people's actions, but also their thoughts and desires.

Naturally, she considers herself an ideal ruler (wise, kind, just, one who makes only the right decisions, etc.). However, this does not mean that she sits around in idleness because she thinks that she is "the best." Having imperialistic ambitions, she knows how to defend them in competitive fighting. She must get the first place always and everywhere. In such "races," this woman will make every effort to prove that she is the best. In order to be number one, in addition to "races" in the environment, she takes cares of making the needed impression—this makes her way to power easier, which in its turn allows her to maintain any image that she likes.

This woman is seriously preoccupied with creating a "bright image," a kind of mirage. She thoroughly makes sure that others perceive her as kind, beautiful, impeccable, and noble. She seeks to look straightforward, openhearted, frank, and open like a flower during the flowering period. A huge amount of energy is spent to ensure that secret sides of her nature never surface and become known to someone. She prefers the image of a holy righteous woman.

On the outside she is smiling, optimistic, well-groomed and tidy, well-brought-up, it is even possible to say that she is tenderly well-meaning and easy in communication. Her voice is usually very pleasant, quiet, and polite. She looks delicate and pampered, but it is not recommended to anyone to mistake her for a soft, comfortable pillow. Quiet voice and angelic appearance, the mask of a polished aristocrat—all this is a beautiful cover and her conscious attempts to appear irresistibly attractive in all respects.

And, there are always plenty of lovers of the beautiful. This woman sets the price herself and it is quite high.

She always clearly knows what she wants and calculates the variants of getting it quite well. This woman is a realist and she firmly stands on the ground with both feet. She is a woman of business—firm and pragmatic. Therefore, at any moment her angelic voice can change to a confident voice, which makes clear, short statements, as if giving orders, and a delicate violet turns into a judgmatic and insidious intriguer or an imperious, fierce fury with eyes glistening of wrath. Multi-faced metamorphoses (pretending) are usual and natural for her because she was born with an amazing gift of transformations. For example, she is able to play a role of a beautiful, submissive lady absolutely accurately. However, this does not mean that in this role she supports or is satisfied by other people's ideas, desires, and decisions. On the contrary, she alone always sets the rules of the game!

This person not only considers herself the head, the leader, but also actively insists on it, while turning into a dictator. She thinks that she knows everything and always. She often assumes the role of a judge, who evaluates someone or something, judges, determines and issues a verdict. As a result of being fully convinced that she is always right, she tries to impose her views on others, edify, moralize and tell them how to live. She intervenes in the lives of others and explains this by that she wants to safeguard from evil, to protect, to make sure that nothing bad happens, and seeks to aid, support someone. She shows that she cares about someone, helps someone, cherishes, fosters, and provides patronage. However, sometimes all this occurs in the form of a dictate, with a stern, imposing look, and a clear and conscious goal—to subjugate everyone.

This woman is a careerist. Career is a mandatory element in her life. And, if there is at least a minimal possibility to make it—she will work on it. She needs a career in order to realize her aptitudes, to get money, fame, and, most importantly, power. A career not only helps her self-realize in some activity, but also to obtain all possible ranks, awards, medals, titles, prestigious prizes, which she finds very attractive, as well as to receive material resources to satisfy all of her pretensions that are very far from modest. Having an immeasurable passion for luxury, this woman serves "the golden calf" with pleasure and sometimes reaches near orgasmic pleasure from possession of material wealth...

DEMO 80

Description Of Men Born On May 20th Of Common Years From The Catalog Of Human Population

Presented demo is a very short description. A complete description consists of a very detailed description of functioning and qualities of personality: a general description and a description on 6 factors (intellectual, nutritional, physical, emotional, sexual, and environmental).

Considered person presents himself as a deity in a luxurious radiance: warm, sunny, ideal. However, this does not mean that he sits around in idleness because he thinks that he is "the best." Having imperialistic ambitions, he knows how to defend them in competitive fighting—there is nothing he enjoys more than competing with someone who is smarter (more handsome, rich, professional, etc.). He must get the first place always and everywhere. In such "races," he will make every effort to prove that he is the best. In order to be number one, in addition to "races" in the environment, he also takes cares of making the needed impression. This man is seriously preoccupied with creating a "bright image," a mirage. He seeks to ensure that others perceive him as kind, impeccable, noble, straightforward, frank, openhearted...

A huge amount of energy is spent to ensure that secret sides of his nature (passion for intriguery, insidiousness, malignity, extreme greediness, dissoluteness, etc.) never surface and become known to someone. He prefers the image of a holy righteous man, a monk, immaculate as Jesus or any other analogous prophet. On the outside, he is smiling, optimistic, well-groomed, well-brought-up (it is even possible to say that he is tender in communication), well-meaning. In short, he is light and pleasant. Usually, his voice is also very pleasant: quiet, polite. Although he might look delicate and pampered, it is not recommended to anyone to mistake him for a soft and comfortable pillow; especially because he is really not like that at all. Quiet voice, angelic appearance, the mask of a simpleton, a well-meaning jollier—all this is for the poor. These are his conscious attempts to seem better, a tool for getting what he wants. And, he always clearly knows what he wants and knows how to calculate the variants of getting the desired. This is a realist, who firmly stands on the ground with both feet: business-minded, firm, and pragmatic. That is why one should not be surprised if at any moment his well-meaning, quiet voice suddenly changes to a confident, imperious voice, which makes clear, short statements, as if giving orders and a "soft pillow" turns into a judgmatic, insidious intriguer with a fierce face and eyes glistening of wrath.

This person thinks of himself as an ideal ruler: wise, kind, just, one who makes only the right decisions. This person not only considers himself the head, the leader, but also actively insists on it ("Come on, everyone listen here!") and sometimes turns into a dictator. Thinking that he has the correct perception of everything, knows everything and always, he assumes the role of a judge, who evaluates, judges, determines and issues a verdict. In general, he takes on too much, thinking that he has the right not only to spread, but also to impose his personal views on others by edifying, moralizing and telling people how they should live. Without any embarrassment, he can intervene in the life of another, allegedly driven by an aspiration to safeguard from the evil, "to put down something soft to fall on," to protect, to aid, to support someone. It might seem that he simply wants to care, cherish, foster, provide patronage, guard, but in reality all this occurs only with one goal—to subjugate everyone. Even his help, even his support can often take place in the form of a dictate. Besides, by nature he is not a bad jailer, and therefore he will easily make a golden cage for anyone, and all this will be done quietly, peacefully, unnoticeably.

With all his might, this man seeks to ensure that life would constantly surprise him, would be supernatural, eccentric, strange and incredible, would amaze him by originality of the occurring and would be similar to a world of wonders. He is persistently drawn to the world of bright shows, outlandish illusions, lies and masks, to the world of great fraudsters, where the hero is the one who deludes masterfully and brilliantly plays a trick on all the rest. He is also drawn to the world of casinos and good fortune, the world of exciting thrillers, mysticism, the world of the eccentric, the world of unusual, weird forms. First of all, a world of show-business (theater, film, television, circus) can become such a world; a world of tricks, strange and absurd escapades; or science, with its unsolvable puzzles and insane theories; or the world of aristocracy and nobility, where every day there are dazzling receptions in various places with people of all sorts and kinds. Or jurisprudence—since that is also nothing but a show, lies, masks. He is also interested in the world of paranormal phenomena: extrasensory experts, magicians, werewolves, mages, evil spirits, nightmares and secrets. He is attracted by any unorthodox, outlandish, fantastic, original teachings. And, it does not matter if they have neither meaning, nor a word of truth because that is exactly what attracts him—lies and trumpery...

DEMO 81

Description Of Women Born On May 21st Of Common Years From The Catalog Of Human Population

Presented demo is a very short description. A complete description consists of a very detailed description of functioning and qualities of personality: a general description and a description on 6 factors (intellectual, nutritional, physical, emotional, sexual, and environmental).

This person presents herself as a deity in a luxurious radiance: warm, sunny, ideal. This woman has a royal attitude and psychology of an empress. Striving for power is a natural state for her because, as she believes, power is money, and all this combined is the basis, the essence of her life space. Her life goal is to make everyone and everything submit to her. It is desirable for power to be total, so that it would be possible to control not only people's actions, but also their thoughts and desires.

Naturally, she considers herself an ideal ruler (wise, kind, just, one who makes only the right decisions, etc.). However, this does not mean that she sits around in idleness because she thinks that she is "the best." Having imperialistic ambitions, she knows how to defend them in competitive fighting. She must get the first place always and everywhere. In such "races," this woman will make every effort to prove that she is the best. In order to be number one, in addition to "races" in the environment, she takes cares of making the needed impression—this makes her way to power easier, which in its turn allows her to maintain any image that she likes.

This woman is seriously preoccupied with creating a "bright image," a kind of mirage. She thoroughly makes sure that others perceive her as kind, beautiful, impeccable, and noble. She seeks to look straightforward, openhearted, frank, and open like a flower during the flowering period. A huge amount of energy is spent to ensure that secret sides of her nature never surface and become known to someone. She prefers the image of a holy righteous woman.

On the outside she is smiling, optimistic, well-groomed and tidy, well-brought-up, it is even possible to say that she is tenderly well-meaning and easy in communication. Her voice is usually very pleasant, quiet, and polite. She looks delicate and pampered, but it is not recommended to anyone to mistake her for a soft, comfortable pillow. Quiet voice and angelic appearance, the mask of a polished aristocrat—all this is a beautiful cover and her conscious attempts to appear irresistibly attractive in all respects.

And, there are always plenty of lovers of the beautiful. This woman sets the price herself and it is quite high.

She always clearly knows what she wants and calculates the variants of getting it quite well. This woman is a realist and she firmly stands on the ground with both feet. She is a woman of business—firm and pragmatic. Therefore, at any moment her angelic voice can change to a confident voice, which makes clear, short statements, as if giving orders, and a delicate violet turns into a judgmatic and insidious intriguer or an imperious, fierce fury with eyes glistening of wrath. Multi-faced metamorphoses (pretending) are usual and natural for her because she was born with an amazing gift of transformations. For example, she is able to play a role of a beautiful, submissive lady absolutely accurately. However, this does not mean that in this role she supports or is satisfied by other people's ideas, desires, and decisions. On the contrary, she alone always sets the rules of the game!

This person not only considers herself the head, the leader, but also actively insists on it, while turning into a dictator. She thinks that she knows everything and always. She often assumes the role of a judge, who evaluates someone or something, judges, determines and issues a verdict. As a result of being fully convinced that she is always right, she tries to impose her views on others, edify, moralize and tell them how to live. She intervenes in the lives of others and explains this by that she wants to safeguard from evil, to protect, to make sure that nothing bad happens, and seeks to aid, support someone. She shows that she cares about someone, helps someone, cherishes, fosters, and provides patronage. However, sometimes all this occurs in the form of a dictate, with a stern, imposing look, and a clear and conscious goal—to subjugate everyone.

This woman is a careerist. Career is a mandatory element in her life. And, if there is at least a minimal possibility to make it—she will work on it. She needs a career in order to realize her aptitudes, to get money, fame, and, most importantly, power. A career not only helps her self-realize in some activity, but also to obtain all possible ranks, awards, medals, titles, prestigious prizes, which she finds very attractive, as well as to receive material resources to satisfy all of her pretensions that are very far from modest. Having an immeasurable passion for luxury, this woman serves "the golden calf" with pleasure and sometimes reaches near orgasmic pleasure from possession of material wealth...

DEMO 82

Description Of Men Born On May 21ˢᵗ Of Common Years From The Catalog Of Human Population

Presented demo is a very short description. A complete description consists of a very detailed description of functioning and qualities of personality: a general description and a description on 6 factors (intellectual, nutritional, physical, emotional, sexual, and environmental).

Considered person presents himself as a deity in a luxurious radiance: warm, sunny, ideal. However, this does not mean that he sits around in idleness because he thinks that he is "the best." Having imperialistic ambitions, he knows how to defend them in competitive fighting—there is nothing he enjoys more than competing with someone who is smarter (more handsome, rich, professional, etc.). He must get the first place always and everywhere. In such "races," he will make every effort to prove that he is the best. In order to be number one, in addition to "races" in the environment, he also takes cares of making the needed impression. This man is seriously preoccupied with creating a "bright image," a mirage. He seeks to ensure that others perceive him as kind, impeccable, noble, straightforward, frank, openhearted...

A huge amount of energy is spent to ensure that secret sides of his nature (passion for intriguery, insidiousness, malignity, extreme greediness, dissoluteness, etc.) never surface and become known to someone. He prefers the image of a holy righteous man, a monk, immaculate as Jesus or any other analogous prophet. On the outside, he is smiling, optimistic, well-groomed, well-brought-up (it is even possible to say that he is tender in communication), well-meaning. In short, he is light and pleasant. Usually, his voice is also very pleasant: quiet, polite. Although he might look delicate and pampered, it is not recommended to anyone to mistake him for a soft and comfortable pillow; especially because he is really not like that at all. Quiet voice, angelic appearance, the mask of a simpleton, a well-meaning jollier—all this is for the poor. These are his conscious attempts to seem better, a tool for getting what he wants. And, he always clearly knows what he wants and knows how to calculate the variants of getting the desired. This is a realist, who firmly stands on the ground with both feet: business-minded, firm, and pragmatic. That is why one should not be surprised if at any moment his well-meaning, quiet voice suddenly changes to a confident, imperious voice, which makes clear, short statements, as if giving orders and a "soft pillow" turns into a judgmatic, insidious intriguer with a fierce face and eyes glistening of wrath.

This person thinks of himself as an ideal ruler: wise, kind, just, one who makes only the right decisions. This person not only considers himself the head, the leader, but also actively insists on it ("Come on, everyone listen here!") and sometimes turns into a dictator. Thinking that he has the correct perception of everything, knows everything and always, he assumes the role of a judge, who evaluates, judges, determines and issues a verdict. In general, he takes on too much, thinking that he has the right not only to spread, but also to impose his personal views on others by edifying, moralizing and telling people how they should live. Without any embarrassment, he can intervene in the life of another, allegedly driven by an aspiration to safeguard from the evil, "to put down something soft to fall on," to protect, to aid, to support someone. It might seem that he simply wants to care, cherish, foster, provide patronage, guard, but in reality all this occurs only with one goal—to subjugate everyone. Even his help, even his support can often take place in the form of a dictate. Besides, by nature he is not a bad jailer, and therefore he will easily make a golden cage for anyone, and all this will be done quietly, peacefully, unnoticeably.

With all his might, this man seeks to ensure that life would constantly surprise him, would be supernatural, eccentric, strange and incredible, would amaze him by originality of the occurring and would be similar to a world of wonders. He is persistently drawn to the world of bright shows, outlandish illusions, lies and masks, to the world of great fraudsters, where the hero is the one who deludes masterfully and brilliantly plays a trick on all the rest. He is also drawn to the world of casinos and good fortune, the world of exciting thrillers, mysticism, the world of the eccentric, the world of unusual, weird forms. First of all, a world of show-business (theater, film, television, circus) can become such a world; a world of tricks, strange and absurd escapades; or science, with its unsolvable puzzles and insane theories; or the world of aristocracy and nobility, where every day there are dazzling receptions in various places with people of all sorts and kinds. Or jurisprudence—since that is also nothing but a show, lies, masks. He is also interested in the world of paranormal phenomena: extrasensory experts, magicians, werewolves, mages, evil spirits, nightmares and secrets. He is attracted by any unorthodox, outlandish, fantastic, original teachings. And, it does not matter if they have neither meaning, nor a word of truth because that is exactly what attracts him—lies and trumpery...

DEMO 83

Description Of Women Born On May 26th Of Leap Years From The Catalog Of Human Population

Presented demo is a very short description. A complete description consists of a very detailed description of functioning and qualities of personality: a general description and a description on 6 factors (intellectual, nutritional, physical, emotional, sexual, and environmental).

A characteristic peculiarity of this individual is that this woman constantly changes little by little. Her changes cannot be defined as sharp. Their algorithm is more like performance of a ritual or a diplomatic reception, where everything happens slowly, without a fuss, and all actions are made with a sense of personal dignity. As a consequence, these changes are almost unnoticeable by others. However, this is not the point. The point is that changes are stably present in her life. And, if there are people, who see (or want to see) a static world in their imagination—this person is constantly involved in internal changes.

All factors of this person work according to this principle—timely (in regard to a situation) changes, and resemble a bird that calmly soars in the sky: its wings practically do not move, but it does not stand still in one place since air masses themselves move it. Only instead of wind and air currents, she has a variety of events, situations from the outside world.

This woman is very situational. Firstly, she always seeks to ensure that in this constantly changing, fluid world she could flexibly integrate into a situation, smoothly "flow into" it. And, she succeeds in this perfectly well. It is not without reason that out of all elements this woman loves water the most. Like water, when she enters a particular field of business or society, she herself changes and inevitably changes something around her, and all this happens quietly and unnoticeably. Her quality of a classifier, who judges everything by analogy, on the basis of examples (historical, cultural, philosophical, anthropological, in other words—how someone once did something , what he said in regard to a particular topic, etc.) helps her in this. She identifies a common sign of similarity, takes that as a model, copies and becomes similar, alike, uniform with the situation. Secondly, she always chooses the right time. This happens without a hurry, slowly, purposefully, but without too much waiting, too many protractions or preparations. She changes her rhythm, speed quietly and smoothly, depending on events, people, and situations. As a result, she is always on time, always fits in well. She will not swim against the current.

This person differs by yet another important characteristic. She stably strives to be in reality instead of living in illusions. She thinks realistically, she is interested in specific affairs, projects that can be implemented. These undertakings will eventually be beneficial, bring tangible dividends. She does not understand useless actions, meaningless body movements.

This person has a subjective view of herself as a person, who is impossible to get ahead of by definition. And, it is necessary to give her credit, as she really does strive to become unattainable by her competitors with all her might! Due to her positive attitude towards work, goal-orientedness, perseverance and persistence, she really does manage to become a very good specialist in any chosen field.

Also, authorities do not exist for her. She herself claims the pedestal, especially in issues that relate to her professional sphere. At the same time, she demands respect, preferably with a touch of worship. These demands do not affect her learning and desire to perfect. As a result, over the years, as she accumulates vast experience, she really turns into a cultured professional, an educated person, who knows a lot and knows how to do a lot. However, there is danger of becoming literally obsessed with the idea of self-perfecting and getting hung up on herself as a super valuable object.

This woman does not believe that geniuses are born. From her point of view, it is unlikely that mastery can come to person without any efforts on his part. Unfortunately, not everyone thinks like this.

Considered person wants to know absolutely clearly what she is doing and for what. That is—she has a habit of acting maximally consciously. This approach bears its fruits—when she begins to do something, she already has stable motives. And, while she executes, she tries to ensure that later on it would not be possible to accuse her of imperfection, lack of knowledge of the issue, negligence, stupidity, dilettantism, etc...

DEMO 84

Description Of Women Born On May 27th Of Leap Years From The Catalog Of Human Population

Presented demo is a very short description. A complete description consists of a very detailed description of functioning and qualities of personality: a general description and a description on 6 factors (intellectual, nutritional, physical, emotional, sexual, and environmental).

A characteristic peculiarity of this individual is that this woman constantly changes little by little. Her changes cannot be defined as sharp. Their algorithm is more like performance of a ritual or a diplomatic reception, where everything happens slowly, without a fuss, and all actions are made with a sense of personal dignity. As a consequence, these changes are almost unnoticeable by others. However, this is not the point. The point is that changes are stably present in her life. And, if there are people, who see (or want to see) a static world in their imagination—this person is constantly involved in internal changes.

All factors of this person work according to this principle—timely (in regard to a situation) changes, and resemble a bird that calmly soars in the sky: its wings practically do not move, but it does not stand still in one place since air masses themselves move it. Only instead of wind and air currents, she has a variety of events, situations from the outside world.

This woman is very situational. Firstly, she always seeks to ensure that in this constantly changing, fluid world she could flexibly integrate into a situation, smoothly "flow into" it. And, she succeeds in this perfectly well. It is not without reason that out of all elements this woman loves water the most. Like water, when she enters a particular field of business or society, she herself changes and inevitably changes something around her, and all this happens quietly and unnoticeably. Her quality of a classifier, who judges everything by analogy, on the basis of examples (historical, cultural, philosophical, anthropological, in other words—how someone once did something , what he said in regard to a particular topic, etc.) helps her in this. She identifies a common sign of similarity, takes that as a model, copies and becomes similar, alike, uniform with the situation. Secondly, she always chooses the right time. This happens without a hurry, slowly, purposefully, but without too much waiting, too many protractions or preparations. She changes her rhythm, speed quietly and smoothly, depending on events, people, and situations. As a result, she is always on time, always fits in well. She will not swim against the current.

This person differs by yet another important characteristic. She stably strives to be in reality instead of living in illusions. She thinks realistically, she is interested in specific affairs, projects that can be implemented. These undertakings will eventually be beneficial, bring tangible dividends. She does not understand useless actions, meaningless body movements.

This person has a subjective view of herself as a person, who is impossible to get ahead of by definition. And, it is necessary to give her credit, as she really does strive to become unattainable by her competitors with all her might! Due to her positive attitude towards work, goal-orientedness, perseverance and persistence, she really does manage to become a very good specialist in any chosen field.

Also, authorities do not exist for her. She herself claims the pedestal, especially in issues that relate to her professional sphere. At the same time, she demands respect, preferably with a touch of worship. These demands do not affect her learning and desire to perfect. As a result, over the years, as she accumulates vast experience, she really turns into a cultured professional, an educated person, who knows a lot and knows how to do a lot. However, there is danger of becoming literally obsessed with the idea of self-perfecting and getting hung up on herself as a super valuable object.

This woman does not believe that geniuses are born. From her point of view, it is unlikely that mastery can come to person without any efforts on his part. Unfortunately, not everyone thinks like this.

Considered person wants to know absolutely clearly what she is doing and for what. That is—she has a habit of acting maximally consciously. This approach bears its fruits—when she begins to do something, she already has stable motives. And, while she executes, she tries to ensure that later on it would not be possible to accuse her of imperfection, lack of knowledge of the issue, negligence, stupidity, dilettantism, etc...

DEMO 85

Description Of Women Born On May 27th Of Common Years From The Catalog Of Human Population

Presented demo is a very short description. A complete description consists of a very detailed description of functioning and qualities of personality: a general description and a description on 6 factors (intellectual, nutritional, physical, emotional, sexual, and environmental).

A characteristic peculiarity of this individual is that this woman constantly changes little by little. Her changes cannot be defined as sharp. Their algorithm is more like performance of a ritual or a diplomatic reception, where everything happens slowly, without a fuss, and all actions are made with a sense of personal dignity. As a consequence, these changes are almost unnoticeable by others. However, this is not the point. The point is that changes are stably present in her life. And, if there are people, who see (or want to see) a static world in their imagination—this person is constantly involved in internal changes.

All factors of this person work according to this principle—timely (in regard to a situation) changes, and resemble a bird that calmly soars in the sky: its wings practically do not move, but it does not stand still in one place since air masses themselves move it. Only instead of wind and air currents, she has a variety of events, situations from the outside world.

This woman is very situational. Firstly, she always seeks to ensure that in this constantly changing, fluid world she could flexibly integrate into a situation, smoothly "flow into" it. And, she succeeds in this perfectly well. It is not without reason that out of all elements this woman loves water the most. Like water, when she enters a particular field of business or society, she herself changes and inevitably changes something around her, and all this happens quietly and unnoticeably. Her quality of a classifier, who judges everything by analogy, on the basis of examples (historical, cultural, philosophical, anthropological, in other words—how someone once did something , what he said in regard to a particular topic, etc.) helps her in this. She identifies a common sign of similarity, takes that as a model, copies and becomes similar, alike, uniform with the situation. Secondly, she always chooses the right time. This happens without a hurry, slowly, purposefully, but without too much waiting, too many protractions or preparations. She changes her rhythm, speed quietly and smoothly, depending on events, people, and situations. As a result, she is always on time, always fits in well. She will not swim against the current.

This person differs by yet another important characteristic. She stably strives to be in reality instead of living in illusions. She thinks realistically, she is interested in specific affairs, projects that can be implemented. These undertakings will eventually be beneficial, bring tangible dividends. She does not understand useless actions, meaningless body movements.

This person has a subjective view of herself as a person, who is impossible to get ahead of by definition. And, it is necessary to give her credit, as she really does strive to become unattainable by her competitors with all her might! Due to her positive attitude towards work, goal-orientedness, perseverance and persistence, she really does manage to become a very good specialist in any chosen field.

Also, authorities do not exist for her. She herself claims the pedestal, especially in issues that relate to her professional sphere. At the same time, she demands respect, preferably with a touch of worship. These demands do not affect her learning and desire to perfect. As a result, over the years, as she accumulates vast experience, she really turns into a cultured professional, an educated person, who knows a lot and knows how to do a lot. However, there is danger of becoming literally obsessed with the idea of self-perfecting and getting hung up on herself as a super valuable object.

This woman does not believe that geniuses are born. From her point of view, it is unlikely that mastery can come to person without any efforts on his part. Unfortunately, not everyone thinks like this.

Considered person wants to know absolutely clearly what she is doing and for what. That is—she has a habit of acting maximally consciously. This approach bears its fruits—when she begins to do something, she already has stable motives. And, while she executes, she tries to ensure that later on it would not be possible to accuse her of imperfection, lack of knowledge of the issue, negligence, stupidity, dilettantism, etc...

DEMO 86

Description Of Women Born On May 28th Of Common Years From The Catalog Of Human Population

Presented demo is a very short description. A complete description consists of a very detailed description of functioning and qualities of personality: a general description and a description on 6 factors (intellectual, nutritional, physical, emotional, sexual, and environmental).

A characteristic peculiarity of this individual is that this woman constantly changes little by little. Her changes cannot be defined as sharp. Their algorithm is more like performance of a ritual or a diplomatic reception, where everything happens slowly, without a fuss, and all actions are made with a sense of personal dignity. As a consequence, these changes are almost unnoticeable by others. However, this is not the point. The point is that changes are stably present in her life. And, if there are people, who see (or want to see) a static world in their imagination—this person is constantly involved in internal changes.

All factors of this person work according to this principle—timely (in regard to a situation) changes, and resemble a bird that calmly soars in the sky: its wings practically do not move, but it does not stand still in one place since air masses themselves move it. Only instead of wind and air currents, she has a variety of events, situations from the outside world.

This woman is very situational. Firstly, she always seeks to ensure that in this constantly changing, fluid world she could flexibly integrate into a situation, smoothly "flow into" it. And, she succeeds in this perfectly well. It is not without reason that out of all elements this woman loves water the most. Like water, when she enters a particular field of business or society, she herself changes and inevitably changes something around her, and all this happens quietly and unnoticeably. Her quality of a classifier, who judges everything by analogy, on the basis of examples (historical, cultural, philosophical, anthropological, in other words—how someone once did something , what he said in regard to a particular topic, etc.) helps her in this. She identifies a common sign of similarity, takes that as a model, copies and becomes similar, alike, uniform with the situation. Secondly, she always chooses the right time. This happens without a hurry, slowly, purposefully, but without too much waiting, too many protractions or preparations. She changes her rhythm, speed quietly and smoothly, depending on events, people, and situations. As a result, she is always on time, always fits in well. She will not swim against the current.

This person differs by yet another important characteristic. She stably strives to be in reality instead of living in illusions. She thinks realistically, she is interested in specific affairs, projects that can be implemented. These undertakings will eventually be beneficial, bring tangible dividends. She does not understand useless actions, meaningless body movements.

This person has a subjective view of herself as a person, who is impossible to get ahead of by definition. And, it is necessary to give her credit, as she really does strive to become unattainable by her competitors with all her might! Due to her positive attitude towards work, goal-orientedness, perseverance and persistence, she really does manage to become a very good specialist in any chosen field.

Also, authorities do not exist for her. She herself claims the pedestal, especially in issues that relate to her professional sphere. At the same time, she demands respect, preferably with a touch of worship. These demands do not affect her learning and desire to perfect. As a result, over the years, as she accumulates vast experience, she really turns into a cultured professional, an educated person, who knows a lot and knows how to do a lot. However, there is danger of becoming literally obsessed with the idea of self-perfecting and getting hung up on herself as a super valuable object.

This woman does not believe that geniuses are born. From her point of view, it is unlikely that mastery can come to person without any efforts on his part. Unfortunately, not everyone thinks like this.

Considered person wants to know absolutely clearly what she is doing and for what. That is—she has a habit of acting maximally consciously. This approach bears its fruits—when she begins to do something, she already has stable motives. And, while she executes, she tries to ensure that later on it would not be possible to accuse her of imperfection, lack of knowledge of the issue, negligence, stupidity, dilettantism, etc...

DEMO 87

Description Of Men Born On May 29ᵗʰ Of Leap Years From The Catalog Of Human Population

Presented demo is a very short description. A complete description consists of a very detailed description of functioning and qualities of personality: a general description and a description on 6 factors (intellectual, nutritional, physical, emotional, sexual, and environmental).

This individual perceives himself as the beginning, the prime cause, the basis of occurring processes. While studying and learning about the world, he seeks to find the only keystone, on which all creation stands. When he comes across something, he tries to understand the origin of the phenomenon, the basis of knowledge, system. In principle, this person might be interested in any scientific, philosophical, esoteric, religious system. However, in the process of examining any issue (an idea, a civilization, a professional field, or a cultural trend), this person wants to get to the fundamental principle, try to find the foundation stone of the whole "construction," and he will certainly be interested in who, when and how founded all this.

Being a fan of the ancient secrets, in his search for the prime cause this person might be interested in ancient writings, look for them in rare editions of books, and might begin to study hieroglyphic texts. While studying any culture, this person will go centuries back, into the mythological layer during his search for the fundamental principle.

This person strictly separates the hidden and the external, the secret and the overt, and believes in miracles. It is his faith in what is called "miracles" (without really fitting this definition) that can significantly help him in the search of what he is looking for because it provides a possibility to go beyond narrow-minded views, materialistic thinking and strictly scientific standpoints.

This individual is a successor of ancestral heritage, doings of the fathers. He might inherit his father's business, or continue the work of founders of some system: scientific, social, cultural, philosophical or any other. However, his personal construction anyway will be based on heritage of founders of the system, just like the Third Reich, was built on ancestral heritage (Aryans). Moreover, he considers it his obligation, his duty to continue, to strengthen in society the undertaking, which the founding fathers began. This man's dream is to start some big affair for the descendants.

Especially with age, this man will have his own style, and carry himself with dignity and grace. He likes to look flawless, perfect both externally and internally. By his qualities, he might remind of the French king Louis XIV, who was also known as the Sun King due to duality of nature and the level, to which he surrounded himself with luxury. In history, he remained unsurpassed in terms of inventiveness in the field of entertainment, as an owner of a vast imagination, excessive luxury in regard to everything: himself, his court and palace, receptions, and entertainment events. Considered individual likes to behave royally, patronizingly and grandly. Also, as the above-mentioned king, he gravitates toward luxury.

The following statement can be considered his principal philosophy: "It's better to be first and best always." In addition, this person really wants to try to "embrace the boundless": research everything, try everything, visit all places, see everything, and know everything. And, he wishes to have a lot of everything, whether it is money, knowledge, friends, baseball caps, information, diamonds, women or mansions. If he decides to buy a "small house," then he thinks that it must be the size of the Hermitage Museum; if he decides to buy a car, then it must be the most expensive one; if he studies, then he thinks that he must learn and know everything. However, this man's desire for luxury is a particular case of his general tendency toward excessiveness.

He does everything without moderation, and when something captures his attention, whether it is work, a person, an event, some action or state—he cannot stop and rushes headlong into it, as if internal brakes do not exist. He thinks that if he is to love, then it must be completely, to hate—with his whole heart, to be bored—desperately, and to fight—until a kill. If it is intellectual work, then it must continue until mental exhaustion; physical exercise—as long as possible; food consumption—until overeating; emotions—until an emotional peak, affect; sex—until a state of madness and satiety; work—to workaholism; career—to maximum social heights. Even the state of lack of money this man is able to bring to desperate poverty. He does not have a good understanding of words 'sufficient', 'plenty', 'enough'...

DEMO 88

Description Of Men Born On May 30th Of Leap Years From The Catalog Of Human Population

Presented demo is a very short description. A complete description consists of a very detailed description of functioning and qualities of personality: a general description and a description on 6 factors (intellectual, nutritional, physical, emotional, sexual, and environmental).

This individual perceives himself as the beginning, the prime cause, the basis of occurring processes. While studying and learning about the world, he seeks to find the only keystone, on which all creation stands. When he comes across something, he tries to understand the origin of the phenomenon, the basis of knowledge, system. In principle, this person might be interested in any scientific, philosophical, esoteric, religious system. However, in the process of examining any issue (an idea, a civilization, a professional field, or a cultural trend), this person wants to get to the fundamental principle, try to find the foundation stone of the whole "construction," and he will certainly be interested in who, when and how founded all this.

Being a fan of the ancient secrets, in his search for the prime cause this person might be interested in ancient writings, look for them in rare editions of books, and might begin to study hieroglyphic texts. While studying any culture, this person will go centuries back, into the mythological layer during his search for the fundamental principle.

This person strictly separates the hidden and the external, the secret and the overt, and believes in miracles. It is his faith in what is called "miracles" (without really fitting this definition) that can significantly help him in the search of what he is looking for because it provides a possibility to go beyond narrow-minded views, materialistic thinking and strictly scientific standpoints.

This individual is a successor of ancestral heritage, doings of the fathers. He might inherit his father's business, or continue the work of founders of some system: scientific, social, cultural, philosophical or any other. However, his personal construction anyway will be based on heritage of founders of the system, just like the Third Reich, was built on ancestral heritage (Aryans). Moreover, he considers it his obligation, his duty to continue, to strengthen in society the undertaking, which the founding fathers began. This man's dream is to start some big affair for the descendants.

Especially with age, this man will have his own style, and carry himself with dignity and grace. He likes to look flawless, perfect both externally and internally. By his qualities, he might remind of the French king Louis XIV, who was also known as the Sun King due to duality of nature and the level, to which he surrounded himself with luxury. In history, he remained unsurpassed in terms of inventiveness in the field of entertainment, as an owner of a vast imagination, excessive luxury in regard to everything: himself, his court and palace, receptions, and entertainment events. Considered individual likes to behave royally, patronizingly and grandly. Also, as the above-mentioned king, he gravitates toward luxury.

The following statement can be considered his principal philosophy: "It's better to be first and best always." In addition, this person really wants to try to "embrace the boundless": research everything, try everything, visit all places, see everything, and know everything. And, he wishes to have a lot of everything, whether it is money, knowledge, friends, baseball caps, information, diamonds, women or mansions. If he decides to buy a "small house," then he thinks that it must be the size of the Hermitage Museum; if he decides to buy a car, then it must be the most expensive one; if he studies, then he thinks that he must learn and know everything. However, this man's desire for luxury is a particular case of his general tendency toward excessiveness.

He does everything without moderation, and when something captures his attention, whether it is work, a person, an event, some action or state—he cannot stop and rushes headlong into it, as if internal brakes do not exist. He thinks that if he is to love, then it must be completely, to hate—with his whole heart, to be bored—desperately, and to fight—until a kill. If it is intellectual work, then it must continue until mental exhaustion; physical exercise—as long as possible; food consumption—until overeating; emotions—until an emotional peak, affect; sex—until a state of madness and satiety; work—to workaholism; career—to maximum social heights. Even the state of lack of money this man is able to bring to desperate poverty. He does not have a good understanding of words 'sufficient', 'plenty', 'enough'...

DEMO 89
Description Of Men Born On May 30th Of Common Years From The Catalog Of Human Population

Presented demo is a very short description. A complete description consists of a very detailed description of functioning and qualities of personality: a general description and a description on 6 factors (intellectual, nutritional, physical, emotional, sexual, and environmental).

This individual perceives himself as the beginning, the prime cause, the basis of occurring processes. While studying and learning about the world, he seeks to find the only keystone, on which all creation stands. When he comes across something, he tries to understand the origin of the phenomenon, the basis of knowledge, system. In principle, this person might be interested in any scientific, philosophical, esoteric, religious system. However, in the process of examining any issue (an idea, a civilization, a professional field, or a cultural trend), this person wants to get to the fundamental principle, try to find the foundation stone of the whole "construction," and he will certainly be interested in who, when and how founded all this.

Being a fan of the ancient secrets, in his search for the prime cause this person might be interested in ancient writings, look for them in rare editions of books, and might begin to study hieroglyphic texts. While studying any culture, this person will go centuries back, into the mythological layer during his search for the fundamental principle.

This person strictly separates the hidden and the external, the secret and the overt, and believes in miracles. It is his faith in what is called "miracles" (without really fitting this definition) that can significantly help him in the search of what he is looking for because it provides a possibility to go beyond narrow-minded views, materialistic thinking and strictly scientific standpoints.

This individual is a successor of ancestral heritage, doings of the fathers. He might inherit his father's business, or continue the work of founders of some system: scientific, social, cultural, philosophical or any other. However, his personal construction anyway will be based on heritage of founders of the system, just like the Third Reich, was built on ancestral heritage (Aryans). Moreover, he considers it his obligation, his duty to continue, to strengthen in society the undertaking, which the founding fathers began. This man's dream is to start some big affair for the descendants.

Especially with age, this man will have his own style, and carry himself with dignity and grace. He likes to look flawless, perfect both externally and internally. By his qualities, he might remind of the French king Louis XIV, who was also known as the Sun King due to duality of nature and the level, to which he surrounded himself with luxury. In history, he remained unsurpassed in terms of inventiveness in the field of entertainment, as an owner of a vast imagination, excessive luxury in regard to everything: himself, his court and palace, receptions, and entertainment events. Considered individual likes to behave royally, patronizingly and grandly. Also, as the above-mentioned king, he gravitates toward luxury.

The following statement can be considered his principal philosophy: "It's better to be first and best always." In addition, this person really wants to try to "embrace the boundless": research everything, try everything, visit all places, see everything, and know everything. And, he wishes to have a lot of everything, whether it is money, knowledge, friends, baseball caps, information, diamonds, women or mansions. If he decides to buy a "small house," then he thinks that it must be the size of the Hermitage Museum; if he decides to buy a car, then it must be the most expensive one; if he studies, then he thinks that he must learn and know everything. However, this man's desire for luxury is a particular case of his general tendency toward excessiveness.

He does everything without moderation, and when something captures his attention, whether it is work, a person, an event, some action or state—he cannot stop and rushes headlong into it, as if internal brakes do not exist. He thinks that if he is to love, then it must be completely, to hate—with his whole heart, to be bored—desperately, and to fight—until a kill. If it is intellectual work, then it must continue until mental exhaustion; physical exercise—as long as possible; food consumption—until overeating; emotions—until an emotional peak, affect; sex—until a state of madness and satiety; work—to workaholism; career—to maximum social heights. Even the state of lack of money this man is able to bring to desperate poverty. He does not have a good understanding of words 'sufficient', 'plenty', 'enough'...

DEMO 90

Description Of Men Born On May 31st Of Leap Years From The Catalog Of Human Population

Presented demo is a very short description. A complete description consists of a very detailed description of functioning and qualities of personality: a general description and a description on 6 factors (intellectual, nutritional, physical, emotional, sexual, and environmental).

This individual perceives himself as the beginning, the prime cause, the basis of occurring processes. While studying and learning about the world, he seeks to find the only keystone, on which all creation stands. When he comes across something, he tries to understand the origin of the phenomenon, the basis of knowledge, system. In principle, this person might be interested in any scientific, philosophical, esoteric, religious system. However, in the process of examining any issue (an idea, a civilization, a professional field, or a cultural trend), this person wants to get to the fundamental principle, try to find the foundation stone of the whole "construction," and he will certainly be interested in who, when and how founded all this.

Being a fan of the ancient secrets, in his search for the prime cause this person might be interested in ancient writings, look for them in rare editions of books, and might begin to study hieroglyphic texts. While studying any culture, this person will go centuries back, into the mythological layer during his search for the fundamental principle.

This person strictly separates the hidden and the external, the secret and the overt, and believes in miracles. It is his faith in what is called "miracles" (without really fitting this definition) that can significantly help him in the search of what he is looking for because it provides a possibility to go beyond narrow-minded views, materialistic thinking and strictly scientific standpoints.

This individual is a successor of ancestral heritage, doings of the fathers. He might inherit his father's business, or continue the work of founders of some system: scientific, social, cultural, philosophical or any other. However, his personal construction anyway will be based on heritage of founders of the system, just like the Third Reich, was built on ancestral heritage (Aryans). Moreover, he considers it his obligation, his duty to continue, to strengthen in society the undertaking, which the founding fathers began. This man's dream is to start some big affair for the descendants.

Especially with age, this man will have his own style, and carry himself with dignity and grace. He likes to look flawless, perfect both externally and internally. By his qualities, he might remind of the French king Louis XIV, who was also known as the Sun King due to duality of nature and the level, to which he surrounded himself with luxury. In history, he remained unsurpassed in terms of inventiveness in the field of entertainment, as an owner of a vast imagination, excessive luxury in regard to everything: himself, his court and palace, receptions, and entertainment events. Considered individual likes to behave royally, patronizingly and grandly. Also, as the above-mentioned king, he gravitates toward luxury.

The following statement can be considered his principal philosophy: "It's better to be first and best always." In addition, this person really wants to try to "embrace the boundless": research everything, try everything, visit all places, see everything, and know everything. And, he wishes to have a lot of everything, whether it is money, knowledge, friends, baseball caps, information, diamonds, women or mansions. If he decides to buy a "small house," then he thinks that it must be the size of the Hermitage Museum; if he decides to buy a car, then it must be the most expensive one; if he studies, then he thinks that he must learn and know everything. However, this man's desire for luxury is a particular case of his general tendency toward excessiveness.

He does everything without moderation, and when something captures his attention, whether it is work, a person, an event, some action or state—he cannot stop and rushes headlong into it, as if internal brakes do not exist. He thinks that if he is to love, then it must be completely, to hate—with his whole heart, to be bored—desperately, and to fight—until a kill. If it is intellectual work, then it must continue until mental exhaustion; physical exercise—as long as possible; food consumption—until overeating; emotions—until an emotional peak, affect; sex—until a state of madness and satiety; work—to workaholism; career—to maximum social heights. Even the state of lack of money this man is able to bring to desperate poverty. He does not have a good understanding of words 'sufficient', 'plenty', 'enough'...

DEMO 91
Description Of Men Born On May 31ˢᵗ Of Common Years From The Catalog Of Human Population

Presented demo is a very short description. A complete description consists of a very detailed description of functioning and qualities of personality: a general description and a description on 6 factors (intellectual, nutritional, physical, emotional, sexual, and environmental).

This individual perceives himself as the beginning, the prime cause, the basis of occurring processes. While studying and learning about the world, he seeks to find the only keystone, on which all creation stands. When he comes across something, he tries to understand the origin of the phenomenon, the basis of knowledge, system. In principle, this person might be interested in any scientific, philosophical, esoteric, religious system. However, in the process of examining any issue (an idea, a civilization, a professional field, or a cultural trend), this person wants to get to the fundamental principle, try to find the foundation stone of the whole "construction," and he will certainly be interested in who, when and how founded all this.

Being a fan of the ancient secrets, in his search for the prime cause this person might be interested in ancient writings, look for them in rare editions of books, and might begin to study hieroglyphic texts. While studying any culture, this person will go centuries back, into the mythological layer during his search for the fundamental principle.

This person strictly separates the hidden and the external, the secret and the overt, and believes in miracles. It is his faith in what is called "miracles" (without really fitting this definition) that can significantly help him in the search of what he is looking for because it provides a possibility to go beyond narrow-minded views, materialistic thinking and strictly scientific standpoints.

This individual is a successor of ancestral heritage, doings of the fathers. He might inherit his father's business, or continue the work of founders of some system: scientific, social, cultural, philosophical or any other. However, his personal construction anyway will be based on heritage of founders of the system, just like the Third Reich, was built on ancestral heritage (Aryans). Moreover, he considers it his obligation, his duty to continue, to strengthen in society the undertaking, which the founding fathers began. This man's dream is to start some big affair for the descendants.

Especially with age, this man will have his own style, and carry himself with dignity and grace. He likes to look flawless, perfect both externally and internally. By his qualities, he might remind of the French king Louis XIV, who was also known as the Sun King due to duality of nature and the level, to which he surrounded himself with luxury. In history, he remained unsurpassed in terms of inventiveness in the field of entertainment, as an owner of a vast imagination, excessive luxury in regard to everything: himself, his court and palace, receptions, and entertainment events. Considered individual likes to behave royally, patronizingly and grandly. Also, as the above-mentioned king, he gravitates toward luxury.

The following statement can be considered his principal philosophy: "It's better to be first and best always." In addition, this person really wants to try to "embrace the boundless": research everything, try everything, visit all places, see everything, and know everything. And, he wishes to have a lot of everything, whether it is money, knowledge, friends, baseball caps, information, diamonds, women or mansions. If he decides to buy a "small house," then he thinks that it must be the size of the Hermitage Museum; if he decides to buy a car, then it must be the most expensive one; if he studies, then he thinks that he must learn and know everything. However, this man's desire for luxury is a particular case of his general tendency toward excessiveness.

He does everything without moderation, and when something captures his attention, whether it is work, a person, an event, some action or state—he cannot stop and rushes headlong into it, as if internal brakes do not exist. He thinks that if he is to love, then it must be completely, to hate—with his whole heart, to be bored—desperately, and to fight—until a kill. If it is intellectual work, then it must continue until mental exhaustion; physical exercise—as long as possible; food consumption—until overeating; emotions—until an emotional peak, affect; sex—until a state of madness and satiety; work—to workaholism; career—to maximum social heights. Even the state of lack of money this man is able to bring to desperate poverty. He does not have a good understanding of words 'sufficient', 'plenty', 'enough'...

DEMO 92
Description Of Men Born On June 1st Of Common Years From The Catalog Of Human Population

Presented demo is a very short description. A complete description consists of a very detailed description of functioning and qualities of personality: a general description and a description on 6 factors (intellectual, nutritional, physical, emotional, sexual, and environmental).

This individual perceives himself as the beginning, the prime cause, the basis of occurring processes. While studying and learning about the world, he seeks to find the only keystone, on which all creation stands. When he comes across something, he tries to understand the origin of the phenomenon, the basis of knowledge, system. In principle, this person might be interested in any scientific, philosophical, esoteric, religious system. However, in the process of examining any issue (an idea, a civilization, a professional field, or a cultural trend), this person wants to get to the fundamental principle, try to find the foundation stone of the whole "construction," and he will certainly be interested in who, when and how founded all this.

Being a fan of the ancient secrets, in his search for the prime cause this person might be interested in ancient writings, look for them in rare editions of books, and might begin to study hieroglyphic texts. While studying any culture, this person will go centuries back, into the mythological layer during his search for the fundamental principle.

This person strictly separates the hidden and the external, the secret and the overt, and believes in miracles. It is his faith in what is called "miracles" (without really fitting this definition) that can significantly help him in the search of what he is looking for because it provides a possibility to go beyond narrow-minded views, materialistic thinking and strictly scientific standpoints.

This individual is a successor of ancestral heritage, doings of the fathers. He might inherit his father's business, or continue the work of founders of some system: scientific, social, cultural, philosophical or any other. However, his personal construction anyway will be based on heritage of founders of the system, just like the Third Reich, was built on ancestral heritage (Aryans). Moreover, he considers it his obligation, his duty to continue, to strengthen in society the undertaking, which the founding fathers began. This man's dream is to start some big affair for the descendants.

Especially with age, this man will have his own style, and carry himself with dignity and grace. He likes to look flawless, perfect both externally and internally. By his qualities, he might remind of the French king Louis XIV, who was also known as the Sun King due to duality of nature and the level, to which he surrounded himself with luxury. In history, he remained unsurpassed in terms of inventiveness in the field of entertainment, as an owner of a vast imagination, excessive luxury in regard to everything: himself, his court and palace, receptions, and entertainment events. Considered individual likes to behave royally, patronizingly and grandly. Also, as the above-mentioned king, he gravitates toward luxury.

The following statement can be considered his principal philosophy: "It's better to be first and best always." In addition, this person really wants to try to "embrace the boundless": research everything, try everything, visit all places, see everything, and know everything. And, he wishes to have a lot of everything, whether it is money, knowledge, friends, baseball caps, information, diamonds, women or mansions. If he decides to buy a "small house," then he thinks that it must be the size of the Hermitage Museum; if he decides to buy a car, then it must be the most expensive one; if he studies, then he thinks that he must learn and know everything. However, this man's desire for luxury is a particular case of his general tendency toward excessiveness.

He does everything without moderation, and when something captures his attention, whether it is work, a person, an event, some action or state—he cannot stop and rushes headlong into it, as if internal brakes do not exist. He thinks that if he is to love, then it must be completely, to hate—with his whole heart, to be bored—desperately, and to fight—until a kill. If it is intellectual work, then it must continue until mental exhaustion; physical exercise—as long as possible; food consumption—until overeating; emotions—until an emotional peak, affect; sex—until a state of madness and satiety; work—to workaholism; career—to maximum social heights. Even the state of lack of money this man is able to bring to desperate poverty. He does not have a good understanding of words 'sufficient', 'plenty', 'enough'...

DEMO 93

Description Of Women Born On June 5ᵗʰ Of Leap Years From The Catalog Of Human Population

Presented demo is a very short description. A complete description consists of a very detailed description of functioning and qualities of personality: a general description and a description on 6 factors (intellectual, nutritional, physical, emotional, sexual, and environmental).

By her behavior, character and essence–this woman is a perpetual servant, a slave. She is always serving, waiting upon, trying to please someone. She has a wonderful ability to foresee desires of other people and act according to their wishes, while very flexibly adjusting to them: "The master is laughing and I'm laughing; the master is sad and I'll be sad with him." This individual is always guided by someone and without a "pointing and directing" force things are difficult for her (both psychologically and materially). She chooses a "master" (or "masters") from the environment and begins to serve and attend to them. All this is supported by plenty of flattery, servility and captation on her part. At the same time, she has a sense of self of a person around whom the universe revolves and considers herself perfect on all factors. How can this be? She thinks that "Everything is possible for money." The thing is that this woman chooses a person to serve and bootlick (whether her husband or her boss) not for nothing. Especially in times when it is necessary to find (keep) a material basis for her existence, this woman will not think for too long—she will act based on the principle: "Anything you want, any whim for your money!" She uses only one criterion: how a person can be useful to her. She thinks that we all live one day at a time and it is necessary to survive this day. However, by and large, her goal is to ensure an easy and preferably rich, comfortable, prosperous life for herself.

The thing is that this woman dreams of making her life a fairytale, to make some fabulous scenario into reality and it necessarily must have a happy ending. She is a fabler: she will make things up for other people (and do it better than Hans C. Andersen!) and will believe in them herself. To fantasize, to build illusory worlds and, of course, to tell great lies are usual things for this woman. And, she does this with or without reason. All the time she says something like this: "Just imagine what happened to me yesterday..." And, the fable begins: allegedly, this and that happened to her, and usually it is something absolutely incredible, something that is simply impossible to believe. What is notable is that her "fairytales" are mainly about how wonderful her life is (or how wonderfully she lived in the past or what surprisingly bright future she has). In essence, these tales are of the same type and fully reflect her real dream and what this woman seeks: princes, Arab sheiks, receptions, diamonds, palaces, ships, private planes, servants; in short, a life similar to Cleopatra's, who bathes in milk daily and drinks ambrosia—either a goddess, or a sovereign. A distinctive characteristic of her behavior is that she does not tell the truth—not a single word. It is not difficult for her to come up with and tell everyone something like this: "Yesterday I received a letter from the Queen of England. We write to each other..." Absurd, but beautiful, she thinks. This woman is convinced that every person can (and must) live like in a fairytale and all means are good for this. For example, everything is possible if you very flexibly penetrate, enter relevant social strata (of wealthy and famous people—presidents, ministers, chairmen) and purposefully get to those places where this can be achieved. "We were born to make a fairytale come true!"

However, in order to actually make her fairytale a reality it is necessary to have money (and quite a considerable amount). Therefore, it is necessary to find them in the environment. To be even more specific, it is necessary to find those, who have money (men) with all the consequences, which result from this. And, this woman finds. If she manages to turn the subject of her interest into her husband, then this woman will do everything to make sure that he feels comfortable and well with her: "What would you like, my dear?" She will do laundry, iron, cook, buy groceries, create comfort in the house, keep it clean (unless the opposite is necessary—to maintain "a mess")! With enthusiasm she will support any hobbies of her spouse, as well as any conversations; she will cherish any of his habits (sexual, nutritional, etc.), satisfy any of his wishes in regard to her appearance and behavior! Is it necessary to be quiet and modest? Sure! Or, on the contrary, is it necessary to express emotions and desires out loud and without hesitation? Of course! Is it necessary to be passionate? Cold and unapproachable? Neat? Dirty? No problem!

This woman is valuable in that she can be any for a person, whose favor and support she wants to have. She is ready to foresee thoughts, fulfill any wishes, and behave in any way that is necessary. And, it does not matter that her "master" is a fool, snotty, flipping, greasy freak—the most important thing is that he gives her money...

DEMO 94

Description Of Women Born On June 6ᵗʰ Of Common Years From The Catalog Of Human Population

Presented demo is a very short description. A complete description consists of a very detailed description of functioning and qualities of personality: a general description and a description on 6 factors (intellectual, nutritional, physical, emotional, sexual, and environmental).

By her behavior, character and essence—this woman is a perpetual servant, a slave. She is always serving, waiting upon, trying to please someone. She has a wonderful ability to foresee desires of other people and act according to their wishes, while very flexibly adjusting to them: "The master is laughing and I'm laughing; the master is sad and I'll be sad with him." This individual is always guided by someone and without a "pointing and directing" force things are difficult for her (both psychologically and materially). She chooses a "master" (or "masters") from the environment and begins to serve and attend to them. All this is supported by plenty of flattery, servility and captation on her part. At the same time, she has a sense of self of a person around whom the universe revolves and considers herself perfect on all factors. How can this be? She thinks that "Everything is possible for money." The thing is that this woman chooses a person to serve and bootlick (whether her husband or her boss) not for nothing. Especially in times when it is necessary to find (keep) a material basis for her existence, this woman will not think for too long—she will act based on the principle: "Anything you want, any whim for your money!" She uses only one criterion: how a person can be useful to her. She thinks that we all live one day at a time and it is necessary to survive this day. However, by and large, her goal is to ensure an easy and preferably rich, comfortable, prosperous life for herself.

The thing is that this woman dreams of making her life a fairytale, to make some fabulous scenario into reality and it necessarily must have a happy ending. She is a fabler: she will make things up for other people (and do it better than Hans C. Andersen!) and will believe in them herself. To fantasize, to build illusory worlds and, of course, to tell great lies are usual things for this woman. And, she does this with or without reason. All the time she says something like this: "Just imagine what happened to me yesterday..." And, the fable begins: allegedly, this and that happened to her, and usually it is something absolutely incredible, something that is simply impossible to believe. What is notable is that her "fairytales" are mainly about how wonderful her life is (or how wonderfully she lived in the past or what surprisingly bright future she has). In essence, these tales are of the same type and fully reflect her real dream and what this woman seeks: princes, Arab sheiks, receptions, diamonds, palaces, ships, private planes, servants; in short, a life similar to Cleopatra's, who bathes in milk daily and drinks ambrosia—either a goddess, or a sovereign. A distinctive characteristic of her behavior is that she does not tell the truth—not a single word. It is not difficult for her to come up with and tell everyone something like this: "Yesterday I received a letter from the Queen of England. We write to each other..." Absurd, but beautiful, she thinks. This woman is convinced that every person can (and must) live like in a fairytale and all means are good for this. For example, everything is possible if you very flexibly penetrate, enter relevant social strata (of wealthy and famous people—presidents, ministers, chairmen) and purposefully get to those places where this can be achieved. "We were born to make a fairytale come true!"

However, in order to actually make her fairytale a reality it is necessary to have money (and quite a considerable amount). Therefore, it is necessary to find them in the environment. To be even more specific, it is necessary to find those, who have money (men) with all the consequences, which result from this. And, this woman finds. If she manages to turn the subject of her interest into her husband, then this woman will do everything to make sure that he feels comfortable and well with her: "What would you like, my dear?" She will do laundry, iron, cook, buy groceries, create comfort in the house, keep it clean (unless the opposite is necessary—to maintain "a mess")! With enthusiasm she will support any hobbies of her spouse, as well as any conversations; she will cherish any of his habits (sexual, nutritional, etc.), satisfy any of his wishes in regard to her appearance and behavior! Is it necessary to be quiet and modest? Sure! Or, on the contrary, is it necessary to express emotions and desires out loud and without hesitation? Of course! Is it necessary to be passionate? Cold and unapproachable? Neat? Dirty? No problem!

This woman is valuable in that she can be any for a person, whose favor and support she wants to have. She is ready to foresee thoughts, fulfill any wishes, and behave in any way that is necessary. And, it does not matter that her "master" is a fool, snotty, flipping, greasy freak—the most important thing is that he gives her money...

DEMO 95
Description Of Women Born On July 4ᵗʰ Of Leap Years From The Catalog Of Human Population

Presented demo is a very short description. A complete description consists of a very detailed description of functioning and qualities of personality: a general description and a description on 6 factors (intellectual, nutritional, physical, emotional, sexual, and environmental).

This woman has only one goal in life: absolute power. Naturally, she is well aware that the highest form of power in society is power over people's minds because this ensures power over people's lives. It is this highest level of influence that this person wants to have. She is focused on reaching high social levels and it is not surprising that in her environment, no matter who she is, this woman always tries to occupy a position of a manager, a leader, a chief or a boss. In other words: if not a queen, then at least someone like the first wife of a padishah, who is kind of a padishah, but tamed and all the power is, in fact, in different hands—in the hands of his wife.

The idea of getting an opportunity to decide destinies of a huge number of people (up to the scale of the global community), to change them—attracts this woman just as much as a magnet attracts a paper clip. However, she is not just a dreamer. For the sake of her dream (raised to the rank of the highest goal), this person will seek to accumulate a variety of resources, including personal qualities: a powerful intellect, the highest level of erudition and a corresponding reputation. And, of course, she will strive to have influential friends and a strong financial base. Certainly this, so to speak, "gentleman's set" will quite strongly depend on the culture and traditions of this woman's country of residence and will quite strongly vary in a wide range of social values. As it is known, in some parts of the world, especially valuable objects of possession and accumulation are information, knowledge, intellectual power—in this case, this person will work on gaining of the status of a smart, educated, erudite, well-informed woman. And, in some other parts of the world, completely different things are much highly valued and demanded—for example, huge herds of cows, goats and sheep, and one who has them is considered the most respected. Well, then this woman will engage in gathering of this type of valuables and begin collecting cattle, including small-size cattle. If in her country of residence morals, ethics, religiosity, or, for example, certain contribution to the life of society are prized above gold, then she thinks: why not acquire all of the above in multitude? And, if the society in which she lives worships the golden calf and money that a person possesses (regardless of other, for

example, personal qualities) automatically increase his or her value, rating, social status, place him or her atop of the social ladder—then, all her efforts will be devoted to acquisition of a solid financial base. However, in any culture this woman will strive to become a notable, authoritative, significant figure and will seek to become the model of best qualities; when looking at this woman, there will be not doubt that she deserves to occupy the highest position in society, to be the ruler, the holder of the highest form of managerial power. Although at times this person might feel despondent (she might experience, so to speak, waves of low-spiritedness, depressed states, in other words, the blues, when suddenly she begins to think of herself as unfortunate, that everything is bad, and so on)—this spleen does not last very long. The blues passes and again this woman is active, mighty and is eager, so to speak, to take the wheel, that is—to regulate huge social areas, decide people's destinies. Again, she turns into a person to whom others listen and one who can really be a real authority to her subordinates, and, of course, one who is capable of changing their fates. By the way, even though by nature she is a leader, she does not wish to be a walking icon, as this person is strongly against being an idol for someone. Also, she does not wish to be a preceptor, a person who knows everything about everything and constantly teaches others how to live, a visionary, or a forecaster. Being the law for her own self and for others is much more important for her.

This woman perceives herself as a great and powerful personality. She thinks that she must be an etalon and everything that relates to her must be of etalon quality. And, she is ready, so to speak, to tear herself apart to achieve this goal. In her individual case, pride and arrogance are normal, natural qualities of personality. Since health allows (and, usually, the state of her health is excellent), why not behave arrogantly, why not walk around with nose pointing up and declare complete permissiveness for her own self? In this sense, she appears as an extremely pampered person: haughty, arrogant, and reckless, especially in his youth. One of the most favorite self-presentations is to show herself as a woman, who is not afraid of anything, to whom everything is available, that she is a law unto herself, that she is a queen and a goddess to herself! It is a common thing for her to show self-will, put on the ritz, be flush with money, and make grand gestures. However, even this is not enough for her: she is convinced that everyone must know how strong and smart she is; in other words—wonderful in all respects! To realize this, she might use public speaking, public promises, and persistent self-advertisement. In other words, this woman, metaphorically speaking, loudly broadcasts how outstanding and wonderful she is...

DEMO 96

Description Of Women Born On July 5th Of Leap Years From The Catalog Of Human Population

Presented demo is a very short description. A complete description consists of a very detailed description of functioning and qualities of personality: a general description and a description on 6 factors (intellectual, nutritional, physical, emotional, sexual, and environmental).

This woman has only one goal in life: absolute power. Naturally, she is well aware that the highest form of power in society is power over people's minds because this ensures power over people's lives. It is this highest level of influence that this person wants to have. She is focused on reaching high social levels and it is not surprising that in her environment, no matter who she is, this woman always tries to occupy a position of a manager, a leader, a chief or a boss. In other words: if not a queen, then at least someone like the first wife of a padishah, who is kind of a padishah, but tamed and all the power is, in fact, in different hands—in the hands of his wife.

The idea of getting an opportunity to decide destinies of a huge number of people (up to the scale of the global community), to change them—attracts this woman just as much as a magnet attracts a paper clip. However, she is not just a dreamer. For the sake of her dream (raised to the rank of the highest goal), this person will seek to accumulate a variety of resources, including personal qualities: a powerful intellect, the highest level of erudition and a corresponding reputation. And, of course, she will strive to have influential friends and a strong financial base. Certainly this, so to speak, "gentleman's set" will quite strongly depend on the culture and traditions of this woman's country of residence and will quite strongly vary in a wide range of social values. As it is known, in some parts of the world, especially valuable objects of possession and accumulation are information, knowledge, intellectual power—in this case, this person will work on gaining of the status of a smart, educated, erudite, well-informed woman. And, in some other parts of the world, completely different things are much highly valued and demanded—for example, huge herds of cows, goats and sheep, and one who has them is considered the most respected. Well, then this woman will engage in gathering of this type of valuables and begin collecting cattle, including small-size cattle. If in her country of residence morals, ethics, religiosity, or, for example, certain contribution to the life of society are prized above gold, then she thinks: why not acquire all of the above in multitude? And, if the society in which she lives worships the golden calf and money that a person possesses (regardless of other, for

example, personal qualities) automatically increase his or her value, rating, social status, place him or her atop of the social ladder—then, all her efforts will be devoted to acquisition of a solid financial base. However, in any culture this woman will strive to become a notable, authoritative, significant figure and will seek to become the model of best qualities; when looking at this woman, there will be not doubt that she deserves to occupy the highest position in society, to be the ruler, the holder of the highest form of managerial power. Although at times this person might feel despondent (she might experience, so to speak, waves of low-spiritedness, depressed states, in other words, the blues, when suddenly she begins to think of herself as unfortunate, that everything is bad, and so on)—this spleen does not last very long. The blues passes and again this woman is active, mighty and is eager, so to speak, to take the wheel, that is—to regulate huge social areas, decide people's destinies. Again, she turns into a person to whom others listen and one who can really be a real authority to her subordinates, and, of course, one who is capable of changing their fates. By the way, even though by nature she is a leader, she does not wish to be a walking icon, as this person is strongly against being an idol for someone. Also, she does not wish to be a preceptor, a person who knows everything about everything and constantly teaches others how to live, a visionary, or a forecaster. Being the law for her own self and for others is much more important for her.

This woman perceives herself as a great and powerful personality. She thinks that she must be an etalon and everything that relates to her must be of etalon quality. And, she is ready, so to speak, to tear herself apart to achieve this goal. In her individual case, pride and arrogance are normal, natural qualities of personality. Since health allows (and, usually, the state of her health is excellent), why not behave arrogantly, why not walk around with nose pointing up and declare complete permissiveness for her own self? In this sense, she appears as an extremely pampered person: haughty, arrogant, and reckless, especially in his youth. One of the most favorite self-presentations is to show herself as a woman, who is not afraid of anything, to whom everything is available, that she is a law unto herself, that she is a queen and a goddess to herself! It is a common thing for her to show self-will, put on the ritz, be flush with money, and make grand gestures. However, even this is not enough for her: she is convinced that everyone must know how strong and smart she is; in other words—wonderful in all respects! To realize this, she might use public speaking, public promises, and persistent self-advertisement. In other words, this woman, metaphorically speaking, loudly broadcasts how outstanding and wonderful she is...

DEMO 97

Description Of Women Born On July 5ᵗʰ Of Common Years From The Catalog Of Human Population

Presented demo is a very short description. A complete description consists of a very detailed description of functioning and qualities of personality: a general description and a description on 6 factors (intellectual, nutritional, physical, emotional, sexual, and environmental).

This woman has only one goal in life: absolute power. Naturally, she is well aware that the highest form of power in society is power over people's minds because this ensures power over people's lives. It is this highest level of influence that this person wants to have. She is focused on reaching high social levels and it is not surprising that in her environment, no matter who she is, this woman always tries to occupy a position of a manager, a leader, a chief or a boss. In other words: if not a queen, then at least someone like the first wife of a padishah, who is kind of a padishah, but tamed and all the power is, in fact, in different hands—in the hands of his wife.

The idea of getting an opportunity to decide destinies of a huge number of people (up to the scale of the global community), to change them—attracts this woman just as much as a magnet attracts a paper clip. However, she is not just a dreamer. For the sake of her dream (raised to the rank of the highest goal), this person will seek to accumulate a variety of resources, including personal qualities: a powerful intellect, the highest level of erudition and a corresponding reputation. And, of course, she will strive to have influential friends and a strong financial base. Certainly this, so to speak, "gentleman's set" will quite strongly depend on the culture and traditions of this woman's country of residence and will quite strongly vary in a wide range of social values. As it is known, in some parts of the world, especially valuable objects of possession and accumulation are information, knowledge, intellectual power—in this case, this person will work on gaining of the status of a smart, educated, erudite, well-informed woman. And, in some other parts of the world, completely different things are much highly valued and demanded—for example, huge herds of cows, goats and sheep, and one who has them is considered the most respected. Well, then this woman will engage in gathering of this type of valuables and begin collecting cattle, including small-size cattle. If in her country of residence morals, ethics, religiosity, or, for example, certain contribution to the life of society are prized above gold, then she thinks: why not acquire all of the above in multitude? And, if the society in which she lives worships the golden calf and money that a person possesses (regardless of other, for

example, personal qualities) automatically increase his or her value, rating, social status, place him or her atop of the social ladder—then, all her efforts will be devoted to acquisition of a solid financial base. However, in any culture this woman will strive to become a notable, authoritative, significant figure and will seek to become the model of best qualities; when looking at this woman, there will be not doubt that she deserves to occupy the highest position in society, to be the ruler, the holder of the highest form of managerial power. Although at times this person might feel despondent (she might experience, so to speak, waves of low-spiritedness, depressed states, in other words, the blues, when suddenly she begins to think of herself as unfortunate, that everything is bad, and so on)—this spleen does not last very long. The blues passes and again this woman is active, mighty and is eager, so to speak, to take the wheel, that is—to regulate huge social areas, decide people's destinies. Again, she turns into a person to whom others listen and one who can really be a real authority to her subordinates, and, of course, one who is capable of changing their fates. By the way, even though by nature she is a leader, she does not wish to be a walking icon, as this person is strongly against being an idol for someone. Also, she does not wish to be a preceptor, a person who knows everything about everything and constantly teaches others how to live, a visionary, or a forecaster. Being the law for her own self and for others is much more important for her.

This woman perceives herself as a great and powerful personality. She thinks that she must be an etalon and everything that relates to her must be of etalon quality. And, she is ready, so to speak, to tear herself apart to achieve this goal. In her individual case, pride and arrogance are normal, natural qualities of personality. Since health allows (and, usually, the state of her health is excellent), why not behave arrogantly, why not walk around with nose pointing up and declare complete permissiveness for her own self? In this sense, she appears as an extremely pampered person: haughty, arrogant, and reckless, especially in his youth. One of the most favorite self-presentations is to show herself as a woman, who is not afraid of anything, to whom everything is available, that she is a law unto herself, that she is a queen and a goddess to herself! It is a common thing for her to show self-will, put on the ritz, be flush with money, and make grand gestures. However, even this is not enough for her: she is convinced that everyone must know how strong and smart she is; in other words—wonderful in all respects! To realize this, she might use public speaking, public promises, and persistent self-advertisement. In other words, this woman, metaphorically speaking, loudly broadcasts how outstanding and wonderful she is...

DEMO 98

Description Of Women Born On July 6th Of Common Years From The Catalog Of Human Population

Presented demo is a very short description. A complete description consists of a very detailed description of functioning and qualities of personality: a general description and a description on 6 factors (intellectual, nutritional, physical, emotional, sexual, and environmental).

This woman has only one goal in life: absolute power. Naturally, she is well aware that the highest form of power in society is power over people's minds because this ensures power over people's lives. It is this highest level of influence that this person wants to have. She is focused on reaching high social levels and it is not surprising that in her environment, no matter who she is, this woman always tries to occupy a position of a manager, a leader, a chief or a boss. In other words: if not a queen, then at least someone like the first wife of a padishah, who is kind of a padishah, but tamed and all the power is, in fact, in different hands—in the hands of his wife.

The idea of getting an opportunity to decide destinies of a huge number of people (up to the scale of the global community), to change them—attracts this woman just as much as a magnet attracts a paper clip. However, she is not just a dreamer. For the sake of her dream (raised to the rank of the highest goal), this person will seek to accumulate a variety of resources, including personal qualities: a powerful intellect, the highest level of erudition and a corresponding reputation. And, of course, she will strive to have influential friends and a strong financial base. Certainly this, so to speak, "gentleman's set" will quite strongly depend on the culture and traditions of this woman's country of residence and will quite strongly vary in a wide range of social values. As it is known, in some parts of the world, especially valuable objects of possession and accumulation are information, knowledge, intellectual power—in this case, this person will work on gaining of the status of a smart, educated, erudite, well-informed woman. And, in some other parts of the world, completely different things are much highly valued and demanded—for example, huge herds of cows, goats and sheep, and one who has them is considered the most respected. Well, then this woman will engage in gathering of this type of valuables and begin collecting cattle, including small-size cattle. If in her country of residence morals, ethics, religiosity, or, for example, certain contribution to the life of society are prized above gold, then she thinks: why not acquire all of the above in multitude? And, if the society in which she lives worships the golden calf and money that a person possesses (regardless of other, for

example, personal qualities) automatically increase his or her value, rating, social status, place him or her atop of the social ladder—then, all her efforts will be devoted to acquisition of a solid financial base. However, in any culture this woman will strive to become a notable, authoritative, significant figure and will seek to become the model of best qualities; when looking at this woman, there will be not doubt that she deserves to occupy the highest position in society, to be the ruler, the holder of the highest form of managerial power. Although at times this person might feel despondent (she might experience, so to speak, waves of low-spiritedness, depressed states, in other words, the blues, when suddenly she begins to think of herself as unfortunate, that everything is bad, and so on)—this spleen does not last very long. The blues passes and again this woman is active, mighty and is eager, so to speak, to take the wheel, that is—to regulate huge social areas, decide people's destinies. Again, she turns into a person to whom others listen and one who can really be a real authority to her subordinates, and, of course, one who is capable of changing their fates. By the way, even though by nature she is a leader, she does not wish to be a walking icon, as this person is strongly against being an idol for someone. Also, she does not wish to be a preceptor, a person who knows everything about everything and constantly teaches others how to live, a visionary, or a forecaster. Being the law for her own self and for others is much more important for her.

This woman perceives herself as a great and powerful personality. She thinks that she must be an etalon and everything that relates to her must be of etalon quality. And, she is ready, so to speak, to tear herself apart to achieve this goal. In her individual case, pride and arrogance are normal, natural qualities of personality. Since health allows (and, usually, the state of her health is excellent), why not behave arrogantly, why not walk around with nose pointing up and declare complete permissiveness for her own self? In this sense, she appears as an extremely pampered person: haughty, arrogant, and reckless, especially in his youth. One of the most favorite self-presentations is to show herself as a woman, who is not afraid of anything, to whom everything is available, that she is a law unto herself, that she is a queen and a goddess to herself! It is a common thing for her to show self-will, put on the ritz, be flush with money, and make grand gestures. However, even this is not enough for her: she is convinced that everyone must know how strong and smart she is; in other words—wonderful in all respects! To realize this, she might use public speaking, public promises, and persistent self-advertisement. In other words, this woman, metaphorically speaking, loudly broadcasts how outstanding and wonderful she is...

DEMO 99

Description Of Women Born On August 28th Of Leap Years From The Catalog Of Human Population

Presented demo is a very short description. A complete description consists of a very detailed description of functioning and qualities of personality: a general description and a description on 6 factors (intellectual, nutritional, physical, emotional, sexual, and environmental).

Considered person aspires to occupy the number one position in society. As she moves towards her dream, she goes not pay attention to authorities or social positions of her opponents. There are serious claims that she is worthy of the palm of superiority due to her exclusivity. She looks as if she belonged to the elite from the beginning. She behaves arrogantly, puts on airs, and cocks her nose: "I am the smartest, I know everything and I know how to do everything!" At any age, whether in childhood or in her youth, she looks like a person, who is endowed with wisdom of old age. She is convinced that nature endowed her with abilities of an unusually talented person, to some degree even superhuman abilities. For the most part this is true, but in potential. She really can make full use of her talents.

This woman might try to self-realize in one field or in several fields at the same time. She is able to concurrently sing, dance, write a dissertation and master the art of hairdressing, for example. If the goal will be selected at the right time, then she will be able to achieve impressive results: a Ph.D., a career of a famous actress, a great hairdresser, an owner of a luxurious yacht, a wife of Nobel Prize winner, etc. In order to do this, there must be a combination of external and internal conditions. Internal conditions are always with her: she is persistent, very hardworking, and knows how to study. However, she needs a person, who knows where to head, can show her the direction, tell her what to do, what to strive for—all these are external conditions that might or might not happen for her. For example, having a good potential for making a career as a scientist and being a student (post-graduate student), this woman is capable of meeting such a supervisor by the will of fates, who, as a luminary of science, will lead some ingenious scientific project. However, it must necessarily be an original, epochal scientific direction (if it comes to science since, in principle, it can be any type of studies), capable of making a radical change in some area of human life, capturing the minds, and seriously affecting the cultural level of a large, if not global, number of people. It might be developments in the field of rocket engineering or in the field of fire safety, electrical kitchen appliances, or in any other field. However, either way, an outstanding person must lead this project and provide original ideas for intellectual work of his whole group (research group, laboratory, etc.). Then, it is possible to say with complete certainty that once she comes across a worthy teaching and a worthy teacher, this woman will become very interested, will join the process and begin to engage in developments persistently and productively. In addition to research, she will literally exert herself to the utmost while promoting and defending this idea. She will tirelessly work toward realization of the project and in the process will be able to provide any services, any kind of help, any type of assistance that are important for the project. She will not only eagerly defend the righteous undertaking of her teacher (supervisor) during any attempts to discredit him, but also will work on ensuring the necessary informational support of the process by extracting knowledge from many different areas.

If she becomes a boss, then her subordinates are not to be envied because she will force them to work with double effort. She herself will literally have to be pulled away from her work. She is ready to work until exhaustion in order to provide a quality product, where everything is complete, clear and understandable. There is a peculiarity: she works even harder, promotes even more successfully if she is engaged with heritage of a genius. That is— if the teacher is no longer alive, then her efforts and productivity increase significantly. Being one of the most devoted students, she is the one, who will become an excellent organizer of the funeral of her teacher and the continuator of his work. She has a propensity to lay the foundation of some philosophical, scientific, ideological thought (sometimes based on someone else's idea). Again, under the supervision of another individual, her thoughts, ideas can be expressed in various articles and books.

Without a goal this woman will be hopelessly lost, spend her life jumping from some interests to other interests without hanging on to anything. In this case, she will remain a moth her whole life and will be a dilettante in everything; there will be a situation called "Life did not work out!" And then, this woman will most likely live and work in a kind of energy-saving mode—without much psychophysiological spending and without much success. Day after day she will engage in some time-work.

On the one hand, this woman knows how to be happy with life in any case. She knows how to appreciate that what she has. Only then, all her self-realization will be limited by absolutely fruitless fantasies, illusions, in which she will picture herself as someone, who already has glory, fame and influence. She will dream about how great it would be to get all this without efforts, for nothing. After dreaming for a while, she will begin to arrange real adventures for herself, which she is capable of under the circumstances, and which will not allow her to become too bored. For this reason: hoorah adventures! And, if no one is offering them, then this woman will quickly organize them (starting with sexual and ending with criminal). However, on the other hand, if she comes across something worthwhile and dares to make use of it, then she will be capable of changing her life sharply, sometimes in a flash. Believing in her lucky star, her fortune, once she acquires a target —she would die rather than yield...

DEMO 100

Description Of Women Born On August 29th Of Common Years From The Catalog Of Human Population

Presented demo is a very short description. A complete description consists of a very detailed description of functioning and qualities of personality: a general description and a description on 6 factors (intellectual, nutritional, physical, emotional, sexual, and environmental).

Considered person aspires to occupy the number one position in society. As she moves towards her dream, she goes not pay attention to authorities or social positions of her opponents. There are serious claims that she is worthy of the palm of superiority due to her exclusivity. She looks as if she belonged to the elite from the beginning. She behaves arrogantly, puts on airs, and cocks her nose: "I am the smartest, I know everything and I know how to do everything!" At any age, whether in childhood or in her youth, she looks like a person, who is endowed with wisdom of old age. She is convinced that nature endowed her with abilities of an unusually talented person, to some degree even superhuman abilities. For the most part this is true, but in potential. She really can make full use of her talents.

This woman might try to self-realize in one field or in several fields at the same time. She is able to concurrently sing, dance, write a dissertation and master the art of hairdressing, for example. If the goal will be selected at the right time, then she will be able to achieve impressive results: a Ph.D., a career of a famous actress, a great hairdresser, an owner of a luxurious yacht, a wife of Nobel Prize winner, etc. In order to do this, there must be a combination of external and internal conditions. Internal conditions are always with her: she is persistent, very hardworking, and knows how to study. However, she needs a person, who knows where to head, can show her the direction, tell her what to do, what to strive for—all these are external conditions that might or might not happen for her. For example, having a good potential for making a career as a scientist and being a student (post-graduate student), this woman is capable of meeting such a supervisor by the will of fates, who, as a luminary of science, will lead some ingenious scientific project. However, it must necessarily be an original, epochal scientific direction (if it comes to science since, in principle, it can be any type of studies), capable of making a radical change in some area of human life, capturing the minds, and seriously affecting the cultural level of a large, if not global, number of people. It might be developments in the field of rocket engineering or in the field of fire safety, electrical kitchen appliances, or in any other field. However, either way, an outstanding person must lead this project and provide original ideas for intellectual work of his whole group (research group, laboratory, etc.). Then, it is possible to say with complete certainty that once she comes across a worthy teaching and a worthy teacher, this woman will become very interested, will join the process and begin to engage in developments persistently and productively. In addition to research, she will literally exert herself to the utmost while promoting and defending this idea. She will tirelessly work toward realization of the project and in the process will be able to provide any services, any kind of help, any type of assistance that are important for the project. She will not only eagerly defend the righteous undertaking of her teacher (supervisor) during any attempts to discredit him, but also will work on ensuring the necessary informational support of the process by extracting knowledge from many different areas.

If she becomes a boss, then her subordinates are not to be envied because she will force them to work with double effort. She herself will literally have to be pulled away from her work. She is ready to work until exhaustion in order to provide a quality product, where everything is complete, clear and understandable. There is a peculiarity: she works even harder, promotes even more successfully if she is engaged with heritage of a genius. That is— if the teacher is no longer alive, then her efforts and productivity increase significantly. Being one of the most devoted students, she is the one, who will become an excellent organizer of the funeral of her teacher and the continuator of his work. She has a propensity to lay the foundation of some philosophical, scientific, ideological thought (sometimes based on someone else's idea). Again, under the supervision of another individual, her thoughts, ideas can be expressed in various articles and books.

Without a goal this woman will be hopelessly lost, spend her life jumping from some interests to other interests without hanging on to anything. In this case, she will remain a moth her whole life and will be a dilettante in everything; there will be a situation called "Life did not work out!" And then, this woman will most likely live and work in a kind of energy-saving mode—without much psychophysiological spending and without much success. Day after day she will engage in some time-work.

On the one hand, this woman knows how to be happy with life in any case. She knows how to appreciate that what she has. Only then, all her self-realization will be limited by absolutely fruitless fantasies, illusions, in which she will picture herself as someone, who already has glory, fame and influence. She will dream about how great it would be to get all this without efforts, for nothing. After dreaming for a while, she will begin to arrange real adventures for herself, which she is capable of under the circumstances, and which will not allow her to become too bored. For this reason: hoorah adventures! And, if no one is offering them, then this woman will quickly organize them (starting with sexual and ending with criminal). However, on the other hand, if she comes across something worthwhile and dares to make use of it, then she will be capable of changing her life sharply, sometimes in a flash. Believing in her lucky star, her fortune, once she acquires a target—she would die rather than yield...

BIBLIOGRAPHY

Vasilyev, V. P. (1866). *Analiz kitayskikh iyeroglifov (Sostavlen dlya rukovodstva studentov professorom S.-Peterburgskogo universiteta Vasilyevym)* [Analysis Of Chinese Hieroglyphs (Prepared By Professor Vasilyev Of University Of St. Petersburg To Guide Students)]. St. Petersburg.

Georgiyevskiy, S. M. (1892). *Mificheskiye vozzreniya i mify kitaytsev (s tablitsami kitayskikh iyeroglifov)* [Mythical Views And Myths Of The Chinese (With Tables Of Chinese Hieroglyphs)]. St. Petersburg: Tipografiya I. N. Skorokhodova.

Hall, M. P. (1928). *The Secret Teachings Of All Ages: An Encyclopedic Outline Of Masonic, Hermetic, Qabbalistic and Rosicrucian Symbolical Philosophy*. San Francisco: H.S. Crocker Company, Inc. Scanned November 2001, by Hare, J. Retrieved September 10, 2014, from http://www.framsteget.net/gratis/TheSecretTeachingsOfAllAges.pdf.

Yanshina, E. M. (Trans.). (1977). *Katalog Gor I Morej (Shan Hai Tszin)* [Catalog of Mountains and Seas (Shan Hai Jing)]. Moscow: Nauka.

Losev, A. F., Meletinskii, E. M., Riftin, B. L., Toporov, V. N., Ivanov, V. V., Averintsev, S. S., ... Afanasyeva, V. K. (1980). S. A. Tokarev (Ed.). *Mify narodov mira* [Myths of the World] (Vols. 1-2.). Moscow: Sovetskaya Entsiklopediya.

Sovetskiy Entsiklopedicheskiy Slovar' (SES) [Soviet Encyclopedic Dictionary]. (2nd ed.). (1982). Moscow: Sovetskaya Entsiklopediya.

Oshanin, I. M. (Ed.). (1983). *Bol'shoy kitaysko-russkiy slovar' (BKRS)* [Large Chinese-Russian Dictionary (BKRS)] (Vols. 1-4.). Moscow: Nauka.

Frazer, J. G. (1984). M. K. Ryklin (Trans.). *The Golden Bough: A Study In Magic And Religion*. Moscow: Politizdat. (Original work published 1890 under the title *The Golden Bough: A Study in Comparative Religion*.)

Pavlenko, N. A. (1987). *Istoriya pis'ma* [History of Writing]. Minsk: Vysheyshaya Shkola.

Starostin, S. A. (1989). *Rekonstruktsiya drevnekitayskoy fonologicheskoy sistemy* [Reconstruction Of The Ancient Chinese Phonological System.]. Moscow: Nauka.

Jung, C. G. (1991). A. M. Rutkevich (Ed.). *Arkhetip i simvol* [Archetype And Symbol]. Moscow: Renessans.

Shchutsky, J. K. (1993). A. I. Kobzev (Ed.). *Kitayskaya klassicheskaya "Kniga peremen"* [Chinese Classical Book of Changes]. (2nd ed.). Moscow: Vostochnaya Literatura.

Gariaev, P. P. (1994). *Volnovoy genom* [Wave Genome]. Moscow: Obshchestvennaya Polza. ISBN 9785856170053 ISBN 9785856171005 [Available at libraries http://www.worldcat.org/title/volnovoi-genom/.]

Lukyanov, A. E. (1994). *Nachalo drevnekitayskoy filosofii: "I tszin", "Dao de tszin", "Lun' yuy"* [The Beginning Of The Ancient Chinese Philosophy: I Ching, Tao Te Ching, Lun Yu]. Moscow: Radiks. ISBN 9785864630266. [Available at multiple libraries http://www.worldcat.org/title/nachalo-drevnekitaiskoi-filosofii-i-tszin-dao-de-tszin-lun-iui/.]

Davydov, A., & corr. of ITAR-TASS Fedoruk, V. (1998). Corr. of RAO L. Verbitskaya & Assoc. Prof. B. Sokolova (Eds.), *Pervyy Rossiyskiy Filosofskiy Kongress: Chelovek – Filosofiya – Gumanizm* [First Russian Philosophical Congress. Human Being – Philosophy – Humanism]: *Vol. 7 Philosophy and Human Problem: Is Shan Hai Jing The Original Catalog Of Psychophysiological Human Structure?* St. Petersburg: Saint Petersburg State University Publishing House, 7, 355-357. ISBN 9785288018947. Presentation at the First Russian Philosophical Congress: Human Being – Philosophy – Humanism (in Russian), St. Petersburg (1997). [Available at: University of Michigan http://mirlyn.lib.umich.edu/Record/003947324 B4231.R6751997 (subscription required), St. Petersburg's Central City Public Library Named After V. V. Mayakovsky http://www.pl.spb.ru/structure/zali/ ББК87Ч-391 (subscription required), and multiple other libraries http://www.worldcat.org/title/chelovek-filosofiia-gumanizm-pervyi-rossiiskii-filosofskii-kongress/]

Otyugov, A. A. (1998). Corr. of RAO L. Verbitskaya & Assoc. Prof. B. Sokolova (Eds.), *Pervyy Rossiyskiy Filosofskiy Kongress: Chelovek – Filosofiya – Gumanizm* [First Russian Philosophical Congress. Human Being – Philosophy – Humanism]: *Vol. 7 Philosophy and Human Problem: Psychological Nature Of Mythological Consciousness.* St. Petersburg: SPSU Publishing House. ISBN 9785288018947. Presentation at the First Russian Philosophical Congress: Human Being – Philosophy – Humanism (in Russian), St. Petersburg. Retrieved from http://mirlyn.lib.umich.edu/Record/003947324 B4231.R6751997 (subscription required). [Also available at other libraries http://www.worldcat.org/title/chelovek-filosofiia-gumanizm-pervyi-rossiiskii-filosofskii-kongress/.]

Torchinov, E. A. (1998). *Religii mira. Opyt zapredel'nogo (transpersonal'nyye sostoyaniya i psikhotekhnika).* [Religions of the World. Experience of the Transcendence (Transpersonal States and Psychotechnique)]. St. Petersburg: Tsentr "Peterburgskoye Vostokovedeniye". ISBN 9785858030782 [Available at libraries http://www.worldcat.org/title/religii-mira-opyt-zapredelnogo-transpersonalnye-sostojanija-i-psihotehnika/.]

Zarochentsev, K. D., & Khudyakov, A.I. (1998). Corr. of RAO L. Verbitskaya & Assoc. Prof. B. Sokolova (Eds.), *Pervyy Rossiyskiy Filosofskiy Kongress: Chelovek – Filosofiya – Gumanizm* [First Russian Philosophical Congress. Human Being – Philosophy – Humanism]: *Vol. 7 Philosophy and Human Problem: The Crisis Of Modern Psychodiagnostics*. St. Petersburg: SPSU Publishing House. ISBN 9785288018947. Presentation at the First Russian Philosophical Congress: Human Being – Philosophy – Humanism (in Russian), St. Petersburg. Retrieved from http://mirlyn.lib.umich.edu/Record/003947324 B4231.R6751997 (subscription required). [Also available at other libraries http://www.worldcat.org/title/chelovek-filosofiia-gumanizm-pervyi-rossiiskii-filosofskii-kongress/.]

Davydov, A., & Fedoruk, V. (1999). *Shan Khay Tszin: Mify Ili Struktura Psikhiki?* [Shan Hai Jing: Myths Or Structure Of Psyche?]. Moscow: *Power Of Spirit*, 32-35.

Davydov, A. (2002). *Katalog Chelovecheskoy Populyatsii* [*Catalog of Human Population*]. Presentation at the International Conference on Prospects of Preservation and Development of Unified Civilization of the Planet: Culture, Ecology, Cosmos (in Russian), Moscow (2002). [Mention in *Parlamentskaya Gazeta*: "...The most luminous were reports by ... A. Davydov about the program that he developed, which opens up the best, but often hidden qualities of a human..." (Umorov, I. (2002). *Chelovechestvu Otpushcheno Tol'ko Tri Goda* [Humanity Has Only Three Years]. Moscow: *Parlamentskaya Gazeta, Sphere of Reason*, 129 (1008), para. 4. Retrieved 13 May 2015 from http://old.pnp.ru/archive/10082921.html.)]

Ezhov, V. V. (2003). *Mify Drevnego Kitaya* [Myths of Ancient China]. (Ill. *Myths of Nations of the World*) Moscow: Astrel.

Wilhelm, R., & Wilhelm H. (2003). V.B. Kurnosova (Trans.). *Ponimaniye «I tszin». Antologiya.* [Understanding The I Ching. Anthology.]. (2nd ed.). *Tradition, Religion, Culture*. Moscow: Aleteya.

Terentev-Katansky, A. (2004). *Illyustratsii k kitayskomu bestiariyu: Mifologicheskiye zhivotnyye drevnego Kitaya* [Illustrations to Chinese Bestiary: Mythological Animals of Ancient China]. St. Petersburg: Forma T.

Nikitina, T. N., & Zaytsev, V.P. (Eds.). (2009). *Slovar' drevnekitayskikh iyeroglifov = 古代漢語字典: s prilozheniyem slovarya naiboleye chastotnykh omografov, vstrechayushchikhsya v drevnekitayskom tekste, sost. Ye. G. Ivanovoy* [The Dictionary Of Ancient Chinese Hieroglyphs = 古代 漢語 字典: With The Appended Dictionary Of Most Frequent Homographs Found In Ancient Chinese Text, Compiled By E. G. Ivanova]. St. Petersburg: Karo. ISBN 9785992504293

Davydov, A., & Skorbatyuk, O. (2014). K. Bazilevsky (Trans.). *AHNENERBE—Your Killer Is Under Your Skin* (Composed 2014. Original work published 2014 in Russian, ISBN 9781311356741.). San Diego, CA: HPA Press. ISBN 9781311266682

Davydov, A., & Skorbatyuk, O. (2014). K. Bazilevsky (Trans.). *IDEOLOGY OF RELIGIONS. Scientific Proof Of Existence Of "God": The Catalog Of Human Population.* (Original work published 2014 in Russian, ISBN 9781311946690.). San Diego, CA: HPA Press. ISBN 9781311413932 ISBN 9780988648593

OUR OTHER BOOKS RELATED TO OUR SCIENTIFIC RESEARCH

Monographic Series

Archetypal Pattern. Fundamentals of Non-Traditional Psychoanalysis.

Davydov, A., & Skorbatyuk, O. (2014). K. Bazilevsky (Ed.). Anonymous (Trans.). *Archetypal Pattern. Fundamentals of Non-Traditional Psychoanalysis*: *Vol. 1. From Carl Gustav Jung's Archetypes of the Collective Unconscious to Individual Archetypal Patterns*. (Composed 2005. Original work published 2013 in Russian, ISBN 9781301447688.). San Diego, CA: HPA Press. ISBN 9781311820082

Davydov, A., & Skorbatyuk, O. (2014). K. Bazilevsky (Trans.). *Archetypal Pattern. Fundamentals of Non-Traditional Psychoanalysis*: *Vol. 2. Can Archetypal Images Contain Chimeras?* (Composed 2005. Original work published 2013 in Russian, ISBN 978130184859.). San Diego, CA: HPA Press. ISBN 9781310658570

Davydov, A., & Skorbatyuk, O. (2014). Arkhetipicheskiy Pattern. Osnovy Netraditsionnogo Psikhoanaliza [Archetypal Pattern. Fundamentals of Non-Traditional Psychoanalysis]: *Vol. 3. Archetype Semantics: How This Corresponds to the Concept of an 'Image'. How Archetypal Are Images?* (Composed 2005.). Marina Del Rey, CA: Catalog Of Human Souls GP. ISBN 9781301337309

Davydov, A., & Skorbatyuk, O. (2014). K. Bazilevsky (Trans.). *Archetypal Pattern. Fundamentals of Non-Traditional Psychoanalysis*: *Vol. 4. Society As A Community Of Manipulators And Their Subjects*. (Composed 2005. Original work published 2013 in Russian, ISBN 9781301399901.). San Diego, CA: HPA Press. ISBN 9781311809353

Catalog of Human Population - Non-Fiction Series

Individual (Subtype) Human Programs

Davydov, A., & Skorbatyuk, O. (2013). *Katalog Chelovecheskikh Dush: Programmnoye Obespecheniye Dushi Muzhchin/Zhenshchin, Rodivshikhsya <Data>* [Catalog of Human Souls: Software of Soul of Men/Women Born On <Date>] (Vols. 1-218. In Russian. Composed 2005-

2013.). Marina Del Rey, CA: Catalog Of Human Souls GP. [Available at http://www.humanpopulationacademy.org/pricing/ in all languages].

Human Manipulation Modes

Davydov, A., & Skorbatyuk, O. (2013-2014). *Katalog Chelovecheskikh Dush: Kak Podchinit' Muzhchin/Zhenshchin, Rozhdonnykh <Data>. Zhenskiy/Muzhskoy Manipulyativnyy Ctsenariy.* [Catalog of Human Souls: How To Subdue Men/Women Born On <Date>. Female/Male Manipulation Scenario.] (Vols. 1-39. In Russian. Composed 2005-2013.). Marina Del Rey, CA: Catalog Of Human Souls GP. [Available at http://www.humanpopulationacademy.org/pricing/ in all languages].

Ideologies

Davydov, A. (2014). K. Bazilevsky (Trans.). *Terrorism: A Concept For The ATC (The Commonwealth Of Independent States Anti-Terrorism Center).* (Composed 2001. Original work published 2014 in Russian, ISBN 9781311277848.). San Diego, CA: HPA Press. ISBN 9781310032189

Davydov, A. (2014). K. Bazilevsky (Trans.). *Ideology Of Monarchy. For Office Of The Head Of The Russian Imperial House, Her Imperial Highness Grand Duchess Maria Vladimirovna.* (Composed 2003. Original work published 2014 in Russian, ISBN 9781310150340.). San Diego, CA: HPA Press. ISBN 9781311970152

Davydov, A., & Skorbatyuk, O. (2014). K. Bazilevsky (Trans.). *Ideology Of Religions. Scientific Proof Of Existence Of "God": The Catalog Of Human Population.* (Original work published 2014 in Russian, ISBN 9781311946690.). San Diego, CA: HPA Press. ISBN 9781311413932 ISBN 9780988648593

Political Science

Davydov, A. (2014). K. Bazilevsky (Trans.). *Essence Of Political Ideologies And Their Role In The Historical Process (Political History Of Russia).* (Composed 2003. Original work published 2014 in Russian, ISBN 9781310199929.). San Diego, CA: HPA Press. ISBN 9781310199929

Davydov, A. (2014). K. Bazilevsky (Trans.). *Influence Of Psychophysiological Specifics Of A Leader On The Style Of Political Decision-Making.* (Composed 2003. Original work published 2014 in Russian, ISBN 9781310037832). San Diego, CA: HPA Press. ISBN 9781310104558

Davydov, A. (2014). K. Bazilevsky (Trans.). *Elitist Political Concepts.* (Composed 2005. Original work published 2014 in Russian, ISBN 9781310223228). San Diego, CA: HPA Press. ISBN 9781310822858

General Non-Fiction

Bazilevsky, K. (2012). *Human Population Academy: Laws of Human Nature Based on Shan Hai Jing Research Discoveries by A. Davydov & O. Skorbatyuk.* San Diego, CA: HPA Press. ISBN 9781301986781 ISBN 9780988648500

Davydov, A. (2013). *Shan Khay Tszin: Mify Ili Struktura Psikhiki?* [Shan Hai Jing: Myths Or Structure Of Psyche?] (Composed 1999. Originally pub. 1999 in Russian in Moscow: *Power Of Spirit*, 32-35.). Marina Del Rey, CA: Catalog Of Human Souls GP. ISBN 9781301590391

Davydov, A. (2013). *"Shan Khay Tszin" i "I Tszin" – Karta Psikhofiziologicheskoy Struktury Cheloveka?* [Shan Hai Jing and I Ching – Map of Human Psychophysiological Structure?] (Composed 2002.). Marina Del Rey, CA: Catalog Of Human Souls GP. ISBN 9781301510009

Davydov, A., & Skorbatyuk, O. (2014). K. Bazilevsky (Trans.). *AHNENERBE: Your Killer Is Under Your Skin* (Original work published 2014 in Russian, ISBN 9781311356741.). San Diego, CA: HPA Press. ISBN 9781311266682

A Man And A Woman – Non-Fiction Series

A Log With Legs Spread Wide

Davydov, A., & Skorbatyuk, O. (2014). K. Bazilevsky (Trans.). *A Log With Legs Spread Wide: Vol. 1. How Men Turn Women Into Nothing.* (Original work published 2014 in Russian, ISBN 9781310388125.). San Diego, CA: HPA Press. ISBN 9781311155771

Davydov, A., & Skorbatyuk, O. (2014). K. Bazilevsky (Trans.). *A Log With Legs Spread Wide: Vol. 2. How Goddesses Are Turned Into Logs. World History Of Turning Women Into Mats.* (Original work published 2014 in Russian, ISBN 9781311238894.). San Diego, CA: HPA Press. ISBN 9781311915603

Davydov, A., & Skorbatyuk, O. (2013). *A Log With Legs Spread Wide: Vol. 3. Women's Thirst For Power Over Men Is The Pathway To Become A*

Garbage. (Original work published 2013 in Russian, ISBN 9781301553075.). Marina Del Rey, CA: Catalog Of Human Souls GP. ISBN 9781301435500

Davydov, A., & Skorbatyuk, O. (2013). *A Log With Legs Spread Wide: Vol. 4. The Head – In The Underpants*. (Original work published 2013 in Russian, ISBN 9781301051281.). Marina Del Rey, CA: Catalog Of Human Souls GP.

Manipulative Games For Women

Davydov, A., & Skorbatyuk, O. (2013). *Manipulyativnyye Igry Dlya Zhenshchin* [Manipulative Games For Women]: *Vol. 1. March 23: Instruction for Exploitation of Men* (2nd ed., in Russian. Original work published 2005, Moscow: SNIALTotems. ISBN 9785716101333). Marina Del Rey, CA: Catalog Of Human Souls GP. ISBN 9781301803521

Davydov, A., & Skorbatyuk, O. (2013). *Manipulyativnyye Igry Dlya Zhenshchin* [Manipulative Games For Women]: *Vol. 2. April 6: Instruction for Exploitation of Men* (2nd ed., in Russian. Original work published 2005, Moscow: SNIALTotems. ISBN 9785716101302). Marina Del Rey, CA: Catalog Of Human Souls GP. ISBN 9781301069286

Davydov, A., & Skorbatyuk, O. (2013). *Manipulyativnyye Igry Dlya Zhenshchin* [Manipulative Games For Women]: *Vol. 3. October 13: Instruction for Exploitation of Men* (2nd ed., in Russian. Original work published 2005, Moscow: SNIALTotems. ISBN 9785716101326). Marina Del Rey, CA: Catalog Of Human Souls GP. ISBN 9781301900824

Davydov, A., & Skorbatyuk, O. (2013). *Manipulyativnyye Igry Dlya Zhenshchin* [Manipulative Games For Women]: *Vol. 4. December 7: Instruction for Exploitation of Men* (2nd ed., in Russian. Original work published 2005, Moscow: SNIALTotems. ISBN 9785716101319). Marina Del Rey, CA: Catalog Of Human Souls GP. ISBN 9781301413065

Secret Sexual Desires

Bazilevsky, K. (2013). *How To Seduce Men/Women Born On <Date> Or Secret Sexual Desires of 10 Million People: Demo From Shan Hai Jing Research Discoveries by A. Davydov & O. Skorbatyuk*. (Vols. 1-10). San Diego, CA: HPA Press.

Bazilevsky, K. (2013). *How To Seduce Men & Women Born On March 5 Or Secret Sexual Desires of 20 Million People: Demo From Shan Hai Jing Research Discoveries by A. Davydov & O. Skorbatyuk*. San Diego, CA: HPA Press. ISBN 9781301087204

Bazilevsky, K. (2013). *Secret Sexual Desires of 100 Million People—Seduction Recipes For Men & Women: Demos From Shan Hai Jing Research Discoveries by A. Davydov & O. Skorbatyuk.* San Diego, CA: HPA Press. ISBN 9780988648579 ISBN 9781301135035 ISBN 9780988648586

A list of other publications related to our scientific research can be found at http://www.humanpopulationacademy.org/publications/.

CONNECT WITH US

1. Visit our official website.

Human Population Academy and Special Scientific Info-Analytical Laboratory—Catalog of Human Souls:
http://www.HumanPopulationAcademy.org

2. Connect with us on social networks.

- ❖ *Facebook* - http://www.facebook.com/HumanPopulationAcademy (Note: you must be logged in to *Facebook* in order to access this page.)
- ❖ *YouTube* - http://www.youtube.com/user/HumanPopulAcademy
- ❖ *Google+* - http://plus.google.com/+HumanpopulationacademyOrghumannature
- ❖ *LinkedIn* - http://www.linkedin.com/company/2484433
- ❖ *Pinterest* - http://pinterest.com/humanpopacademy/
- ❖ *Twitter* - http://twitter.com/HumanPopAcademy

3. Contact us.

You can find out how to contact us at the Human Population Academy's website under Contacts (see http://www.humanpopulationacademy.org/breakthrough-discovery/contacts/).

ABOUT US

Special Scientific Info-Analytical Laboratory—Catalog of Human Souls was founded by Andrey Davydov. The laboratory is engaged in research and decryption of the ancient Chinese monument Shan Hai Jing, as well as other ancient texts, and creation of the *Catalog of Human Population*. The technology of uncovering individual structures of psyche of *Homo sapiens* for this Catalog was developed by Andrey Davydov; it is not based on any existing domestic or foreign research, methods or theoretical concepts. The laboratory is a partner with the Human Population Academy.

Human Population Academy was founded by Kate Bazilevsky. The Academy's mission is to inform all of over 7 billion humans living on Earth about the discovery of the *Catalog of Human Population*. The Academy educates about the *Catalog of Human Population* (*Catalog of Human Souls*) and provides access to informational materials from this Catalog to the public.

LEADERSHIP

ANDREY DAVYDOV

Research Supervisor of the Special Scientific Info-Analytical Laboratory—Catalog of Human Souls

Andrey Davydov is an expert in Chinese culture, researcher of ancient texts, the author of scientific discovery of the *Catalog of Human Population* and the technology of decryption of the ancient Chinese monument Shan Hai

Jing as the *Catalog of Human Population*. He authored over 300 published books, including scientific monographs and ideologies. In 2012, he was granted political asylum in the USA due to persecution by a group of employees of the Federal Security Service of Russian Federation (FSB, formerly KGB), who decided to expropriate his research product—the *Catalog of Human Population*.

OLGA SKORBATYUK

Senior Analyst at the Special Scientific Info-Analytical Laboratory—Catalog of Human Souls

Olga Skorbatyuk is a professional psychologist, one of the developers of the *Catalog of Human Population*, the founder of Non-Traditional Psychoanalysis, and co-author of over 300 books and scientific articles. She was granted political asylum in the USA together with A. Davydov.

KATE BAZILEVSKY

Founder of the Human Population Academy, Junior Analyst at the Special Scientific Info-Analytical Laboratory—Catalog of Human Souls

Kate Bazilevsky is the director of the Human Population Academy, a Junior Analyst at the Catalog of Human Souls laboratory, an author and a translator of books about the *Catalog of Human Population*. She holds a degree in MIS and psychology. She founded the Human Population Academy in 2011 and a publishing company called HPA Press in 2012.